Gendered Defenders

NEW SUNS:

RACE, GENDER, AND SEXUALITY IN THE

SPECULATIVE

Susana M. Morris and Kinitra D. Brooks, Series Editors

Gendered Defenders

Marvel's Superheroines in
Transmedia Spaces

*Edited by Bryan J. Carr and
Meta G. Carstarphen*

THE OHIO STATE UNIVERSITY PRESS
COLUMBUS

Library of Congress Cataloging-in-Publication Data
Names: Carr, Bryan, editor. I Carstarphen, Meta G., 1954– editor.
Title: Gendered defenders : Marvel's heroines in transmedia spaces / edited by Bryan
    J. Carr and Meta G. Carstarphen.
Other titles: New suns: race, gender, and sexuality in the speculative.
Description: Columbus : The Ohio State University Press, [2022] I Series: New
    suns: race, gender, and sexuality in the speculative I Includes bibliographical
    references and index. I Summary: "Examines representations of Marvel
    superheroines such as Carol Danvers, Jessica Jones, Shuri, Ms. Marvel, Black
    Widow, Pepper Potts, and Squirrel Girl across multiple media formats to
    understand and critique real-world gender dynamics"—Provided by publisher.
Identifiers: LCCN 2022028047 I ISBN 9780814215272 (cloth) I ISBN 0814215270
    (cloth) I ISBN 9780814282472 (epub) I ISBN 0814282474 (epub)
Subjects: LCSH: Women superheroes in literature. I Women superheroes on
    television. I Women superheroes in motion pictures. I Women superheroes in
    mass media. I Comic books, strips, etc.—Social aspects. I Women in popular
    culture. I Mass media and women. I Women—Social conditions.
Classification: LCC PN6714 .G45 2022 I DDC 302.23082—dc23/eng/20220818
LC record available at https://lccn.loc.gov/2022028047
Other identifiers: ISBN 9780814258521 (paper) I ISBN 0814258522 (paper)

Cover design by Black Kirby
Text composition by Stuart Rodriguez
Type set in Palatino

CONTENTS

ACKNOWLEDGMENTS

A project on the scale and scope of *Gendered Defenders* requires the effort of many dedicated and talented individuals. We thank all the contributors to this volume for their insights and hard work. Each author and/or team of authors brought their love of the genre along with insightful, and exciting, feminist perspectives about the character, the story lines, and the media contexts. They were gracious and open to our prodding and editorial input, as they pushed themselves against the boundaries of common genre perceptions.

We are also so grateful for the support and guidance from OSUP Acquisitions Editor Ana Jimenez-Moreno, who quickly understood our vision for this project and carefully guided us through the many stages of completion. We thank Rebecca Bostock and the entire production team at The Ohio State University Press, whose combined talents helped create a distinctive design for this volume. This includes the talented team at Black Kirby for the design of a striking and provocative book cover. We also extend our deep appreciation for Ajia Meux, a doctoral student in the Gaylord College at the University of Oklahoma, for her keen eye and careful review in copyediting the original manuscript. We also thank Kristen Ebert-Wagner for her work in copyediting the final manuscript. Our index is the product of B. Narr's time and talents, for which we are grateful.

Our respective institutions, the University of Wisconsin–Green Bay and the University of Oklahoma–Norman, supported us and, by extension, this project. We are also grateful for a grant from the Gaylord College of Journalism and Mass Communication's Faculty Development Fund, which supported the completion of this project.

To all our students—past, present, and future—we appreciate your questions and enthusiastic reception to classes and projects that indulged our mutual fascination with superheroes and what they meant to us collectively. Finally, we are indebted beyond measure to our families (pets included!) for their love, patience, and indulgence of our research work.

PART 1

Introduction

Framing Our Starting Places and Conceptual Origins

CHAPTER 1

Who Has Power, and How Do We Read It?

Bryan J. Carr and Meta G. Carstarphen

Black Widow. Captain Marvel. Shuri. Pepper Potts. Jessica Jones.

These names, not long ago, were obscurities known primarily to only the most dedicated fans of superhero comics. Like their male counterparts, they may have starred in critically acclaimed comics stories, but they lacked the mainstream salience—and the opportunity to create it—that their male contemporaries like Spider-Man, Wolverine, and the Hulk were granted. In recent years, however, that has changed. Each of the characters listed above, and the others mentioned in this volume, have been at the center of wildly popular television programs and films via the Marvel Cinematic Universe (MCU) transmedia experiment.

With this, of course, come some difficult truths—these characters have generally entered the public consciousness well after their male counter-parts, for a confluence of reasons at both the production and the story-telling levels. While Marvel as a brand loves to tout its female characters and creators, the company's history in front of and behind the scenes is still extremely male-dominated. And as the Marvel universe of characters becomes more relevant, this disparity becomes more apparent. While these heroines have power on the page and on the screen, the power surrounding them is concentrated elsewhere.

The fantastical metaphor of the superhero belies its importance to human morale and identity. Superheroes and heroines, after all, embody the desirable personalities and characteristics we possess, just amplified. Writer Danny Fingeroth suggests that superheroes and heroines symbolize "what we believe is best in ourselves" and act as a "standard to aspire to as well as an individual to be admired."[1] Even fictional villains allow us to experience the feeling of breaking the law without personal consequence. Noted comics writer Grant Morrison makes a similar argument, speculating that the superhero (regardless of gender) holds significant psychic resonance in a world without an optimistic view of the future, providing the reader a surrogate "spiritual leadership"; the best superheroines, for all their supernatural exploits, are connected to universal human experiences.[2] This representation matters, especially to those who may often feel marginalized in culture and society. As Cheo Hodari Coker, executive producer of the MCU Netflix series *Luke Cage*, said in an interview with the *Los Angeles Times* about fellow Marvel property *Black Panther*: "We're now finally having the opportunity to see heroes that look, sound, and feel like us. . . . Growing up, I always loved Luke Skywalker, I always loved Han Solo, but there was always a disconnect because I knew that I could never really be them."[3]

Superheroes and heroines, then, serve a powerful rhetorical purpose, offering their fans the ability to transcend the mundane and embrace multilayered identities that act in ways we can only imagine while still speaking to these universally held experiences and situations. One of these universal experiences that human beings share is the longing to be part of something larger than themselves. Philosopher and author Joseph Campbell described this experience through his exploration of "monomyths," or those larger-than-life ideas that help explain the human relationship both to divinity and to other people. Campbell discovered that although details of specific myths varied across culture and country, universal themes and motifs emerged. Across cultures, genre, and media, we have countless iterations of the "hero with a thousand faces," to paraphrase the title of one of his most influential works.

In *A Rhetoric of Motives*, Kenneth Burke too imagines a new ordering scheme of language and ideas. At the top he places Ideology, followed by Myth. In the Burkeian view, myth is simply not an archetype; nor is it the ultimate hegemonic ideal. Myth is not simply a unified and unchanging set of narratives, as we learn to identify it through such schemas as Greek

1. Fingeroth, *Superman on the Couch*, 14–15.
2. Morrison, *Supergods*, xvii.
3. Kelley, "At the 'Black Panther' Premiere."

or Norse mythology, with their fixed casts of members, participants, and rituals. Rather, Burke argued that mythic images and vocabularies must be "continually reenacted" to account for the addition of new voices or perspectives.[4] Arguably, the contemporary media representations of superheroes and heroines, from the early twentieth-century comic strips to the transmedia-connected universes of today, reinforce and reify these mythic ideas for new audiences. Superheroines, in whatever form they take, not only provide myths of good, evil, and community for readers to engage with but do so through a uniquely gendered lens.

Again, these myths carry power outside their context of origin. Stergios Botzakis speaks to the power and importance of popular culture when he suggests that users of the medium look to it for respite from real-world concerns, for companionship, or as a lens through which they can view their real-world lives.[5] Some popular culture consumers also associate popular culture artifacts with particular moments or experiences in their lives and in doing so ascribe even greater meaning and value to them.[6] Popular culture has value and power because it can be a conduit through which an individual adapts and forms their own identity ("I am a gamer," "I am a Trekkie," etc.) as well as a means of finding commonality and relationships with others and metaphors that provide strength and catharsis in one's own life.

The exquisitely manufactured and presented structure of the Marvel "product" lends itself naturally to this close association between media and self. What we consider in this volume to be the Marvel "product" is a larger cultural hydra composed of many heads. Consider that a Marvel character can appear in multiple comics, video games, mobile apps, television programs, and films with varying levels of consistency and intertextuality between them. The Marvel product is, by definition, a transmedia product because it creates an ecosystem encouraging fans to follow their favorite characters and stories from one media form to another. As Henry Jenkins suggests, "Transmedia storytelling represents a process where integral elements of a fiction get dispersed systematically across multiple delivery channels for the purpose of creating a unified and coordinated entertainment experience. Ideally, each medium makes its own unique contribution to the story."[7]

Jenkins's definition is widely considered foundational in transmedia studies, and it is not difficult to see how franchises like *Star Trek* and *Star*

---

4. Burke, *Rhetoric of Motives*, 118.
5. Botzakis, "Adult Fans."
6. Harrington and Bielby, "Life Course Perspective."
7. Jenkins, "Transmedia Storytelling 101."

Wars reward fans by spreading elements of one consistent narrative across multiple media forms. One can enjoy the streaming *Star Trek: Discovery* series on its own, but if they are familiar with the other series in the franchise—notably the original 1960s series—they will see direct follow-ups to plot points introduced in those shows that carry the narrative from years past forward, and they can enjoy novels and comics and other tie-in properties that expand the world of the primary show and provide greater context to character actions and personalities. In this way, the story is parceled out in different capacities, but everything ties together in a coherent sequential narrative.

Yet, in an age of horizontal integration, where companies like Disney and AT&T become empires through acquiring intellectual property to be leveraged across multiple media channels, our definition of transmedia must evolve from simply being one consistent fiction across multiple channels toward multiple channels of adaptation that influence the larger *cultural sense* of the fiction and the place it inhabits in the popular zeitgeist. Marvel is perhaps one of the strongest examples of our proposed repositioning of transmedia storytelling.

Consider the film *Guardians of the Galaxy*. A few years before its 2014 release, Marvel relaunched the 2008 version of the team of intergalactic scoundrels (which was, itself, a reboot of a very different group of characters from the 1970s) to align more closely with the broad strokes of what the films were doing, matching the composition of characters on the team with those selected for the film and allowing them to partner with Iron Man to become part of the mainstream Marvel Universe, and so forth. After the film's release, those same characters were redesigned and reimagined yet again so that readers who had enjoyed the film would find familiarity on the page. Star-Lord went from relatively obscure also-ran galactic hero to his current incarnation as a pop-music-obsessed ne'er-do-well in the name of corporate synergy. As Jenkins notes, this is one of the core motivating factors for such storytelling, as it allows the holder of media franchises to expand those intellectual properties across a variety of horizontally held platforms.[8]

This transmedia popularity plays out in many ways when it comes to the superheroines under the Marvel banner. In 2014, as part of the original *Spider-Verse* comics event, Marvel introduced an alternate universe version of Peter Parker's late girlfriend Gwen Stacy, who herself gained superpowers while that universe's version of Peter Parker was killed, an inversion of the "main" Marvel Universe story and a sort of reclamation of the character.

8. Jenkins, "Transmedia Storytelling 101."

While the comic was considered a one-off tie-in to the larger event, after fans flooded the internet with art, costumes, and tributes to the character, Marvel not only greenlit Stacy's own comic series but also put the character at the forefront of many of its consumer goods as well as featured roles in the *Marvel Rising* animated series and *Into the Spider-Verse* film. Fans can create their own interpretations of these characters, and fan reactions may in turn influence what the rights holders do.

These interpretations are important and, if anything, help create the ersatz mythological qualities of the characters. We can reinvent the stories of King Arthur or the Journey to the West in a myriad of ways, just as we can reimagine Spider-Man over and over again, after all. However, unlike those stories, the Marvel heroines are decidedly not in the public domain. Rather, they are wholly corporate-owned brands that can be used to sell everything from gum to toys to even an achingly artificial sense of feminist empowerment, as the next chapter illuminates. While the characters are the sum of a variety of different interpretations, media, and styles, this transmedia element largely serves to create different applicable visions of the characters for different audiences as market circumstances warrant.

The Way Forward

To delve into the issue of how Marvel both shapes and reflects outside culture, and to determine the academic and social value of superheroines, this book investigates some of the most unique and powerful superpowered women throughout the near-century-long publishing history of the company as well as its more contemporary and globalized transmedia efforts. Across the book's chapters, we hope to offer context for and answers to address the paradox of why Marvel and other companies that stand to benefit from embracing female audiences seem to hold them at arm's length.

More than this, however, this book has at its core this thesis: the evolution of Marvel's female characters mirrors the development, struggles, and triumphs of women in the real world. More than perhaps any other superhero company, Marvel has at the center of its mission the charge of representing a version of our world drenched in the fantastic—its heroes operate primarily out of the real city of New York, address social and political issues, mourn when we mourn and celebrate when we celebrate. Superheroes and superheroines are a means of reconstructing and redeveloping cultural and mythological languages, but they are the product of human creators influenced by the cultural contexts in which they operate. Therefore, the standards and language of our mythic heroes change as we change, and these characters bear with them the standards of culture as they are ported from one global market to another.

Objectively determining the most popular and relevant characters is ultimately difficult in such a subjective creative medium, and undoubtedly the reader will have their own suggestions about characters who were left out. However, we have given our authors freedom to investigate the characters that speak most to them and their research interests and offer a unique and important lens through which we can interrogate larger issues about feminism and gender roles in the real world. Above all else, these characters help tell the story of a culture—and an archetype—that has changed over time.

The opening chapter by Bryan J. Carr attempts to quickly explain how Marvel's approach to female characters and readers has changed over the years in ways both progressive and regressive, and Meta G. Carstarphen explores how these stories reflect the need for a new trans/linear approach to feminism.

This book is organized into four broad parts. The first is "Introduction: Framing Our Starting Places and Conceptual Origins." As the title implies, we lay the foundation for this volume by offering key definitions and historical contexts. In "Who Has Power, and How Do We Read It?," editors Carr and Carstarphen discuss power and identity as represented in fictional genres such as comics and other media. Next, in "Too Long a Boys' Club: The Superhero Industrial Complex and the Marvel Heroine," Carr traces key turning points in the growth of superheroes in comics, their expansion into other media, and the identity questions they provoke. Last, Carstarphen's "Trans/Linear Feminism: Finding a New Space to Call Home" presents a new construct for connecting feminist theory to imaginative media.

Part 2, "Phenomenal Women: Gender and Feminism," explores how Marvel's superheroines are positioned in unique moments in time, reinvented and reclaimed to challenge problematic existing narratives. In other words, this part focuses on Kairos, a rhetorical principle suggesting that there is an ideal time and place for messages and ideas. In an ongoing, persistent fictional universe that must periodically refresh itself to address continuity problems and inconsistent plotlines, the door is also periodically opened to re-evaluate existing concepts and present them in a new light. It is in this way that the Marvel Universe periodically readapts to the contemporary feminist culture in which it operates. Few characters symbolize this better than Carol "Captain Marvel" Danvers, and J. Richard Stevens and Anna C. Turner explore the character's tumultuous and often regressive development relative to the evolution of feminist thought over the span of nearly half a century. In the second chapter, Kathleen M. Turner Ledgerwood explores Agent Peggy Carter across comics, film, and her titular television program through standpoint theory and makes a case for her unique status as a transgenerational feminist character. Wrapping up part 2, Amanda K. Kehrberg explores how the rejection of traditional superhero trappings allows Jessica Jones to recontextualize what it means to perform the role of "superhero" across television, video games, and comics.

In part 3, "Embodied Power: Otherness, the Body, and the Superheroine," our contributors explore the "body" of the superheroine. These authors consider the innate duality of the heroine and the complexity of feminine identity and probe how various identity characteristics affect both character and reader. Rachel Grant opens this part by exploring the character of Shuri and how she reflects postcolonial feminism and Pan-African identity while challenging colonialist mindsets. Maryanne A. Rhett writes about Kamala Khan, one of the most popular young Marvel heroines and the inheritor of the "Ms. Marvel" title. Khan's portrayal as a teenage girl trying to fit in while also living as a practicing Pakistani American Muslim offers an instructive approach to feminist thought as seen through an Islamic lens. In the final chapter of this section, Stephanie L. Sanders posits an alternate timeline for former NYPD cop and cybernetic "Daughter of the Dragon" Misty Knight. Here, Knight changes jobs from superheroine to campus diversity officer and must negotiate her way through gendered and racialized roles for which her superhero training did not prepare her.

Finally, in part 4, "Answering the Call: Marvel Superheroines as Responses to Cultural Change," authors explore how the Marvel Comics brand has evolved in response to cultural and social forces to reinvent and create new heroines that speak to more relevant lived experiences. The Marvel Comics brand has been around since 1936; however, it has seen significant changes over that time. These chapters explore how the dynamic of the Marvel heroine changes over time in response to cultural forces. Julie A. Davis and Robert Westerfelhaus interrogate the intersection between the sexualization of Natasha "Black Widow" Romanoff and how the context of her role as a former Soviet spy has changed as global geopolitics have. Next, Mildred F. Perreault and Gregory P. Perreault explore how Pepper Potts's professional and personal femininity is performed across transmedia channels and through fan reinterpretations. CarrieLynn D. Reinhard then chronicles the peculiar case of Doreen "Squirrel Girl" Greene, a parody character who went from a running gag to a STEM-oriented transmedia superheroine in her own right. Finally, Annika Hagley wraps up with a return to the character Carol Danvers, who began these chapters, through a powerful exploration of feminist trauma theory in a post-9/11 context.

In the end, our goal in this book is to ask what Marvel's superheroines can teach us about our culture (popular and otherwise) and how these teachings reflect the real, lived experiences of women. We also wish to provide a means through which we can go beyond the surface-level readings of superhero texts to explore the complex subtextual power relationships behind them. We hope with this volume to provide a work that stands at the intersection of the complex constellation of womanhood. In doing so, we invoke mythological, practical, social, feminist, and rhetorical perspectives, hoping that they can collectively shape and inspire larger discussions and investigations.

Bibliography

Botzakis, Stergios. "Adult Fans of Comic Books: What They Get Out of Reading." *Journal of Adolescent & Adult Literacy* 58, no. 1 (2009): 50–59.

Burke, Kenneth. *A Rhetoric of Motives*. Berkeley: University of California Press, 1969.

Fingeroth, Danny. *Superman on the Couch: What Superheroes Really Tell Us about Ourselves and Our Society*. New York: Continuum International, 2004.

Harrington, C. Lee, and Denise Bielby. "A Life Course Perspective on Fandom." *International Journal of Cultural Studies* 13, no. 5 (2010): 429–50.

Jenkins, Henry. "Transmedia Storytelling 101." *Henry Jenkins: Confessions of an Aca-Fan* (blog), March 21, 2007. http://henryjenkins.org/blog/2007/03/transmedia_storytelling_101.html.

Kelley, Sonaiya. "At the 'Black Panther' Premiere, Representation Is Everything." *Los Angeles Times,* January 30, 2018. https://www.latimes.com/entertainment/movies/la-et-mn-black-panther-world-premiere-20180130-story.html.

Morrison, Grant. *Supergods*. New York: Spiegel & Grau, 2011.

CHAPTER 2

Too Long a Boys' Club

The Superhero Industrial Complex and the Marvel Heroine

Bryan J. Carr

Near the end of Marvel Studios' blockbuster *Avengers: Endgame,* Carol "Captain Marvel" Danvers appears to a battered and terrified Peter "Spider-Man" Parker, asking him to hand over the hero's makeshift Infinity Gauntlet in the hopes of getting the device and its reality-altering stones to a time tunnel and away from the murderous despot Thanos, who wants to once again use it to erase the heroes and the innocents they protect from reality. Worried, Parker looks at the encroaching, ravenous armies of Thanos and tells the elder hero, "I don't know how you're gonna get it through all that."[1] On cue, fellow Marvel heroines Wanda Maximoff, Okoye, Valkyrie, Pepper Potts, Mantis, Shuri, Gamora, Nebula, and The Wasp appear to reassure Parker that Danvers is not alone and that they will clear a path for her. In a dramatic shot, all the heroines are placed in the frame as they march toward their foes, using energy blasts and martial artistry to take down the hordes, with Danvers flying through.

As executive producer Trin Tranh indicated in an interview with *Slashfilm,* the scene, which got its own glowing featurette on home video copies of *Endgame,* was clearly meant to act as a moment of empowerment and a celebration of Marvel's cadre of female heroes—in Tranh's words: "I've never

---

1. Russo and Russo, *Marvel's Avengers.*

seen that many women arrive on set just to see that moment. Because they were so proud they were involved in it, but they were so happy that they're able to see something like that. To sort of pay tribute to our female heroines in the MCU and give them a moment was very personal to me."[2] Co-writer Christopher Markus concurred in the same interview: "All the women—and there were a great many of them—from the crew and the offices all came and they were like 'This is fucking awesome,' and it was."

The scene may have played well in multiplexes around the country in the moment, but many ultimately found it empty. Critic Caroline Siede said that the scene "misses the mark so badly it could only come from a studio that made 20 movies before it got to one with a female lead and then acted like we should all be grateful for its trailblazing feminism."[3] Indeed, *Captain Marvel*, the Marvel Cinematic Universe's first female-led film, had been released only a few months prior to the hero's big appearance in *Endgame*. Similar scenes of the majority-male cast banding together were treated with substantially less knowing fanfare. As Siede adds: "That's the MCU in a nutshell: When 10 women are briefly onscreen together it's a Big Moment. When eight men have extended scenes together it's just business as usual."[4] *Rotten Tomatoes* editor Jacqueline Coley winced during a discussion of the scene, agreeing with the sentiment that the scene tried too hard and adding: "It was so female thirsty, either give me a female *Avengers* or don't."[5] The scene was even the inspiration for a season-long running gag in the violent superhero satire *The Boys*, where the evil Vought Corporation that owns the show's morally bankrupt superheroes forces a similar sequence into its own big-budget film with an accompanying "Girls Get It Done" marketing campaign (that one of its featured heroines is revealed over the course of the series to be a Nazi arguably adds to the gag).[6]

Regardless of one's opinions on the scene itself, in the context of the film—which features significantly less screen time for its female heroes and includes a scene where founding Avenger Black Widow sacrifices herself to preserve her male counterpart Hawkeye and gives him a chance to return to his family—it is easy to see how it might ring hollow.[7] Of course, this is far from the only indignity inflicted on Widow in the MCU. Consider also a scene in *Avengers: Age of Ultron* where she laments that her inability to have

2. Siede, "Avengers."
3. Siede, "Avengers."
4. Siede, "Avengers."
5. "Avengers: Endgame Discussion."
6. Abramovitch, "We're Living in the Dumbest Dystopia."
7. Sperling, "Pow Per View."

children as a result of forced sterilization makes her a "monster" on par with the Hulk.[8] Coupled with Marvel's reticence toward female leads in its films up to that point, the "girl power" moment feels, at best, like pandering—and while recent additions to the canon like a standalone *Black Widow* film, the Scarlet Witch series *WandaVision,* and the Gemma Chan–led ensemble of *The Eternals* have shown a renewed commitment to the company's female heroes, these changes still have come late in the franchise's existence.

The debate over the scene ultimately serves as an illustrative microcosm of larger questions surrounding female heroes across the superhero industry, of which Marvel is the biggest brand component. The genre, for many years, had been and still is too often considered one primarily for boys and young men, to the extent that the companies behind these characters have often pretended that their female characters and fans simply do not exist. The marketing blitz for the *Age of Ultron* and *Guardians of the Galaxy* films featured little to no merchandise for their respective female heroes Black Widow and Gamora—a surprising omission for a company so commodity-friendly as Disney, and one that prompted backlash from fans and the film's cast.[9] *Iron Man 3* director Shane Black revealed in an interview that Marvel's corporate arm demanded that he scale back his original plan to have a prominent female villain in the film because "the toy won't sell as well if it's a female."[10] According to an anonymous former Marvel marketing specialist, this was not an isolated opinion and extended to the parent company, which saw Marvel as delivering a desired predominantly male demographic to complement its existing and all-powerful Disney Princess line and other merchandise aimed primarily at young girls.[11] Initial attempts at making Marvel apparel for young women in the juniors-focused "Marvel HERoes" line landed with a thud thanks to sexist T-shirt slogans like "My Boyfriend is a Superhero" and "I Only Date Heroes" over images of exclusively male characters.[12] While the *Captain Marvel* film and the merchandise for the as-of-this-writing unreleased *Black Widow* standalone film have changed this model by offering a wide array of merchandise, the message for many years was clear—superheroes are for boys and for boys alone.

Yet, this sentiment is consistently not supported by evidence. In fact, while data are notoriously difficult to come by unless released by the publishers, all evidence indicates that girls and women like science fiction and

8. Whedon, *Marvel's Avengers.*
9. MacDonald, "Report."
10. McMillan, "'Iron Man 3' Female Villain."
11. Mouse, "Invisible Women."
12. Mouse, "Invisible Women."

superheroes just as much as, if not more than, their male counterparts—regardless of what media executives might think. Digital retailers like ComiXology have reported record growth among female readers, and in January 2021 over half of Facebook users who engaged with superhero content on the site were female.[13] Competitor DC Comics found success with its DC Super Hero Girls line in the mid-2010s, with graphic novels featuring kid-friendly versions of the popular female heroes regularly outselling adult male-oriented prestige DC titles like *Suicide Squad, Watchmen,* and *Preacher.*[14] Finally, while it took all too long to actually arrive in theaters, Marvel's first female-led feature in the form of *Captain Marvel* eclipsed DC's *Wonder Woman* financially as the highest-grossing film starring a female superhero, taking in over a billion dollars worldwide and proving that an audience for Marvel's female heroes clearly existed.[15] So if that market is there, why has Marvel been so hesitant until just recently to sell to it?

Here it is important to understand that when we refer to the "superhero industrial complex," it is not just comics, film, or merchandise but rather the combined economic and marketing power of all the above as well as broader licensing and multimedia concerns. A transmedia approach to understanding these characters requires that we look not only at one medium but rather at how the multitude of reference points draw an outline of these characters and who they are for. So too should we understand that this multifaceted approach to intellectual property allows for entrée points into these fictional worlds that are not uniform. Many of Marvel's staunchest fans, male or female, have never picked up a comic book but instead follow their favorites across films, TV shows, and video games. In that light, it is hard to draw a direct, connective line between the circumstances of the industry and the representation of its female characters. Still, comics provide a necessary starting point for understanding the complex confluence of circumstances that result in the current intersection between Marvel's female characters and their fans.

A "Herstory" of Marvel

While the Marvel behemoth has in many ways evolved beyond its comics publishing arm, this aspect of the company remains significant to its his-

---

13. O'Connell, "Women Are the Changing Face"; Schenker, "Demo-Graphics."
14. Pulliam-Moore, "DC Super Hero Girls"; Surrey, "DC Entertainment's Super Hero Girls."
15. Rubin, "'Captain Marvel.'"

tory and the present discussion. The comics arm of Marvel dates back to the 1930s in its original incarnation as Timely Comics, but for our purposes its rise to the forefront of the popular consciousness with the Fantastic Four and the then new "Marvel Comics" branding is of primary interest—as it is here that characters like The Incredible Hulk, Spider-Man, Captain America, and the X-Men all come to establish the Marvel brand in the hearts and minds of readers. The brand, which came to stand for stories featuring comparatively complex and down-to-earth heroes struggling with their own real-world problems and social issues, became wildly popular with college students and in the counterculture movement as a result of the stories' more liberalized and humanist tendencies.[16] The characters grappled with real-world social and political problems: Iron Man grappled with his legacy as an arms manufacturer, Spider-Man struggled with relationships and money, and the X-Men served as a malleable metaphor for generations of struggles for equality. These aspects still exist in Marvel stories in a meaningful way to this day and speak to the enduring cultural power of the company.

The story of the Marvel women, as you will see throughout this volume, is comparatively more complex. This volume spends a great deal of time discussing the fictional characters that make up the stories Marvel tells across its transmedia output, so let us take a moment and look at the flesh-and-blood women behind the scenes first. Women have been a crucial part of the history of Marvel off the page, from editors like Jo Duffy, Katie Kubert, Emily Shaw, and Sana Amanat to artists and creators like Gail Simone, Kelly Sue DeConnick, Sara Pichelli, G. Willow Wilson, Roxane Gay, and the Japanese art team Gurihiru (many of whom are associated with many of the characters in this book). Despite this, that history is still predominantly male-centric. Women played a significant role in the comics industry during World War II, taking over many art, writing, and publishing duties—but were ultimately replaced by their male counterparts as they returned home.[17] Some who stayed in the industry served as secretaries who also took on responsibilities like inking, lettering, and editing comic stories—acts often largely unrecognized for many years until Trina Robbins began the "Friends of Lulu" project highlighting the work of female cartoonists and creators.[18] Today, while the number of female creators has increased, data from May 2019 showed that only 14.8 percent of the total credits in Marvel's output in the early months of that year went to female creators (with 0.08 percent of the credits going to nonbinary individuals), with women drasti-

16. Howe, *Marvel Comics*; O'Neil, "How the Cold War."
17. Wright, *Comic Book Nation*, 33.
18. Katz, "Women and Mainstream Comic Books," 101.

cally underrepresented in every capacity except the assistant editor position and most severely underrepresented in art duties.[19] These numbers, the most recent available as of this writing, reflect a steady and consistent trend at Marvel—women are a presence, but they are dwarfed in representation by their male counterparts.

Numbers tell only part of the story, of course. The work of these women and its impact on the characters and stories discussed in this book cannot be overstated. While Marvel has never had a female publisher, its business was nonetheless influenced by a female publisher: DC's Jenette Kahn. Kahn was hired by DC Comics as publisher in 1976. In addition to aggressively positioning the company's characters in films and other media, Kahn also famously pushed to move the company toward a "creative rights" model that announced a royalty plan for creators whose comics sold over 100,000 copies and led to greater creative morale. Marvel would echo that plan soon after, in no small part because Kahn was aggressive in trying to poach its talent.[20] Other women had a tremendous impact on how Marvel approached its female characters and marketed them in a transmedia context. Gail Simone parlayed her early success writing internet humor columns and the website *Women in Refrigerators*, a blog chronicling the women who were raped, maimed, and killed to further the stories of male heroes, into a wildly successful writing career and started an important discussion about the way female heroes were treated in comics.[21] Sara Pichelli's art was crucial to launching the now wildly popular character of Miles Morales, whom she co-created in the original *Ultimate Spider-Man* series.[22] Without the guiding hand of Kelly Sue DeConnick, Captain Marvel's relaunch and subsequent success would have been substantially less likely—the costume the character sports in the film and merchandise is a riff on a comics redesign that DeConnick cleverly forced Marvel's hand to pay for.[23] As more women were encouraged to join the field, the industries surrounding it also came to include more women. Former DC Comics editor Heidi MacDonald launched *The Beat,* to this day arguably the definitive blog for comics news, in 2004.[24] Victoria Alonso, the executive vice president of production for Marvel Studios, was instrumental in working for years to get the company's female

19. Hanley, "Women in Comics."
20. Tucker, "Slugfest," 142; Wright, *Comic Book Nation,* 262.
21. Abad-Santos, "Gail Simone."
22. Dominguez, "Miles Morales Co-creator."
23. Polo, "Captain Marvel's Mohawk Costume."
24. Weldon, *The Caped Crusade,* 261–62.

heroes on screen, as well.[25] In short—Marvel (and the comics industry) as we understand it in the contemporary context would not exist today without the women working behind the scenes and on the page.

The Characters

Scholars and long-term comics readers can likely identify distinct eras of Marvel's female heroes. In the 1960s and 1970s, Marvel's heroines were certainly women of action—Sue Storm helped villains alongside her ersatz family in the pages of *Fantastic Four,* and the Black Widow vexed Iron Man first as a villainous femme fatale and later as an ally. But this era of Marvel woman was just as likely to be a bystander or doe-eyed love interest. Millie the Model starred in her own line of romantic comedy books; Gwen Stacy was Peter Parker's first and idealized love, and her death at the hands of the Green Goblin would haunt him for years of storylines to come; and Pepper Potts (whom you will read about in Mildred and Gregory Perreault's chapter later in this book) dreamed of nothing but trying to marry her dashing billionaire boss, Tony Stark (if only he would stop running off each time his bodyguard Iron Man showed up).

From the 1970s onward, female heroes began taking a greater role in the action. The powerful weather-controlling mutant Storm regularly led the X-Men on missions. Colleen Wing and Misty Knight fought crime as the Daughters of the Dragon, and Bruce Banner's cousin Jennifer Walters balanced her career as a lawyer with her responsibilities of breaking bad guys (and occasionally, in John Byrne's run on the series, the fourth wall) as She-Hulk. Carol Danvers used her cosmic powers to do battle as Ms. Marvel, but as you will see in J. Richard Stevens and Anna Turner's chapter, Marvel editorial once again had severe differences of opinion on how to handle a female hero that led to unfortunate and ill-advised results. In the 1970s an unfortunate Avengers storyline pitted the male superheroes against their female allies—as the women call out their male team members' chauvinism and sexism, it is ultimately revealed that they were duped by a villain posing as a "female liberator."[26] In 1972 Marvel attempted a line of comics aimed at female readers, produced by female artists and writers, that revived some of their defunct female characters like Shanna the She-Devil

---

25. Modiano, "Marvel Exec Victoria Alonso."
26. Wright, *Comic Book Nation,* 250.

and created new ones like The Cat and Night Nurse. The books did not sell well and were canceled shortly thereafter.[27]

In recent years the company has taken steps to diversify its publishing line with a more intersectional approach to identity. The 2014 introduction of the teenage Pakistani American superheroine Kamala "Ms. Marvel" Khan, the co-creation of Marvel editor Sana Amanat and writer G. Willow Wilson, is arguably the watershed moment. Kamala Khan's polymorphic abilities represented the superpower not only to grow and extend her limbs but also to change her body as she grappled with her own sense of identity as a Muslim teenager in Jersey City. The character appeared across Marvel's transmedia output after her debut, appearing not only in the comics but also in the *Marvel Rising* animated series and video games like 2020's *Marvel's Avengers,* in which she took the lead role.[28] Other characters like the queer Latina superheroine America Chavez, the computer science major Squirrel Girl, tween supergenius Moon Girl, and many other characters have been part of the company's efforts to attract a female audience. In some cases, female heroes even took over for their male counterparts. Long-time love interest Jane Foster took over the role of Thor in 2014 and remained in the role for a long period as she battled the foes of Asgard along with a terminal cancer diagnosis. Carol Danvers was promoted from Ms. Marvel to the rank of Captain in 2012, and an alternate-universe Gwen Stacy who not only was alive and well but had spider-powers of her own became a surprise smash hit for Marvel in the form of Ghost Spider, a.k.a. "Spider-Gwen"—a character who would appear in the Academy Award–winning film *Spider-Man: Into the Spider-Verse,* in 2018.

The Economics of Marvel Heroines

Women and girls have always enjoyed comics. For a long time, everyone did. During the so-called Golden Age of the medium, comic books reaped the benefits of being an affordable entertainment medium in an age before television dominated the American psyche, enjoyed by readers of all ages and genders. That began to change thanks, in large part, to psychologist Frederic Wertham's crusade against the medium in the 1950s. Wertham's publication of the 1954 book *Seduction of the Innocent* was a watershed text in American pop culture history that nonetheless made inaccurate and under-researched claims and broad, sweeping generalizations about the moral

27. Wright, *Comic Book Nation,* 251.
28. Crystal Dynamics, *Marvel's Avengers.*

purity of the medium. The result was the Comics Code Authority, a self-regulating industry body put in place to police the content in comic books. The Code ostensibly served to protect readers (and more importantly publishers) from the social consequences of objectionable content like sex and violence.[29] In practice, however, their policies were extremely restrictive, leading to less creative and more repetitive stories that were overly simplistic in their narratives and morality. While this led to something of a resurgence for the superhero genre (largely because it was easy to uphold the Code's requirements in the genre), it also led to many creators leaving or simply eschewing work for the big comics publishers like Marvel altogether in favor of less restrictive, independent paths to publication.[30]

As newsstand sales continued to decrease both directly and indirectly because of these changes, the means through which fans accessed their favorite comics also changed. As the underground comix movement showed, there was money in taking comics directly to the consumer without a newsstand distributor in the middle setting the terms of the arrangement. In the 1970s Marvel and other publishers shifted toward a direct sales model where their books were placed primarily in stores specializing in comics retail.[31] While this had immediate financial benefits (and lower risk) for the company, it also created a culture in which the stores were inhabited only by the most hardcore fans—fans who were often overwhelmingly male, resulting in a form of gatekeeping that made many female readers feel unwelcome and uncomfortable. Such gatekeeping still often extends online with antiprogressive and antifeminist rhetoric like that seen in the 2018 "Comicsgate" movement that harassed many prominent female fans and creators on social media.[32] Far from being only gatekeeping, male fans criticizing women brought into the medium for their lack of knowledge or authenticity as fans, the product itself can also be off-putting for girls and women looking to enjoy the medium. The way female heroes are drawn in comics is a recurring issue. Writer Barbara Kesel has noted that many young women feel "universally repulsed" by the exaggerated proportions and scant outfits of mainstream superhero stories.[33] Artist June Brigman laments that "skimpy outfits and big boobs" have become visual shorthand for "a sexy woman" in comics regardless of the aesthetic quality of the art.[34]

29. Abad-Santos, "Insane History."
30. Wright, *Comic Book Nation*.
31. Tucker, *Slugfest*, 134–36.
32. Riesman, "Comicsgate"; Schenkel, "I Guess Comics."
33. Katz, "Women," 114.
34. Katz, "Women."

This gatekeeping extends to decisions at Marvel's creative corporate level as well. In 2015 Marvel artist Frank Cho was criticized for drawing a sexually provocative version of Spider-Gwen for a fan. After the controversy, Cho doubled down by drawing other female characters in the same pose on other books and posting them online.[35] In 2017 Marvel vice president David Gabriel was roundly criticized for statements insinuating that underwhelming sales of some comics could be blamed on their more diverse casts and that readers and retailers "didn't want diversity" (Marvel was ultimately the top comics publisher that year, commanding over 36 percent market share in what was a down year for the industry as a whole).[36]

For these reasons, and the comparative friendliness of bookstores and in-school book fairs, comics outside the superhero genre tend to resonate not only with female readers but with readers more generally. While specialty comic stores still accounted for $525 million of the industry's total $1.2 billion take in 2019, traditional booksellers and other channels eclipsed them at $570 million that year.[37] Nestled in the data is growth for digital storefronts like ComiXology that offer consumers the same comics they can get at a store, delivered immediately to their tablets or other reading devices. While digital sales account for only a small percentage of the market overall, there is data to suggest that many of the people reading digital comics are outside the traditional or stereotypical white-male-dominated market. Indeed, comics featuring women and people of color do well on digital platforms. A 2015 sale on the ComiXology platform resulted in female-led comics taking seven of the top ten Marvel best-seller spots on the platform.[38] Insinuations that female heroes do not sell and female readers do not read comics are, ultimately, ill informed at best.

The Role of Transmedia in the Marvel Superheroine

You would be forgiven for wondering why so much time is spent on the nuances and intricacies of the comics industry in a book ultimately about transmedia depictions of fictional superheroes. Yet the comics, while certainly not the primary generator of revenue for Marvel and Disney, particularly compared with the merchandise and film side of the equation, act as the de facto intellectual property mill for the company, where new stories

---

35. Asselin, "Outrage and Complacency."
36. Abad-Santos, "Outrage"; Schedeen, "Marvel Comics."
37. Griepp and Miller, "Comics and Graphic Novel Sales."
38. Grieep and Miller, "Comics"; Polo, "Comixology's Numbers."

and heroes are developed and can be routinely harvested for other media. At all levels of the company, until recently, female readers and characters were a novelty rather than a priority. Even now, the company struggles to make those steps as it tries to reconcile a film division aimed at the broadest possible audiences with a tremendous female following with a comics division still aimed at an older male audience and an overly conservative executive leadership that is slow to change.

For this reason, it is helpful to once again think about the way we defined *transmedia* at the beginning of this volume. Instead of telling one story in pieces across multiple media, what Marvel does is create an ecosystem in which every piece of media adds to a larger, metatextual definition of who its characters are and what they represent. Captain Marvel in the comics must be careful not to stray too wildly from what fans might expect in the films, for instance—which is why casting her as the primary ideological antagonist in the *Civil War II* storyline that came out near the film's release seemed so ill advised. Marvel's ecosystem requires a series of contact points at which consumers must spend money, and keeping consumers invested in that ecosystem requires at least some degree of consistency in adaptation. However, those contact points remain influenced by recalcitrant attitudes toward gatekeeping and gender roles that can often backlash, the loudness of which is often inversely proportional to its size. If *Captain Marvel* sold a billion dollars in tickets at the box office, how big can the group of fans vocally upset about it truly be? Yet these attitudes are nonetheless the source of occasional reactionary panic among the top tier of Marvel's executive offices (and illustrate a lack of knowledge about their genre's own history—for instance, much of what is now considered superhero and science fiction fandom is owed to the women who wrote zines and fanfiction about the original *Star Trek* series in the 1960s and, in so doing, helped keep it on the air).[39] What is more important, however, is this: female fans keep coming to the material; the movies, comics, and merchandise keep selling; and the characters continue to resonate despite an institutional structure seemingly designed to make that extremely difficult.

Marvel's heroines are an example of how the definition of feminism and female identity is refracted and changed across the prism of a transmedia ecosystem. They are also an example of how gender roles are negotiated and challenged. But that alone is not reason enough to put a volume like this together. Rather, the meaning of these heroines transcends any one portrayal or depiction and reflects the lived experiences of real women on a

---

39. McNally, "Women Who Love 'Star Trek.'"

broader metatextual level. This essay—and this book—argues that the Black Widow, Gamora, Captain Marvel, and all their powerful sisters represent a phenomenon that is profoundly relevant to our understanding of identity, feminism, power, and gender. The imaginative presence and reconstitution of these superheroines in this historical moment invite more probing analyses of both our understanding of myth and of the realities they can mask at a time where the investigation of power and womanhood in our media has never been more relevant.

Bibliography

Abad-Santos, Alex. "How Gail Simone Changed the Way We Think About Female Superheroes." *Vox*, October 17, 2014. https://www.vox.com/2014/10/17/6981457/gail-simone-dc-comics-female-superheroes.

———. "The Insane History of How American Paranoia Ruined and Censored Comic Books." *Vox*, March 13, 2015. https://www.vox.com/2014/12/15/7326605/comic-book-censorship.

———. "The Outrage Over Marvel's Alleged Diversity Blaming, Explained." *Vox*, April 8, 2017. https://www.vox.com/culture/2017/4/4/15169572/marvel-diversity-outrage-gabriel.

Abramovitch, Seth. "'We're Living in the Dumbest Dystopia': 'The Boys' Boss on His Superhero Hit." *Hollywood Reporter*, October 15, 2020. https://www.hollywoodreporter.com/live-feed/superheroes-are-inherently-maga-the-boys-boss-on-his-zeitgeisty-hit.

Asselin, Janelle. "Outrage and Complacency: Responses to Frank Cho's Spider-Gwen Cover." *Comics Alliance*, April 15, 2015. https://comicsalliance.com/responses-to-frank-cho-spider-gwen-cover/.

"Avengers: Endgame Discussion (Spoilers): Big Moments, Shocks, Surprises" [Video]. *Rotten Tomatoes*, April 27, 2019. https://www.youtube.com/watch?v=C2ze5ibWJZ8&t=1562s&ab_channel=RottenTomatoes.

Crystal Dynamics. *Marvel's Avengers*. Square Enix, 2020. Multiplatform.

Dominguez, Noah. "Miles Morales Co-creator Shares Her Contribution to Into the Spider-Verse." *CBR.com*, December 29, 2018. https://www.cbr.com/miles-morales-sara-pichelli-into-the-spider-verse/.

Griepp, Milton, and John Jackson Miller. "Comics and Graphic Novel Sales Top $1.2 Billion in 2019." *Comichron*, n.d. https://comichron.com/yearlycomicssales/industrywide/2019-industrywide.html.

Hanley, Tim. "Women in Comics, by the Numbers: Winter 2019." *The Beat: The Blog of Comics Culture*, May 16, 2019. https://www.comicsbeat.com/women-in-comics-numbers-winter-2019/.

Howe, Sean. *Marvel Comics: The Untold Story*. New York: Harper Perennial, 2012.

Katz, Jill S. "Women and Mainstream Comic Books." *International Journal of Comic Art* 10, no. 2 (2008): 101–47.

MacDonald, Heidi. "Report: One Marvel Exec Blocked Making Black Widow Toys." *The Beat: The Blog of Comics Culture*, September 2, 2015. https://www.comicsbeat.com/report-one-marvel-exec-blocked-making-black-widow-toys/.

McMillan, Graeme. "'Iron Man 3' Female Villain Was Nixed over Toy Fears, Says Director." *Hollywood Reporter,* May 16, 2016. https://www.hollywoodreporter.com/heat-vision/original-iron-man-3-villain-894649.

McNally, Victoria. "Women Who Love 'Star Trek' Are the Reason That Modern Fandom Exists." *Revelist,* September 8, 2016. https://www.revelist.com/tv/star-trek-fandom-50th/4643.

Modiano, Alexander. "Marvel Exec Victoria Alonso Welcomes a Female 'Future of Hollywood' at Archer Film Festival." *Hollywood Reporter,* May 23, 2019. https://www.hollywoodreporter.com/news/marvel-exec-victoria-alonso-welcomes-female-future-hollywood-at-archer-film-festival-1213370.

Mouse, Annie N. "Invisible Women: Why Marvel's Gamora & Black Widow Were Missing from Merchandise, and What We Can Do About It." *The Mary Sue,* April 7, 2015. https://www.themarysue.com/invisible-women/.

O'Connell, A. J. "Women Are the Changing Face of Comics Fandom." *The Establishment,* December 8, 2015. https://medium.com/the-establishment/women-are-the-changing-face-of-comic-fandom-2170006efd01.

O'Neil, Tegan. "How the Cold War Saved Marvel and Birthed a Generation of Superheroes." *The AV Club,* March 31, 2016. https://www.avclub.com/how-the-cold-war-saved-marvel-and-birthed-a-generation-1798246215.

Pearson, Ben. "'Avengers: Endgame' Final Battle Oral History: How the Biggest Scene in Comic Book Movie History Came Together." *Slashfilm,* November 1, 2019. https://www.slashfilm.com/avengers-endgame-final-battle-oral-history/2/.

Polo, Susana. "Captain Marvel's Mohawk Costume Is the Result of a Comic Creator's Bet." *Polygon,* December 3, 2018. https://www.polygon.com/2018/9/18/17873482/captain-marvel-trailer-costume-mohawk-kelly-sue-deconnick.

———. "Comixology's Numbers Indicate Female Characters Dominate Digital Comics Sales." *Polygon,* April 14, 2015. https://www.polygon.com/2015/4/14/8410771/digital-comics-female-characters.

Pulliam-Moore, Charles. "*DC Super Hero Girls* Is DC's Most Popular New Series." *Io9,* July 14, 2017. https://io9.gizmodo.com/dc-super-hero-girls-is-dcs-best-selling-new-series-1796936850.

Riesman, Abraham. "Comicsgate Is a Nightmare Tearing Comics Fandom Apart—So What Happens Next?" *Vulture,* August 29, 2018. https://www.vulture.com/2018/08/comicsgate-a-comic-book-harassment-campaign-is-growing.html.

Rubin, Rebecca. "'Captain Marvel' Smashes $1 Billion Milestone at Global Box Office." *Variety,* April 3, 2019. https://variety.com/2019/film/news/captain-marvel-1-billion-box-office-1203175093/.

Russo, Joseph, and Anthony Russo, dirs. *Marvel's Avengers: Endgame.* Burbank, CA: Marvel Studios, 2019.

Schedeen, Jesse. "Marvel Comics Is the Top-Selling Publisher of 2017." *IGN,* January 16, 2018. https://www.ign.com/articles/2018/01/16/marvel-comics-is-the-top-selling-publisher-of-2017.

Schenkel, Katie. "'I Guess Comics Aren't for Me'—My Own Story of Childhood Gatekeeping and Why Just Making Girl-Friendly Comics Is Not Enough." *The Mary Sue,* September 4, 2014. https://www.themarysue.com/comics-gatekeeping-why-making-girl-comics-isnt-enough/.

Schenker, Brett. "Demo-Graphics: Comic Fandom on Facebook—US Edition." *Graphic Policy,* January 4, 2021. https://graphicpolicy.com/2021/01/04/demo-graphics-comic-fandom-facebook-us-edition-16-2-2/.

Siede, Caroline. "*Avengers: Endgame* Doesn't Earn Its Big 'Girl Power' Moment." *The AV Club*, April 29, 2019. https://film.avclub.com/avengers-endgame-doesn-t-earn-its-big-girl-power-mom-1834366317.

Sperling, Daniel. "Pow per View: Captain America Beats Iron Man and Thor for the Most Camera Time in A-List-Filled Movie Avengers: Endgame." *The Sun*, April 24, 2019. https://www.thesun.co.uk/tvandshowbiz/8932134/captain-america-most-screen-time-avengers-endgame/.

Surrey, Miles. "DC Entertainment's Super Hero Girls Could Be Over $1 Billion Brand for Warner Bros." *Yahoo News*, May 25, 2016. https://news.yahoo.com/dc-entertainments-super-hero-girls-155700356.html.

Tucker, Reed. *Slugfest: Inside the Epic 50-Year Battle Between Marvel and DC*. New York: Hachette, 2017.

Weldon, Glen. *The Caped Crusade: Batman and the Rise of Nerd Culture*. New York: Simon & Schuster, 2016.

Whedon, Joss, dir. *Marvel's Avengers: Age of Ultron*. Burbank, CA: Marvel Studios, 2015.

Wright, Bradford W. *Comic Book Nation*. Baltimore, MD: Johns Hopkins University Press, 2001.

CHAPTER 3

Trans/Linear Feminism

Finding a New Space to Call Home

Meta G. Carstarphen

White hair in unruly waves cuffs her rich brown face. She flies in on a majestic angle, adorned in the purple and gold colors of royalty. "Glorious," she says, as much to herself as to T'Challa, the Black Panther. "I have been away from Africa far too long."[1]

Ororo, or as she is more commonly known, Storm, has arrived in Wakanda to enact heroism in a place she calls home. Fans who know parts of her story have watched Storm enact her powers within the pages of comic book fantasies as well as in big-screen renditions of the *X-Men* cinematic series. Her powers to subdue forceful weather conditions, or to call them into furious being, have yet to find a central role in the ever-expanding Marvel Universe of superbadness. Is she a mutant, or something more? Is she a descendant of royalty, or is she an obedient, pliant member of a team, fighting for a seemingly moveable standard of justice, with changing alliances and loyalties?

Storm, like every other character of the superhuman imagination, gets to become reinvented through the craftsmanship of her creators, as well as within the parameters of the various media that give her identity and the

---

1. Priest, Velluto, and Almond, "Stürm and Drang."

illusion of substance. But Storm, like every female superhero of the imagined universe, lives and exists because of the willingness of fans to embrace the impossible, the improbable, and to make it palpable.

I use a brief snippet of Storm's story as emblematic of a larger narrative that envelops both character and audience and, more specifically, a female reader-responder. I argue that a narrative such as Storm's exists because of the lived experiences of actual women. I make this claim in spite of the specific areas of control over her story that have been clearly managed by individual writers, artists, creators, and corporate marketing campaigns. And because of this, I want to suggest that women, in turn, can view superheroine texts in a fashion singularly distinctive from male readers, if they choose to. That choice, which I describe as a *trans/linear feminism*, manifests as our agency to imagine power in ways that remain palpable, yet unseen.

Digital Feminism: Filling Spaces in Bits and Pieces

Digital spaces offer many compartments in which to experience and share identity. In one example, the social media profiles of Chinese women portray public-facing narratives that connect Confucian principles of gentle engagement with feminist empowerment and subtle resistance.[2] These autonomous descriptors, created by individual women united ethereally by a common ethos, speak of both a unity and a dis/unity of being. The "she" of each profile expresses agency in communicating the who she imagines herself to be, while at the same time forming a piece of a cultural chorus. This feminism expresses a core tenet of feminist theory, writ large. Recognizable in Virginia Woolf's plea for a "room of her own,"[3] as well as in Alice Walker's search for her mother's "garden,"[4] in which she found her own creative space of celebration, voice is everything.

And yet, digital spaces present additional hazards for women to be known and their voices to be heard. Online harassment abounds, and online trolls threaten harm and abuse. These realities become more complex for women of color using digital channels to communicate their views, opinions, research, and truths. Ethical boundaries blur, as some audiences use these materials in the "commons" of digital discourse to borrow, without the protections of limited attribution or credit.[5] Assessing value for intellec-

---

2. Chang, Ren, and Yang, "Virtual Gender Asylum?"
3. Woolf, *Room of One's Own.*
4. Walker, *Our Mothers' Gardens.*
5. Adair and Nakamura, "Digital Afterlives."

tual work is, at best, fraught with hazards and systemic fault lines. At the center of this question is whether the labor of women—especially women of color—will be valued, credited, and rewarded.

Digital feminism suggests that it is marked by a performance and articulation of feminist ideals through acts that can be marked by what we have recognized as feminism. These include networking with others who self-identify as allies or joining groups with agendas consistent with ideals of the movement and participating through social media in women-centered social justice campaigns.[6]

Feminism made visible in digital spaces also invites uncomfortable comparisons and latent biases. The technology of representation has morphed, especially in the twenty-first century, into multiple channels and applications. TikTok, Instagram, Twitter, Snapchat, WhatsApp, Facebook's latest version, and those apps yet to be discovered have created audiences across global boundaries more effortlessly than legacy media of print, film, and video. Yet, despite this diverse reach, we tend to operate, as one scholar observes, as if a strict dichotomy exists between the technologically savvy women in developed countries and those technologically bereft women in less dominant regions.[7] And while we can materially measure "haves" and "have-nots," we have no formula for measuring ingenuity and creativity.

A Linear Trap of Feminist Historiography

Quickly, name three famous women. The speed and comfort with which you can evoke an answer may depend on the layered information you have already subsumed. The histories you have read, the images and pictures you have seen, and the media you consume necessarily play a decisive role in the imagined answers. And yet, the question itself invites a list of rhetorical questions: *What does it mean to be famous? What does it mean to be a woman? And what does it look like to be both?*

Certainly, the media we access contribute to how we might answer these questions and more. The women who could be, and should be, recognized often result as a measure of public acclaim that a woman receives. The calculus of fame can be misleading, indeed. The challenge, ultimately, is a test not of knowledge but of equivalency. The challenge is to escape the linear trap of a feminist historiography and envision a way in which the activism

---

6. Briana Barner in Elfman, "Necessity of Digital Feminism."
7. Gajjala, "Woman and Other Women."

of an Ida B. Wells-Barnett, a Dolores Huerta, a Grace Lee Boggs, a Gloria E. Anzaldúa, and so many others can be known as deeply, and widely, as a Susan B. Anthony.

Trans/Linear Feminism and Why We Need Superheroines

One way of knowing the female subject beyond traditional boundaries is what I call a trans/linear feminism. A trans/linear feminism allows for narratives of female agency to go above, beyond, and even through traditional constraints, while mapping out a personal journey that progresses from one point to another. Such a feminism calls for a sensibility that such stories already exist, at any given moment and time, in varied spaces and places. By breaking the hegemony of a master, linear narrative, what might the universe of feminist thought and action resemble?

Each chapter in this volume illustrates in a singular way the path to refreshing and revitalizing our understanding of the feminist identity. Such a perspective is multifaceted, complex, and mediated. In truth, trans/linear feminists in popular culture exist, perhaps, because our longings for transformational experiences and meaningful impact are larger than ordinary experience. The idea of a woman with superpowers who still inhabits a world identifiable to other women because of her "ordinariness" is compelling. And necessary. Her duality reflects the real challenges of women juggling duty and agency, as well as restriction and freedom, in their daily lives. Trans/linear feminism helps interpret those spaces between the limited parameters of sequential living compared with the variability of past choices and future uncertainties.

So, what more are we to make of these trans/linear females in the superheroine imagination? They present themselves to us as multidimensional fantasy figures, made palpable by their realistic and mediated representation. And it may be challenging to pinpoint what exactly makes those depictions seem real to us. Perhaps the answers lie within the craft of their storytelling that can mine historical depths, summon futuristic scenarios, and occupy neat spaces that both define and defy present realities. These are the trans/linear readings that help define the feminine spaces they occupy, by highlighting how identity manifests in speculative fiction *and* in feminist theory. When these two realms interact dynamically, we can revel in stories and narratives that both animate us and inspire us.

Finally, we must interpret such stories through historical lenses. For even though the characters, spaces, and narratives we learn to love about these superheroes are not real, they seem somehow realistic. Trans/linear feminism provides identities that not only allow us to cross the boundaries of fact and fiction comfortably; they allow us to move through past, present, and future sensibilities adeptly. And as readers and audiences who embrace these stories, we connect with trans/linear identities, from the wellsprings of our own social histories and lived experiences.

Consider, again, the example of Storm. Her narrative journey may, on the surface, explore the trials of feeling "othered" as she maneuvers between mutant and human identities. Her African heritage is complex and at odds with Western-defined representations where there is, for instance, no clear role for a queen in diaspora, a goddess, and a woman with a radical sense of right and wrong. Storm, moved to anger, finds her strength by unleashing her powers and channeling righteous fury into power, visibly manifested. Social justice movements where women have fearlessly led and contributed provide stunningly dynamic contexts for reading such a story through new, empowering perspectives. We offer the contributions to this book in this vein, where the deft interpretations of feminist perspectives, along with the urgent narratives of imaginary women, can offer new ways of seeing ourselves, and the world around us.

Complex stories *can* move us through past, present, and future sensibilities adeptly. And we, as readers and audiences who embrace these stories, are empowered to travel new and unknown places, too. In the end, we connect with trans/linear identities from the wellsprings of our own social histories and lived experiences. All of our lives are richer for the journey.

Bibliography

Adair, Cassius, and Lisa Nakamura. "The Digital Afterlives of *This Bridge Called My Back*: Woman of Color Feminism, Digital Labor, and Networked Pedagogy." *American Literature* 89, no. 2 (2017): 255–78.

Barker, Kim, and Olga Jurasz. "Online Misogyny: A Challenge for Digital Feminism." *Journal of International Affairs* 72, no. 2 (2019): 95–113.

Chang, Jiang, Hailong Ren, and Qiguang Yang. "A Virtual Gender Asylum? The Social Media Profile Picture, Young Chinese Women's Self-Empowerment, and the Emergence of a Chinese Digital Feminism." *International Journal of Cultural Studies* 21, no. 3 (2018): 325–40.

Elfman, Lois. "The Necessity of Digital Feminism." *Women in Higher Education* 26, no. 6 (2017): 6. https://doi.org/10.1002/whe.20445.

Gajjala, Radhika. "Woman and Other Women: Implicit Binaries in Cyberfeminisms." *Communication & Cultural Studies* 11, no. 3 (2014 2014): 288–92.

Priest, Christopher, Sal Velluto, and Bob Almond. "Stürm and Drang—A Story of Love and War: Book One—Echoes." *Black Panther*, no. 26. Digital. New York: Marvel Comics, 2015, Marvel Unlimited / ComiXology.

Walker, Alice. *In Search of Our Mothers' Gardens*. New York: Harcourt Brace Jovanovich, 1984.

Woolf, Virginia. *A Room of One's Own*. Boston: Mariner Books / HarperCollins, 1989.

PART 2

Phenomenal Women

Gender and Feminism

CHAPTER 4

Marvel's Carol Danvers

Evolving Past the Second-Wave Feminist Icon

J. Richard Stevens and Anna C. Turner

Created in 1968 as a feminist character, Carol Danvers has endured several reconfigurations over the years in order to adjust to changing narrative needs. Historically written and drawn almost exclusively by men, Danvers's narratives were assigned to female writers by Marvel Comics starting in 2012, beginning a series of changes that altered nearly every aspect of the character's appearance, history, and even personality. Danvers's evolution from a male-gaze feminist icon into a more contemporary feminist space is considered a vanguard of the concerted effort by Marvel to increase the number of female heroes in its publications and raise their profile to more explicitly address the interests of a rising female readership.

This chapter tracks the publication history of Carol Danvers, documenting the particular struggles to adapt her to changing notions of gender and feminism. In order to erase previous narrative choices, the character had her mind erased as an explicit attempt to eradicate previous problematic elements from the character's publication history that make her inclusion in the Marvel Cinematic Universe (MCU) awkward. The frequent mind erasures allow Danvers to serve as a long-standing feminist symbol without becoming mired in the gendered politics of any particular age.

Remembering Pasts Forgotten

> Believe it or not, I've been so busy fighting crooks the past few days—I
> haven't thought about my black-out spells—or about my complete lack of
> memory! Maybe I've had a mental block against thinking about my past—
> but the fact remains: I DON'T KNOW WHO I AM![1]

The history of Carol Danvers as Ms. Marvel begins with frequent memory
loss, a trope that not only allows the character to cope with changing gendered contexts but also invites the readers to forget the many transitions
the character endured in pursuit of feminist icon status. To say that Carol
Danvers is Marvel Comics' most long-standing feminist superhero would
be technically a true statement, provided the claimant was prepared to com-
bine many loose definitions of feminism into his or her statement. The constructed feminist narratives that appeared in 2019's *Captain Marvel* presented
a particular configuration of feminist texts, but the Marvel Comics character the film version is supposedly adapted from endured several retroactive
continuity (retcon) reconfigurations through the years, including significant alterations to the character's appearance, history, and even personality.
This chapter reviews the evolving feminist history of the Danvers character,
tracking editorial decisions Marvel writers made for the character over the
years, as Captain Marvel became the feminist icon Marvel so desperately
needs to engage the growing female audience of its film properties, comic
books, and merchandise.

In 2014 Marvel Studios announced what would become the 2019 film
as an upcoming film project for the Carol Danvers version of Captain Marvel. This announcement followed a series of articles and social media posting criticism of the then fourteen Marvel Studios film portrayals of female
characters, including incidents of actors slut-shaming a female character,[2]
continued observations about the lack of any female-led solo film,[3] a relative
lack of merchandising for female characters,[4] and general concerns about
the trend toward oversexualized presentations of female characters.[5] Part of
that struggle is likely owed to Disney's gendered conception of Marvel film
projects, most prominently on display when Disney purchased Marvel in
2009 to fill a "boy need."[6]

---

1. Conway (w), Buscema (p), and Sinnott (i), *Ms. Marvel* 1, no. 1, p. 15.
2. Yamato, "Avengers."
3. Brown, *Modern Superhero*, 51.
4. Baker-Whitelaw, "Why Is Gamora"; Stewart, "Marvel."
5. Gentry, "Women of Marvel."
6. Carlson, "Marvel."

Captain Marvel premiered the weekend of March 8, 2019, eventually earning more than $1 billion at the box office for Marvel Studios. Set as an origin story for the MCU version of the character, Carol Danvers is abducted by the Kree (who suppress her memories of her human life as an air force test pilot) to serve as a member of Starforce, an elite team of hypermasculine Kree commandos. An encounter with the Skrulls brings her suppressed memories closer to the surface and deposits her on Earth, where Danvers discovers her true heritage with the help of Nick Fury and Maria Rambeau.

Captain Marvel presents Danvers as the most powerful hero in the MCU but also explores her identity through the lens of feminist community. Dr. Wendy Larson (a gender-swapped Mar-Vell) serves a key role in Danvers's origin story, as Larson's cosmic-cube-fueled ship explodes, infusing Danvers's body with the power of the space stone. Torn between her Kree and human identities, Danvers finds her identity repeatedly challenged and reconstructed by her memories of the dead Mar-Vell, the words of her lifelong friend Maria Rambeau, and her connection to Maria's young daughter, Monica.

By the film's conclusion, Danvers overcomes existential challenges to herself and the earth by confronting representations of sexism in her remembered past and by continuing to symbolically rise when she is knocked down, embodying an inspiring resistance to social norms and male domination. She single-handedly defeats the Kree (and rejects their constant pressure to "prove herself" by "controlling emotions") and sets off with Skrull refugees to find them a new home. Danvers would play a significant role in *Avengers: Endgame,* released the following month, in which her status as the most powerful hero in the MCU is reinforced.

The struggle between MCU executive producer Kevin Feige and Marvel CEO Ike Perlmutter over the film has been widely chronicled,[7] with Perlmutter's 2014 email suggesting he thought female-led films were too risky,[8] and the reorganization of Marvel within the Disney corporation to allow Feige's *Black Panther* and *Captain Marvel* projects to move forward.[9] During production, actor Brie Larson claimed that feminism was the original intent of the film: "I had a meeting with Marvel and what we discussed is they wanted to make a big feminist movie."[10] Right-wing trolls and alt-right groups launched repeated antifeminist attempts to undermine the film's success before the film premiered.[11]

---

7. Knoop, "Kevin Feige."
8. Dockterman, "Marvel CEO."
9. Holloway and Donnelly, "Marvel Promotion."
10. Boone, "Brie Larson.'"
11. Salam, "Trolls."

As *Captain Marvel* released, reviews offered assessments of feminist frames in the film, with some reviewers touting the lack of romantic interest, the strong female friendship frames, empathetic themes, Danvers's conquering of self-doubt, and empowerment plotlines.[12] Others stressed the text of Danvers's repeatedly overcoming male voices criticizing her efforts as "too emotional" as a distinctly feminist frame.[13] Of course, qualitatively evaluating feminism hinges on one's definition, and though the MCU film draws on character elements from the Marvel comics, Carol Danvers has represented many different feminisms over the years, none precisely like what appeared on screen.

The Second-Wave Ms. Marvel

Introduced as an act of superficial second-wave feminism, Carol Danvers has evolved through the years amid different waves and symbols of feminism. The second wave is considered to have begun with the publication of Betty Friedan's *The Feminine Mystique,* in which Friedan characterizes the introduction of superficial feminism in entertainment media as "trying to acknowledge the impending release of female sexual and political energy, while keeping it all safely in a straightjacket."[14] Carol Danvers fits this tension.

Created by Roy Thomas and Gene Colan, Carol Danvers originally appeared in *Marvel Super-Heroes* volume 1, issue 13 (March 1968), as a supporting character. In his mission to spy on earth, Mar-Vell adopts the guise of deceased scientist Walter Lawson but increasingly works against Kree interests to protect humans. The character of Carol Danvers served dramatic tension in Mar-Vell's narratives: a love interest, a threat to his mission, and a damsel in distress in the original Captain Marvel's self-titled series.

Introduced as head of NASA security, Danvers is initially described as "man or woman, . . . the finest head of security a missile base could want!"[15] Holding a typically male position of authority gives Danvers a kind of symbolic feminism; however, her real narrative role in the series was to serve as a damsel in distress for Captain Marvel, as she did in issues 1, 7, 9, 10, 13, 14, 16, 17, and 18 of the first volume of *Captain Marvel*. This function matches

---

12. Brusuelas, "Feminist Reviews."
13. Savyasachi, "Captain Marvel."
14. Friedan, *Feminine Mystique,* 124.
15. Thomas (w), Colan (p), and Reinman (i), *Marvel Super-Heroes* 1, no. 13.

MARVEL'S CAROL DANVERS • 37

what Julie D'Acci described as a backlash of "the jiggle era," where empowered women often wound up as "women in distress."[16]

In fact, it is as a damsel-in-distress that she receives her powers. In *Captain Marvel* volume 1, issue 18, Danvers's genes are fused with Mar-Vell's genetic material in an explosion, granting Danvers the powers of flight, invulnerability, strength, and a precognitive "sixth sense" that served as a superhuman form of "women's intuition";[17] thus, even her powers are derived from Mar-Vell.[18] Mike Madrid described this origin in his 2009 book as the decision by Marvel to "snap off a rib from one of their male characters to create their Eve."[19] Danvers dresses in a version of Mar-Vell's costume and uses a version of his superhero name.

Danvers became Ms. Marvel in the first issue of her self-titled series. The "Ms." title served as a symbolic connection to second-wave feminism,[20] with Danvers battling in her civilian identity for equal pay status.[21] In her day job, Danvers is the editor of a women's magazine and battles with publisher J. Jonah Jameson for control of the framing of "women's issues."

Within the narrative, Danvers is unaware of her Ms. Marvel adventures; she transforms by experiencing fainting spells and later awakens having forgotten what transpired. Thus, the strength exhibited as a modern professional woman is often undercut by her need to retire from stressful situations to transform, leading to missed deadlines and unfinished tasks (undermining her position as a strong career woman). Like many superheroes, her alter-ego adventures present to the reader the unfairness of her workplace struggles, but her male colleagues do not suffer the additional burden of representation that her gender imparts. Danvers eventually gains control of her two identities, but her derivative relationship with Captain Marvel, the bare midriff of her uniform, the fainting spells, and her inability to "move far from traditionally female roles"[22] made Danvers's original incarnation a considerably weak feminist symbol. She would receive a new costume in *Ms. Marvel* volume 1, issue 20, to get some identity of her own, but she would eventually be fired from her job.

---

16. D'Acci, *Defining Women*, 15.

17. 1970s Marvel writers seemed to think "women's intuition" was a female marker of superheroism. Earlier that decade the "Femme Force," a group of female S.H.I.E.L.D. agents with extrasensory perceptions, appeared in *Captain America* 1, no. 144.

18. Thomas (w), Kane, Buscema, Romita (p), and Adkins (i), *Captain Marvel* 1, no. 18.

19. Madrid, *Supergirls*, 175.

20. Wheeler, "New Ms. Marvel."

21. White, "Marvel Women."

22. Inness, *Tough Girls*, 145.

The *Ms. Marvel* series soon ended because of poor sales, but Danvers's adventures continued in the pages of *The Avengers*, a team she later officially joined.[23] As a member of the Avengers, Danvers mysteriously becomes pregnant and gives birth within hours to a being who rapidly grows into an adult.[24] Her "son," a being known as Marcus, explains that he abducted Danvers, used mind control to seduce her, impregnated her with his own essence, and then wiped her memory before returning her to Earth to give birth to him. Danvers is initially repulsed but agrees by the conclusion of the story to accompany Marcus back to his dimension.

This story arc was controversial among several fans and commentators, most notably the thinly veiled rape portrayed in the story:

> It was rape and obvious rape at that. The writer had to go an extra, knowing step to add that line about mind control. If he'd just left that off, it would have merely been a fanboy romance, where the blonde and buxom heroine is swept off her feet by flowers and candy (no need for romance or love), and readily agrees to anything and everything the hero (or fanboy in clever disguise) wants.
>
> But time went by and NO ONE said anything about the rape! Not one word besides how some readers were so happy that Ms. M had finally found a good man. I wanted to barf.[25]

Ms. Marvel writer Chris Claremont also expressed his outrage: "How callous! How cruel! How unfeeling! Considering that [the Avengers] must have seen Ms. Marvel only a couple of days before, or even a couple of months before. She wasn't pregnant then. How could she be eight months pregnant now?"[26]

Claremont removed that episode from Danvers's remembered (in-continuity) character history by having her mind erased by the mutant Rogue in *Avengers Annual*, issue 10.[27] Using her abilities to drain and "bor-

---

23. Michelinie (w), Byrne (p), and Jansen (i), *The Avengers* 1, no. 183.

24. Shooter et al. (w), Pérez (a), and Green (i), *The Avengers* 1, no. 200.

25. Strickland, "The Rape of Ms. Marvel." Strickland's critique originally appeared in published form in the magazine *LOC: On Comics Opinion and Comics Review*, no. 1 (January 1980), but years later Strickland posted the article to her website with additional commentary, which is why that version of the article is cited.

26. Sanderson, *The X-Men Companion II*, 23.

27. This annual, cited as the first appearance of the mutant and future X-Man Rogue, was the continuation to Claremont's story for *Ms. Marvel* 1, no. 25, which was not published before the series was canceled. That story (and the historic first appearance of Rogue) was finally printed in 1992 in the pages of Claremont, Furman (w), Vosburg, Gustovich (p), and Patterson (i), *Marvel Super-Heroes* 3, no. 11.

row" the powers of anyone she touches, Rogue holds on to Danvers too long, permanently absorbing her powers and erasing Danvers's memory. Claremont later had Danvers erase records of the existence of Ms. Marvel,[28] removing all accounts of the rape storyline from Marvel Comics continuity. Danvers turns to telepath Charles Xavier to recover some of her memories. She expresses outrage at the Avengers for allowing her to depart with her rapist, and she joins the X-Men for a series of adventures. Beginning with *Uncanny X-Men* volume 1, issue 164, Danvers gains cosmic powers and becomes the galactic hero Binary.[29]

In the 1990s Danvers returned to her black Ms. Marvel costume, but with the new name Warbird. She briefly rejoins the Avengers but sees her powers diminished and increasingly turns to alcohol to cope.[30] Insecurities mount, and Danvers attacks Tony Stark in a drunken rage,[31] harms one of the Inhumans when fighting intoxicated,[32] and is court-martialed by the Avengers.[33] Danvers later endures a judicial hearing on destruction of property caused while intoxicated[34] and is ordered to rejoin the Avengers to avoid jail time.[35]

These events produced another stain on the already tenuous reception of Ms. Marvel as a second-wave feminist icon.[36] But beginning in 2006, Marvel writers mounted a concerted effort to recover the Danvers character from her troubled past. In *The New Avengers* volume 2, issue 15, Danvers declines an invitation by Captain America to rejoin the Avengers, pledging that she intends to reclaim her status and "re-earn my wings as a superhero" before returning to the Avengers.[37]

Two months later a second volume of *Ms. Marvel* premiered. Writer Brian Reed reformulated Danvers as a high-flying adrenaline junkie.[38] Visually, the series presented Danvers quite literally within the "Bad Girl" frame, complete with the stereotypical "huge, gravity-defying breasts, mile-long legs, perpetually pouty lips, and perfectly coiffed big hair."[39] These markers

---

28. Claremont (w), Cockrum (p), and Wiacek (i), *The Uncanny X-Men* 1, no. 158.
29. Claremont (w), Cockrum (p), and Wiacek (i), *The Uncanny X-Men* 1, no. 164.
30. Busiek (w), Pérez (p), Vey, and Wiacek (i), *The Avengers* 3, no. 4.
31. Busiek, Howell (w), Chen (p), Canon, and Parsons (i), *Iron Man* 3, no. 7.
32. Ostrander, Edkin (w), Aucoin (p), and Faber (i), *Quicksilver* 1, no. 10.
33. Busiek (w), Pérez (p), and Vey (i), *The Avengers* 3, no. 7.
34. Busiek (w), Immonen (p), and von Grawbadger (i), *The Avengers* 3, no. 26.
35. Busiek (w), Pérez (p), and Vey (i), *The Avengers* 3, no. 27.
36. Brown, *Dangerous Curves*; D'Amore, "Invisible Girl's"; D'Amore, "Accidental Supermom"; Emad, "Wonder Woman's Body"; Gibson, "Who Does She Think She Is?"; Madrid, *Supergirls*; Murray, "Feminine Mystique"; Robinson, *Wonder Women*; and Stuller, *Ink-Stained*.
37. Bendis (w) and Cho (a), *The New Avengers* 1, no. 15, p. 9.
38. Reed (w), De La Torre (a), and Palmiotti (i), *Ms. Marvel* 2, no. 1.
39. Brown, *Dangerous Curves*, 55.

allowed Danvers to be coded postfeminist by the stereotypes of her swimsuit costume and the amount of skin she showed[40] while still performing the recognizably male superhero trope to her core audience:

> The comic book industry was so dominated by men for so long and so little attention was paid to the polysemy of comic book texts that most of the differentiation of female characters remained at the visual level; the code, message and way of thinking were clearly male and simply transposed into the mouths and minds of heroines.[41]

The series catered to its male audience with revealing presentations of Danvers's anatomy, a characterization of her personality more masculine than feminine, a common trait of female superheroes:

> Any feminist critic could demonstrate that most of these characters fail to inscribe any specific female qualities: they behave in battle like male heroes with thin waists and silicone breasts.[42]

These frames also support a postfeminist reading, that "feminism can now safely be relegated to the past,"[43] and the notion that feminism is something women should be liberated from in order to focus on consumption and sexuality.[44] The increased narrative emphasis on appearance, clothing, consumer culture, and sexuality are hallmarks of postfeminist discourse,[45] normally functioning to provide superficial symbols of empowerment disconnected from feminist critique. In this manner, "feminism itself is no longer needed—it has become a spent force."[46]

However, late in the 2006 *Ms. Marvel* series, the narrative would introduce a retcon story arc that reclaimed more of the classic second-wave feminist discourse, as Danvers is reimagined to have suffered a brutal POW experience that ended her air force flying career and launched her career in intelligence.[47] From this moment onward, Danvers's military framing would provide a growing retcon context of prior second-wave feminist struggles to

40. Tasker and Negra, *Interrogating Postfeminism*, 8.
41. Bongco, *Reading Comics*, 111.
42. Reynolds, *Super Heroes*, 80.
43. Budgeon, "Contradictions," 281.
44. Whelehan, *Overloaded*.
45. Kinser, "Negotiating Spaces," 134–35.
46. Sarikakis and Tsaliki, "Post/Feminism," 112.
47. Reed (w) and Marz (a), *Ms. Marvel* 2, no. 31; Reed (w), Siqueria (p), and Santos (i), *Ms. Marvel* 2, no. 32.

frame her status as a feminist icon. But taken as a whole, the thirty-five-year literary history of Carol Danvers leading up to the emergence of the MCU narratives is fraught with uncomfortably gendered texts. Though some symbolic forms of second-wave feminism appear within the text, her fainting spells, the derivative origin of her powers, her revealing costume—to say nothing of her instances of memory loss, struggles with alcoholism, and rape—presented significant challenges for film adaptation. Danvers also struggles with relationships with other women, and she constantly seeks approval from the male members of the Avengers, particularly Captain America.

But 2012 represented a turning point, as the character was reformulated as Captain Marvel. Over the next few years, Carol Danvers appeared in four new "Captain Marvel" titles (as well as a number of miniseries and team titles), each adding new elements to her narrative, as the character was slowly reconstructed to fit more modern feminist sensibilities.

Repositioning Carol Danvers's Feminism

A seventh Marvel series titled *Captain Marvel* released in 2012, with Carol Danvers appearing on the cover in a costume more reminiscent of a military flight suit than of a spandex costume. Above the logo appeared a new tagline: "Earth's Mightiest Hero."[48] Prior to the series, the promotional materials generated strong reactions. In the first issue's editorial section, the editor printed four submitted fan drawings of the new costume. In the letter column section of issue 2 appeared two strong objections to the new costume by (male) fans. The 2012 series signaled a new approach to the character, intentionally targeted at female readers and fans.

The first issue features Danvers idolizing Helen Cobb, a pilot who set fifteen speed records in the 1950s and was a member of the Mercury 13 space program before the glass ceiling prevented her selection for spaceflight. Cobb passes away in the issue, and Danvers scatters her ashes into space.[49] Writer Kelly Sue DeConnick explained she had "pitched Carol as Chuck Yeager," drawing more heavily on her air force background to instill

---

48. Note also that the 2012 series was the first time the character's ongoing stories were written by a female writer. Though Gerry Conway is credited as the writer of *Ms. Marvel* no. 1, the title page notes "with more than a little aid and abetment from Carla Conway."

49. DeConnick (w) and Soy (a), *Captain Marvel* 7, no. 1.

a new spirit in the character: "Carol has a similar appeal to me. She's got that thing—that need to faster, further, higher, more . . . always more."[50]

The series focused on Danvers coming to terms with a tumor growing within her brain, forcing her to choose between using her powers and preserving her personality. After spending several issues holding her powers in check, Danvers chooses to save New York City by flying into outer space to break her connection to an alien machine.[51] As a result, her brain hemorrhages, and she loses her memories. Carol Danvers is once again freed from the consequences of her negative publication history (this time, her history with alcoholism) through memory loss, and all the trauma and controversial events from her past are pushed aside. Danvers rebuilds her memories through conversations with a little girl that idolizes her:

> She's trying to figure out who she is and how to move forward, recreating everything for herself, and the deepest connection she has at that point is with this little girl. So she starts to relearn her personal history through the eyes of this 8-year-old girl who sees her in the best possible light—that is what she is trying to be now. That's how she understands herself.[52]

This decision not only gave DeConnick a way to banish problematic elements of Danvers's past; it also provided the chance to bring Danvers into closer alignment with the "Carol Corps" fan base, a cluster of vocal fans DeConnick had cultivated from the earliest announcement of Danvers's transition to Captain Marvel. As one writer observed:

> Carol Danvers isn't suddenly popular after languishing in relative obscurity because she's now Captain Marvel. She's popular because Kelly Sue DeConnick has tapped into a market demographic that's been not only ignored but actively abused by publishers and fans alike.[53]

The series' final issue, 17, culminates in a celebration of fan involvement. As Captain Marvel is attacked by a gathering of drones using their microwave weaponry against her, individuals in the crowd begin to yell "I am Captain Marvel!" to redirect the targeting systems of the drones and diffuse the beam. Recovered, Danvers destroys the remaining drones.

---

50. Hudson, "Kelly Sue."
51. DeConnick (w) and Andrade (a), *Captain Marvel* 7, no. 17.
52. Ching, "'Captain Marvel' returns."
53. Rosburg, "Wrong Lessons."

Issue 17 also features Kamala Khan, shown pinning one of Captain Marvel's cards to a bulletin board. Khan premiered as the new Ms. Marvel a few months later, and the relationship between her and Danvers would provide a powerful framework for both characters and their respective fans. More importantly, this intergenerational and intersectional dialogue allowed Danvers's second-wave boomer feminism to interact with Khan's postfeminist millennial attitudes. This interaction proved important because the kind of postfeminist rhetoric typically employed through millennial discourse "actively draws on and invokes feminism as that which can be taken into account in order to suggest that equality is achieved, in order to install a whole repertoire of meanings which emphasize that it is no longer needed, a spent force."[54] New female superheroes tend to consider their forerunners as "Camp Mothers,"[55] appreciating the style but not the substance of the earlier feminist struggles. As Brown explained:

> For better or worse, the girl action heroine represents a kind of post-feminist character who operates in a world where earlier feminist concerns are seen as outdated. This is an era in which the media embrace a rhetoric that declares girls are unquestionably empowered. Girls can be anything they want, and they can do anything they want.[56]

The retconned adjustments to Danvers's publication history instilled a stronger sense of second-wave feminism just as Khan's adventures were exploring millennial concerns from a postfeminist perspective. Therefore, bringing the two characters into direct dialogue was essential to establishing each as a source of cultural authority, engaging—in dialogue—concerns that are normally dismissed.

Another significant retcon occurred in the preview issue (0) of *The Mighty Captain Marvel*. Within the comic, Danvers's comic book origin is reframed yet again, altering her air force career and intelligence career into a drive toward space. Danvers is presented as one of the first female astronauts (if not the first), and the text implies that it was on a space mission that she received her powers. For the first time, Danvers's origin story is presented without Mar-Vell's presence at all, as if her powers came directly to her in space.[57] In one comics page, her history with Mar-Vell is seemingly erased,

---

54. McRobbie, "Postfeminism," 30.
55. Hopkins, *Girl Heroes*.
56. Brown, *Dangerous Curves*, 142.
57. Stohl (w), Rosanas, and Laiso (a), *The Mighty Captain Marvel* 1, no. 0, p. 13.

and references to this male presence in her origin (as well as the damsel-in-distress framing and the "imprinted DNA" explanation for her powers) are wiped from publication history and contemporary continuity.

At the end of the 2016 *Captain Marvel* series, Danvers uncovers and battles the self-proclaimed Master of the World from among her staff. As she fights, she verbally clarifies her understanding of her own leadership style and the isolation it brought (which she believes suited her personality) and appears to find renewed purpose through the conflict:

> A leader has to project confidence. Fight for what she believes in. But never stop questioning, wondering how to be better. You take in everything . . . and make your call. You thought isolating me would make me weaker? Buddy, you don't know me too well. All my life I've had to rely on myself, trust my instincts and convictions when others doubted me, and be prepared to back them up. You didn't hurt me with what you did. You gave me what I needed to win.[58]

This rhetoric frames Marvel's new approach to the character in comics. Danvers prevails in the battle, and then wrestles with her status as a symbol as she encounters a large crowd of adoring fans. Thinking she doesn't deserve the praise, she instead gives waves to honor their trust, and then silently commits to earn it every day.[59]

For a new reader (particularly a member of the Carol Corps), the four new *Captain Marvel* series (2012, 2014, 2016, and 2019) push into near-inaccessible archives of unmentioned history the literary histories of rape, alcoholism, fainting, dual identities, alien births, and her earliest portrayals as a damsel in distress. Instead, the four more recent series become the more accessible foundational text for new readers, and for the MCU source text. Even Danvers's connection to the original male Captain Marvel fades into a vague conception. Captain Marvel emerges as "Earth's Mightiest Hero," now a former astronaut, and increasingly one of the most influential characters in mainstream Marvel continuity. This transition occurred carefully and in stages, as female creators and fans alike participated in an unlikely reconstruction of Marvel's first premiere female superhero—just in time for her cinematic feature film.

---

58. Gage, Gage (w), Silas (a), *Captain Marvel 8*, no. 10, p. 11.
59. Gage, Gage (w), Silas (a), *Captain Marvel 8*, no. 10, p. 23.

Continuing Constructions of Feminism

The commercial and cultural success of *Captain Marvel* presented Marvel Comics with an opportunity to rework part of Danvers's publication history into a prosocial feminist continuity more in line with the feature film narrative. In 2018 the five-issue limited series *The Life of Captain Marvel* released, with Danvers returning to her childhood home in Maine to cope with anxiety.[60] While there, Danvers confronts the memories of sexism displayed by her father, and she battles a Kree soldier who is hunting Danvers's mother, only to discover that her mother had secretly been an empowered Kree warrior all along.[61] The Mar-Vell DNA element of Danvers's origin story would be literally removed with this discovery, since Danvers's powers had been (retroactively) hereditary, not from the accident with Mar-Vell. This removes Mar-Vell as the derivative source of her powers, giving Danvers the female agency that lacking in her earliest stories.

These revelations also reposition Captain Marvel's publication origin at the same moment the film reinterprets it: the idea that her powers derive from an infusion of male Kree DNA are removed from the storyline. In mainstream Marvel Comics continuity, Danvers has now inherited her mother's abilities, which were merely activated by the events in *Captain Marvel* volume 1, issue 18. In the film, the powers originate with an explosion involving energy drawn from an infinity stone. Though the narratives stress different origins of her powers, both connect to female community for identity (in the film, Dr. Wendy Larson appears as a role model and surrogate maternal figure for Danvers; in the comics, Danvers's powers come directly from her mother).

These moves suggest that Carol Danvers will be a continued site of constructed feminism, adaptable to incorporating reactions to feminist critiques that banish problematic framing through retcon reconfiguration. This enterprise might occur most often in the printed text, but the effort is transmedia and multimodal, coordinating frames across media. For example, just before the release of the 2019 *Captain Marvel* film, Marvel Comics released the first issue of the newest volume of the *Captain Marvel* comic series;[62] the first issue of this eleventh series topped sales charts for individual issue sales across all publishers.[63] In the first arc of the series, Danvers and a select

---

60. Stohl (w), Pacheco, Sauvage (p), and Fonteriz (i), *The Life of Captain Marvel* 2, no. 1.
61. Stohl (w), Pacheco, Sauvage (p), and Fonteriz (i), *The Life of Captain Marvel* 2, no. 5.
62. Thompson (w) and Carnero (a), *Captain Marvel* 11, no. 1.
63. Miller, "January 2019."

team of female heroes are transported to a dystopian future reality in which they band together to fight literal chauvinism in the form of Mahkizmo (the Nuclear Man), who seeks to enslave all women to reinforce his patriarchal hold on society. Female teamwork and resolving old interpersonal resentments prove to be the key to defeating literal male domination and restoring the female heroes to the present comics continuity in an explicit message to new readers who might wander into a comic shop after seeing the film.

Since that repositioning, Carol Danvers's adventures have continued in the Marvel Universe across several printed titles. She loses James Rhodes, but gets him back; she battles a doppelganger in a derivative hero named Star; she leaves Earth to become an Accuser for the Kree/Skrull Empire, and discovers she has a half-sister. But as each Marvel event or Danvers solo-series story unfolds, Danvers's profile in the Marvel Comics Universe rises. No longer a supporting role, Danvers as a character serves as a marque brand for the printed continuity, ever adapting to fit the narrative (and feminist) needs of the moment. Meanwhile, the cinematic sequel *The Marvels*, written by *WandaVision* writer Megan McDonnell and directed by Nia DaCosta, is scheduled for release on February 17, 2023. With announcements that Kamala Khan (the current Ms. Marvel, played by Iman Vellani) and Monica Rambeau (WandaVision's Teyonah Parris) will be making appearances in it, one can imagine that the screen version of the character will again be exploring feminist community, likely in ways that will further evolve the character. Thus, though the articulations of feminist critiques continue to evolve to describe the economic, social, and cultural dimensions of gendered experiences and discourse, Carol Danvers remains an adaptation (and possible mind-wipe) away from evolving into a space to continue the conversation across media forms.

Bibliography

Baker-Whitelaw, Gavia. "Why Is Gamora Missing from 'Guardians of the Galaxy' Merchandise?" *TheDailyDot*, August 6, 2014. http://www.dailydot.com/parsec/fans-notice-lack-of-gamora-merchandise/.

Bendis, Brian Michael (w), and Frank Cho (a). *The New Avengers* 1, no. 15. New York: Marvel Comics, 2006.

Bongco, Mila. *Reading Comics: Language, Culture, and the Concept of the Superhero in Comic Books.* New York: Garland, 2000.

Boone, John. "Brie Larson on 'Captain Marvel' and Starring in Marvel's 'Big Feminist Action Movie' (Set Visit)." *Entertainment Tonight*, December 4, 2018. https://www.etonline.com/brie-larson-on-captain-marvel-and-starring-in-marvels-big-feminist-action-movie-set-visit-114994.

Brown, Jeffrey A. *Dangerous Curves: Action Heroines, Gender, Fetishism, and Popular Culture.* Jackson: University Press of Mississippi, 2011.

———. *The Modern Superhero in Film and Television: Popular Genre and American Culture.* New York: Routledge, 2016.

Brusuelas, Candice. "Feminist Reviews: Captain Marvel." *Medium,* March 23, 2019. https://medium.com/@cbrucewillis/feminist-reviews-captain-marvel-4341e894cfdb.

Budgeon, Shelley. "The Contradictions of Successful Femininity: Third-Wave Feminism, Postfeminism and 'New' Femininities." In *New Femininities: Postfeminism, Neoliberalism and Subjectivity,* edited by Rosalind Gill and Christina Scharff, 279–92. New York: Palgrave Macmillan, 2011.

Busiek, Kurt, Richard Howell (w), Sean Chen (p), Eric Cannon, and Sean Parsons (i). "Bad Moon Rising." *Iron Man* 3, no. 7. New York: Marvel Comics, 1998.

Busiek, Kurt (w), Stuart Immonen (a), and Wade von Grawbadger (i). " . . . Under the Cover of Night!" *The Avengers* 3, no. 26. New York: Marvel Comics, 2000.

Busiek, Kurt (w), George Pérez (p), and Al Vey (i). "The Court Martial of Carol Danvers." *The Avengers* 3, no. 7. New York: Marvel Comics, 1998.

———. "New Order." *The Avengers* 3, no. 27. New York: Marvel Comics, 2000.

Busiek, Kurt (w), George Pérez (p), Al Vey, and Bob Wiacek (i). "Too Many Avengers!" *The Avengers* 3, no. 4. New York: Marvel Comics, 1998.

Carlson, Nicholas. "Marvel Solves Disney's $50 Billion Boy Problem." *Business Insider,* August 31, 2009. http://www.businessinsider.com/marvel-solves-disneys-50-billion-boy-problem-2009-8.

Ching, Albert. "'Captain Marvel' Returns in a Cosmic Journey to Find Herself." *UpRoxx,* February 16, 2014. http://uproxx.com/hitfix/captain-marvel-returns-in-a-cosmic-journey-to-find-herself/.

Claremont, Chris (w), Dave Cockrum (p), and Bob Wiacek (i). "Binary Star!" *The Uncanny X-Men* 1, no. 164. New York: Marvel Comics, 1982.

———. "The Life That Late I Led . . ." *The Uncanny X-Men* 1, no. 158. New York: Marvel Comics, 1982.

Claremont, Chris (w), and Michael Golden (a). "By Friends—Betrayed!" *Avengers Annual* 1, no. 10. New York: Marvel Comics, 1981.

Claremont, Chris, Simon Furman (w), Mike Vosburg, Mike Gustovich (p), and Bruce Patterson (i). "Cry, Vengeance!" *Marvel Super-Heroes* 3, no. 11. New York: Marvel Comics, 1992.

Conway, Gerry, Carla Conway, (w), John Buscema (p), and Joe Sinnott (i). "This Woman, This Warrior!" *Ms. Marvel* 1, no. 1. New York: Marvel Comics, 1977.

D'Acci, Julie. *Defining Women: Television and the Case of Cagney & Lacey.* Chapel Hill: University of North Carolina Press, 1994.

D'Amore, Laura Mattoon. "The Accidental Supermom: Superheroines and Maternal Performativity, 1963–1980." *The Journal of Popular Culture* 45, no. 6 (2012): 1226–48. http://www.americanpopularculture.com/journal/articles/fall_2008/d'amore.htm.

———. "Invisible Girl's Quest for Visibility: Easy Second Wave Feminism and the Comic Book Superheroine." *Americana: The Journal of American Popular Culture, 1900 to Present* 7, no. 2 (Fall 2008).

DeConnick, Kelly Sue (w), and Filipe Andrade (a). *Captain Marvel 7*, no. 17. New York: Marvel Comics, 2014.

DeConnick, Kelly Sue (w), and Dexter Soy (a). *Captain Marvel 7*, no. 1. New York: Marvel Comics, 2012.

Dockterman, Eliana. "Marvel CEO Says in Leaked Email That Female Superhero Movies Have Been a 'Disaster.'" *Time*, May 5, 2019. https://time.com/3847432/marvel-ceo-leaked-email/.

Emad, Mitra C. "Reading Wonder Woman's Body: Mythologies of Gender and Nation." *Journal of Popular Culture* 39, no. 6 (2006): 954–84.

Friedan, Betty. *The Feminine Mystique*. New York: Norton, 1963.

Friedrich, Gary (w), and John Romita Sr. (a). "Hydra Over All." *Captain America 1*, no. 144. New York: Marvel Comics, 1971.

Gage, Christos N., Ruth Fletcher Gage (w), and Tony Silas (a). "Lonely at the Top, Part 5." *Captain Marvel 8*, no. 10. New York: Marvel Comics, 2017.

Gentry, Sage. "The Women of Marvel and Geek Subculture." *Sequart*, July 2, 2015. http://sequart.org/magazine/58745/the-women-of-marvel-and-geek-subculture/.

Gibson, Mel. "Who Does She Think She Is? Female Comic Book Characters, Second-Wave Feminism and Feminist Film Theory." In *Superheroes and Identities*, edited by Mel Gibson, David Huxley, and Joan Ormond, 135–46. Oxford: Routledge, 2015.

Holloway, Daniel, and Matt Donnelly. "Does Kevin Feige's Marvel Promotion Mean Ike Perlmutter's Endgame?" *Variety*, October 22, 2019. https://variety.com/2019/biz/news/kevin-feige-ike-perlmutter-marvel-disney-1203377802/.

Hopkins, Susan. *Girl Heroes: The New Force in Popular Culture*. Melbourne, Australia: Pluto Press, 2002.

Hudson, Laura. "Kelly Sue DeConnick on the Evolution of Carol Danvers to Captain Marvel." *Comics Alliance*, March 19, 2012. http://comicsalliance.com/kelly-sue-deconnick-captain-marvel/.

Inness, Sherrie A. *Tough Girls: Women Warriors and Wonder Women in Popular Culture*. Philadelphia: University of Pennsylvania Press, 1999.

Kinser, Amber E. "Negotiating Spaces for/through Third-Wave Feminism." *NWSA Journal* 16, no. 3 (Autumn 2004): 124–53.

Knoop, Joseph. "Kevin Feige Confirms Rumors of Ike Perlmutter's Opposition to MCU Diversity." *IGN*, November 11, 2019. https://www.ign.com/articles/2019/11/12/kevin-feige-ike-perlmutter-controversy-diversity-mcu-marvel.

Madrid, Mike. *Supergirls: Fashion, Feminism, Fantasy, and the History of Comic Book Heroines*. Minneapolis: Exterminating Angel Press, 2009.

McRobbie, Angela. "Postfeminism and Popular Culture: Bridget Jones and the New Gender Regime." In *Interrogating Postfeminism: Gender and the Politics of Popular Culture*, edited by Diane Negra and Yvonne Tasker, 27–39. Durham, NC: Duke University Press, 2007.

Michelinie, David (w), John Byrne (p), and Klaus Jansen (i). "The Redoubtable Return of Crusher Creel!" *The Avengers 1*, no. 183. New York: Marvel Comics, 1979.

Miller, John Jackson. "January 2019 Comic Book Sales to Comics Shops." *Comichron*, 2019. https://www.comichron.com/monthlycomicssales/2019/2019-01.html.

Murray, Ross. "The Feminine Mystique: Feminism, Sexuality, Motherhood." *Journal of Graphic Novels and Comics* 2, no. 1 (2011): 55–66.

Ostrander, John, Joe Edkin (w), Derec Aucoin (p), and Rich Faber (i). "Live Kree or Die! Part 3: Blue Moon." *Quicksilver* 1, no. 10. New York: Marvel Comics, 1998.

Reed, Brian (w), Roberto De La Torre (p), and Jimmy Palmiotti (i). "Best of the Best." *Ms. Marvel* 2, no. 1. New York: Marvel Comics, 2006.

Reed, Brian (w), and Marcos Marz (a). "Secret Agent Danvers Part 1: Ascension." *Ms. Marvel* 2, no. 31. New York: Marvel Comics, 2008.

Reed, Brian (w), Paulo Siqueria (p), and Amilton Santos (i). "Secret Agent Danvers Part 2: Vitamin." *Ms. Marvel* 2, no. 32. New York: Marvel Comics, 2009.

Reynolds, Richard. *Super Heroes: A Modern Mythology*. Jackson: University Press of Mississippi, 1992.

Robinson, Lillian S. *Wonder Women: Feminisms and Superheroes*. New York: Routledge, 2004.

Rosburg, Caitlin. "Marvel Learned the Wrong Lessons from the Carol Corps." *The A.V. Club*, April 27, 2015. http://www.avclub.com/article/marvel-learned-wrong-lessons-carol-corps-218003.

Salam, Maya. "Trolls Tried to Sink 'Captain Marvel.' She Triumphed." *New York Times*, March 15, 2019. https://www.nytimes.com/2019/03/15/arts/captain-marvel-trolls.html.

Sanderson, Peter. *The X-Men Companion II*. Stamford, CT: Fantagraphic Books, 1982.

Sarikakis, Katharine, and Liza Tsaliki. "Post/Feminism and the Politics of Mediated Sex." *International Journal of Media and Cultural Politics* 7, no. 2 (August 2011): 109–19.

Savyasachi, Bageshri. "Captain Marvel: The Female Superhero We Deserve." *Feminism in India*, March 12, 2019. https://feminisminindia.com/2019/03/12/captain-marvel-review-female-superhero/.

Shooter, Jim, George Pérez, Bob Layton, David Michelinie (w), George Pérez (a), and Dan Green (i). "The Child Is Father To . . . ?" *The Avengers* 1, no. 200. New York: Marvel Comics, 1980.

Stewart, Sara. "Marvel and Its Sexist Superhero Movies Hit a New Low." *New York Post*, May 7, 2015. http://nypost.com/2015/05/07/marvel-and-its-sexist-superhero-movies-hit-a-new-low/.

Stohl, Margaret (w), Emilio Laiso, and Ramon Rosanas (a). *The Mighty Captain Marvel* 1, no. 0. New York: Marvel Comics, 2017.

Stohl, Margaret (w), Carlos Pacheco, Marguerite Sauvage (p), and Rafael Fonteriz (i). "Part One: Trapped." *The Life of Captain Marvel* 2, no. 1. New York: Marvel Comics, 2018.

———. "Part Five: Championed." *The Life of Captain Marvel* 2, no. 5. New York: Marvel Comics, 2019.

Strickland, Carol A. "The Rape of Ms. Marvel." *carolastrickland.com*, January 1980. http://www.carolastrickland.com/comics/msmarvel/index.html.

Stuller, Jennifer K. *Ink-Stained Amazons and Cinematic Warriors: Superwomen in Modern Mythology*. New York: I. B. Tauris, 2010.

Tasker, Yvonne, and Diane Negra. "Introduction: Feminist Politics and Postfeminist Culture." In *Interrogating Postfeminism: Gender and the Politics of Popular Culture*, edited by Yvonne Tasker and Diane Negra, 1–25. Durham, NC: Duke University Press, 2007.

Thomas, Roy (w), Gene Colan (p), and Paul Reinman (i). "Where Stalks the Sentry." *Marvel Superheroes* 1, no. 13. New York: Marvel Comics, 1968.

Thomas, Roy (w), Gil Kane, John Buscema, John Romita Sr. (p), and Dan Adkins (i). "Vengeance Is Mine!" *Captain Marvel* 1, no. 18. New York: Marvel Comics, 1969.

Thompson, Kelly (w), and Carmen Canero (a). "Re-Entry." *Captain Marvel* 11, no. 1. New York: Marvel Comics, 2019.

Wheeler, Andrew. "Marvel Unveils New Ms. Marvel: A Muslim Pakistani-American Teenager." *Comics Alliance*, November 5, 2013. https://comicsalliance.com/marvel-comics-ms-marvel-g-willow-wilson-alphona-muslim-teen/.

Whelehan, Imelda. *Overloaded: Popular Culture and the Future of Feminism*. London: Women's Press, 2000.

White, Brett. "Marvel Women of the 70's: Ms. Marvel." *Marvel.com*, July 9, 2014. https://news.marvel.com/comics/22834/marvel_women_of_the_70s_ms_marvel/. Page discontinued.

Yamato, Jen. "The Avengers' Black Widow Problem: How Marvel Slut-Shamed Their Most Badass Superheroine." *Daily Beast*, April 28, 2015. http://www.thedailybeast.com/articles/2015/04/28/the-avengers-black-widow-problem-how-marvel-slut-shamed-their-most-badass-superheroine.html.

CHAPTER 5

"I Know My Value"

The Standpoint Evolution of Agent Carter as a Transmedia and Transgenerational Feminist

Kathleen M. Turner Ledgerwood

In *Captain America: The First Avenger*, Agent Carter first appears in the Marvel Cinematic Universe (MCU) as she inspects the new recruits for the Strategic Scientific Reserve (SSR) and introduces herself. One of the recruits begins to heckle Carter about her British accent, calling her Queen Victoria. Carter gives him a nonchalant look and asks for his name before calmly ordering him, "Step forward, Hodge. Put your right foot forward." Hodge continues to insult her with an insubordinate, sexually harassing comment: "Mmm . . . we gonna wrassle? 'Cause I got a few moves I know you'll like." Hodge winks at her right before she punches him in the face, knocking him to the ground.[1] The viewer immediately senses that Agent Carter is not the average woman of the 1940s. Not only is it clear that she is the head of operations for the SSR, it is also clear that she will deal swiftly with bullies and misogynists. This chapter uses standpoint theory to demonstrate that Agent Carter is a feminist across generations and across platforms, making her a true transgenerational and transmedia feminist.

In the Marvel transmediated world, Agent Margaret "Peggy" Carter appears first in Captain America comics in 1966.[2] Her first appearance in the

---

1. *Captain America: The First Avenger.*
2. Lee (w), Austin (p), and Kirby (i), "Hostage."

Marvel comics depicts Agent Carter, known only as Agent 13 or Mademoiselle, as a strong woman fighting in World War II. As she fights alongside Captain America, a romance develops between them. With the rise of the MCU, Agent Carter appears in *Captain America: The First Avenger* (2011) when Steve Rogers volunteers to become a science experiment, which endows him with the superpowers to become Captain America. Agent Carter's role in the Captain America movie led to the eponymous television show. Across all these narratives, Agent Carter is a character who, though she has no superpowers, has an extraordinary ability to defeat villains.[3] Carter proves herself to have a good grasp of science, to be a great covert agent in the SSR, and she becomes a founder of S.H.I.E.L.D. There is only one instance of Carter having super-skills in the alternate universe presented in *Exiles*, issue 3, by Saladin Ahmed and Javier Rodriquez, where Carter is Captain America.[4] Thus, Carter participates in several workplace arenas that are stereotypically male-dominated. Across all the transmedia depictions of Agent Carter, she is faced with gender stereotypes often leaving people grossly underestimating her. However, Carter is a fan favorite and is often cited by fans as a feminist heroine they hope to learn more about. Standpoint theory helps us understand the role of Agent Carter in building her own standpoint as a feminist across transmedia representations; it also helps illustrate why the show resonated more with feminist and female fans, who appreciated Agent Carter as MCU's first female heroine with her own production.

Since Nancy Hartstock defined standpoint theory in 1983, it has been much debated and discussed by feminist theorists and has undergone several theoretical and epistemological permutations. Hartstock and many interdisciplinary feminist theorists have contributed to and used standpoint theory, including Evelyn Fox Keller, Sandra Harding, Dorothy Smith, Patricia Hill Collins, and Brooke Lenz. These scholars, working mostly independently, agree that marginalized groups of people have less investment in supporting the status quo and a unique position from which to analyze the cultural systems within which they are marginalized. By examining specific subject positions, we can learn more about dominant social structures. Beginning from the position of a marginalized subject, difference (as characterized by socioeconomic status, age, race, gender, ability, sexuality, etc.) becomes an operational variable through which we gain a better understanding of the sociopolitical historicity of experience and can better analyze the dominant

---

3. "Character Close-Up."
4. Ahmed (w), Rodriquez (p), and Lopez (i), *Exiles*, no. 3.

culture. The idea of the "outsider within" status is particularly beneficial when considering certain marginalized subject positions.

Even though standpoint theory has largely been practiced in the social sciences, as Brooke Lenz argues, standpoint theory can be particularly useful in literary criticism, "particularly as the field is already structured to consider the experiences and perspectives of literary characters as both specific to those individuals and indicative of larger social realities."[5] The outsider-within standpoint allows readers and viewers to see truths and realities that may not be apparent to someone more fully assimilated into dominant ideologies. As we watch or read about characters who have an outsider-within standpoint, we are often able to view a growing consciousness of these characters, which makes clearer to the reader-viewer the ways in which categorical structures privilege some while oppressing others. In the case of Agent Peggy Carter, she is one of a very few female special agents in a male-dominated workplace, making her a marginalized worker, and she is further marginalized in the MCU for being British in the US. Nevertheless, as a white woman, she does occupy a system of privilege, but in the television show and the comics, as her political consciousness grows, her standpoint shifts to an ally for Black men across transmedia narratives. Therefore, through analyzing Agent Carter's shifting standpoint in the transmediated representations of her, the reader-viewer is better able to understand the historical and social matrices of oppression and can then use this understanding to connect to their own standpoint in the current historical-political culture in which we live. Thus, through an analysis of our past, we are able to see that the struggle for equality still exists, and we are better able to develop our own standpoints in relation to Agent Carter.

Even though Agent Carter has been a Marvel character since 1966, appearing in numerous comics, movies, and television shows, few scholars have written about the depictions of her character. In the book chapter "Marvel's *Agent Carter*: [Peggy Punches Him in the Face]," Cat Mahoney argues that Agent Carter in the MCU appears to be feminist but actually is not because the historical setting only serves to reify a postfeminist attitude, or the belief that the work of feminism is done. Thus Mahoney argues that "Peggy is not a feminist."[6] Mahoney claims this purely based on the belief that as a present-day audience, we cannot look upon the character of Agent Peggy Carter as anything more than a historical representation of how far women have come in the struggle for equality. However, I argue that

---

5. Lenz, "Postcolonial Fiction," 100.
6. Mahoney, "Marvel's *Agent Carter*," 96.

looking across the mediated depictions of Carter's character clearly demonstrates a feminist perspective and transcends multiple waves of feminist
movements through her transmediated character. The portrayal of a token
woman in a man's workplace cannot help but touch on sexual discrimi-
nation and workplace issues. Agent Carter demonstrates that certainly the
battle for women to be seen and respected as equals is not over; feminism's
work is not "done." We still have a long way to go; therefore, Agent Carter
as a transmedia character speaks at once to both how far we have come and
how far we still have to go.

Most discussions surrounding Agent Carter come from fan sites and
popular media reviews. Several male fan critics, like Abraham Riesman and
Marc Buxton, explain that they thought of Peggy Carter as a very minor
character that no one would remember from the comics.[7] Riesman argues,
"Prior to 2011, most geeks would've been hard-pressed to name a single
story arc involving her."[8] He continues to claim that the portrayal of Hayley
Atwell in the MCU "only bears a passing resemblance" to the Agent Carter
in the Captain America and Tales of Suspense comics because she is British
in the MCU and American in the original comics.

Indeed, most male writers in popular venues underestimate Carter and
her role in comics, and they often point only to Agent Carter's low ratings as
a television show. In stark contrast, female writers, fans, and media critics
laud the television show and how Marvel spun the MCU character out of
this powerful, secondary character from the comics. In her farewell to Agent
Carter, staff writer and media critic Meagan Damore writes that the show's
cancellation was "a tragic blow" because "MCU is sorely lacking in well-
rounded female leads."[9] Similarly, other female media writers explain not
only that Agent Carter was an important character in the MCU but also that
this show was groundbreaking and important to the franchise. These different responses in media criticism illustrate why standpoint theory illuminates
the transmediated character of Peggy Carter. In reading through reviews
and fan sites, it becomes clear that criticism takes a different standpoint,
depending on the gender identity of the critic. Women seem more apt to
point out how strong Carter is and how important the show is for focusing
on a well-developed female character, while men use different rhetoric to
discuss this "minor" and relatively "unimportant" character. The standpoint
of being a woman reading and watching a strong and powerful woman in
the Marvel universe means that we are better able to understand her impor-

---

7. Riesman, "Brief History"; Buxton, "Agent Carter Comics."
8. Reisman, "Brief History."
9. Damore, "Goodbye, 'Agent Carter.'"

tance as a character in a patriarchal world, and in a male-dominated fan base where female "rights" to fandom are often questioned.

The important role that *Marvel's Agent Carter* plays in the MCU cannot be denied. As Matt Chapman explains, this show "marked the first time Marvel Studio had given us a female lead for one of its projects."[10] Similarly, female media critics, including Maureen Ryan, explain how much the show means for diversity in the "superhero portfolio":

> Gender is an important consideration for Marvel as well. It shouldn't keep the show on the air simply because it has a female lead, but because Peggy Carter is a wonderfully nuanced and complex female character, one who's imbued with exceptional charisma and charm by star Hayley Atwell. Having just one major female lead in the Marvel TV universe—Jessica Jones—is not enough, and settling for that state of affairs smacks of tokenism. That is not the route a company that's been hammered for its lack of female representation wants to take.[11]

Ryan also mentions that the show in season 2 giving "a prominent role to a black actor—would serve as proof of the hunger for the kinds of characters that have been underrepresented in the past."[12]

Peggy Carter first appeared in 1966 in *Tales of Suspense*, issue 77.[13] She appears in a flashback twenty years in the past during World War II, where she was fighting and became a love interest of Captain America. In this issue she is called Agent 13, and even Captain America does not know her real name. After appearing in this brief flashback, Carter disappears and re-emerges in 1973.[14] At the beginning of this issue, Captain America is fighting alongside his latest love interest, S.H.I.E.L.D. agent Sharon Carter. As they fight beside one another and profess their love for each other, Sharon reveals to Captain America that "Peggy Carter—that girl you loved in World War II"—is her sister. Captain America learns what happened to Peggy Carter after World War II from Sharon. After this issue, Carter becomes a recurring secondary character in Captain America's comics, often fighting by his side as a S.H.I.E.L.D. Agent, but she is never again Captain America's love interest. Throughout these comics, Peggy Carter changes in appearance,

---

10. Chapman, "Agent Carter Season 3."
11. Ryan, "Battle On."
12. Ryan, "Battle On."
13. Lee (w), Austin (p), and Kirby (i), "Hostage."
14. Englehart (w), Buscema (p), and Verpoorten (i), "Cap Goes Mad!"

which might explain why some readers failed to recognize her as an often-returning secondary character in the Captain America comics.

In *Tales of Suspense,* issue 77, Peggy Carter first appears in a flashback right after the Partisans defeat a group of Axis forces. Two frames show Carter and Captain America expressing their feelings for one another. In the first frame, Carter is facing Captain America, holding his shoulders, and exclaims, "You were wonderful! I'll never forget these weeks with Captain America fighting at our side!" Captain America replies, "I won't forget them either! But . . . you've got to leave the partisans! This isn't woman's work!" In the next frame, Carter has turned away from Captain America, and we see a close-up of their faces with Captain America over her shoulder. Carter says, "I can't leave! This war is everybody's war . . . I was needed . . . and I answered the call . . . just as you did, in your own way!" Captain America replies, "I know! And I know I haven't the right to speak to you this way! It's just that you . . . you've come to mean so much to me . . . !"[15] From early in her appearance in Marvel comics, Peggy is questioned for doing things that are not "woman's work." Even though Carter is a skilled fighter in the resistance in Nazi-occupied France, Captain America asks her to leave out of concern because she means "so much" to him. In these frames, Carter shows that she has developed a standpoint beyond viewing herself in stereotypical roles for women. As Sandra Harding claims, "Standpoints are critically and theoretically constructed discursive positions, not merely perspectives or views that flow from their authors unwittingly because of their biology or location in geographical or other such social relations."[16] Carter chose to fight in Nazi-occupied France, and she equates her call to action with Captain America's, seeing no difference between their duty due to gender stereotypes. Thus, in a historic moment when women were not fighting on the front lines, Carter joins the fight and excels in the Partisans.

Later, when the character of Peggy returns in the comics, her standpoint as a strong woman ready to fight is further developed. In her reappearance story line, Captain America finds her in the lair of the villain Doctor Faustus.[17] Captain America marvels at being reunited with the woman who was "the first girl" he "ever loved" and "the last, until Sharon!" But as soon as he finds her again, Dr. Faustus's men burst into the room, and Carter immediately knocks one out while making a quip about his uniform. Captain America thinks about how he needs to protect her because she's older now and has been suffering in an undiagnosed mental state; she still seems to think it

15. Lee (w), Colan (a), Austin (p), and Michaels (i), "Hostage." Ellipses in original.
16. Harding, *Is Science Multicultural?*, 17.
17. Englehart (w), Buscema (p), and Verpoorten (i), "Cap Goes Mad!"

is World War II. Later in this comic, though, Carter saves Captain America by knocking Faustus out with a candle holder.[18] This moment makes it clear that the intersectional oppression because of her age and gender will not keep her from saving the day. Peggy Carter has been suffering mentally since the war, and her sister Sharon says that it is because Captain America was lost in 1945 and presumed dead. Peggy Carter herself never weighs in on her mental issues, though, and recovers fully before she appears in future Captain America comics, becoming an agent of S.H.I.E.L.D. and working to fight evil. But when Captain America refuses to reveal his face and true identity while telling Carter not to wait for him and explaining that he will no longer be Captain America, Peggy does walk away crying and Steve Rogers thinks to go after her, but does not because he is attacked by the Golden Arrow.[19] By *Captain America* issue 184, Peggy Carter is a S.H.I.E.L.D. agent assigned to missions with Captain America, who has returned. They fight and work together, without any romantic relationship. Most notably, in this issue, Carter and her partner, Gabe Jones, come to help Captain America guard Red Skull's targets for assassination. As Carter is guarding the premises, Red Skull grabs her from behind and says, "Foolish female! That the Americans would send a woman into combat does not surprise me." But Peggy slams her foot down on his and retorts wittily as she hits him: "What does Nazi stand for again, Hans? 'National Chauvinism'? You're dealing with a qualified SHIELD Agent—not Betty Grable!" Red Skull eventually punches Peggy in the face before making his escape.[20] Not only does Carter battle Red Skull physically in this moment, she also battles his chauvinist ideas about women, asserting her standpoint that she is a different woman, whom he will have to physically battle, because she does not exist for a man's visual pleasure, like in narrative cinema.

In the next issue, Carter is shown with a black eye from her hand-to-hand combat with Red Skull, and she and Jones are still working with Captain America and Falcon on their mission. But Red Skull has become very angry about Peggy Carter. He's had success killing his targets, but he cannot get over the fact that he thinks that Peggy Carter (a white woman) and Gabe Jones (a Black man) had "more than just comradery there," and he decides to "crush those two 'lovers'!"[21] Thus, leaving his mission behind, he decides to pursue Carter and Jones. In this same issue, Jones asks Carter whether she still has feelings for Captain America, and she replies that she

---

18. Englehart (w), Buscema (p), and Verpoorten (i), "Cap Goes Mad!"
19. Englehart (w), Buscema (p), Colletta (i), "Slings."
20. Englehart (w), Trimpe (p), Giacola (i), and Esposito (i), "Cap's Back!"
21. Englehart (w), Buscema (p), Robbins (p), and Giacola (i), "Scream."

does not, in part because he still looks twenty-five while she is forty-seven. Jones was with the Howlers before joining S.H.I.E.L.D., and as he and Carter fight side by side, she remarks on how she's treated because of misogyny, and he remarks on how he is treated because of racism. Red Skull's men kidnap Jones and Carter, and Red Skull tortures them both for seven hours; they resist his torture and Carter even spits in his face when he threatens her with seven days of torture.[22] In these issues, Carter and Jones begin to share their standpoints with one another and to see how their struggles with oppression are similar. It expands Carter's standpoint, and she spits in the face of these oppressive systems, demonstrating a growing consciousness in her character's standpoint.

Male media critics who write about the comics and the MCU often give more credit to Sharon Carter in early comics. But in actuality in these comics, Sharon leaves S.H.I.E.L.D. and the fight for justice, and she urges Captain America to do the same. As Captain America talks to her about how easy his life has been since giving up his superhero status, he begins to say something about how, on the other hand, it was not difficult to be a superhero when he was with her sister Peggy. But his thought-provoking comparison of the two sisters is cut short when Golden Arrow attacks him for the first time.[23] In these issues, Rogers seems easily distracted from Peggy, and Sharon Carter cries over Captain America returning to being a superhero.[24] This demonstrates a difference in relationships that the MCU adaptations of Carter seem to try to correct; Steve Rogers and Peggy Carter love and can be themselves with each other, in ways they might not be able to without a well-developed feminist standpoint.

In the relaunched *Captain America,* issue 1 (2011), Peggy Carter dies, which removes her briefly from the comic realm while her character was written into the MCU. The interest in Carter only grew after her appearances in MCU, and around the time of the television show's first season, Marvel comics hired Kathryn Immonen and Michael Komarck to create *Operation S.I.N.* (2015), which ran for five issues and presented some of "the untold" Peggy Carter stories in a noir style similar to the television show. Around the same time, and with the same author and artist team, Marvel released a fiftieth anniversary of S.H.I.E.L.D. issue, *Agent Carter: S.H.I.E.L.D. 50th Anniversary,* issue 1 (2015), which details how she recruited Dum Dum Dugan into S.H.I.E.L.D. Thus, Agent Carter remained a focus in comics.

22. Englehart (w), Buscema (p), Robbins (p), and Giacola (i), "Scream."
23. Englehart (w), Buscema (p), and Colletta (i), "Slings and Arrows."
24. Englehart (w), Buscema (p), Robbins (p), and Giacola (i), "Scream."

In the MCU, Peggy Carter (Hayley Atwell) first appears in *Captain America: The First Avenger* (2011). She is a commander in the SSR, and by the end of the movie, it is clear that she is Steve Rogers's love interest, and at the end of the film, he is lost and presumed to be dead. She reappears in a bonus feature released on the *Iron Man 3* Blu-Ray, "Marvel One-Shot: Agent Carter." In this short film, she is working at the SSR and is seen beating up men and catching bad guys. Agent Carter's character then reappears in *Captain America: Winter Soldier* (2014) before the television show focused on her, *Marvel's Agent Carter* (2015–16), started on ABC. The *Agent Carter* television show marked the first Marvel Studio production to focus on a female lead. Agent Carter continues to play an increasingly important role in the MCU through her work in founding S.H.I.E.L.D. and through the love that Captain America feels for her, even after her death in *Captain America: The Winter Soldier* (2016).

In *Marvel's Agent Carter*, Carter is the only female SSR agent working as an investigator and field agent; thus, she occupies a role consistent with the token woman in the workplace. As Turner and Dunn explain, the "token woman in the workplace" in television narratives has the consistent trope and narrative device of "the display of gender difference and the challenge that the working woman makes toward stereotypical female gender roles."[25] This token standpoint is presented early in the first episode when Carter's red hat is moving among a sea of dark male hats and suits on her way to work.[26] Carter deals early on in the show with the chief trying to keep her out of briefings; with other agents sending her on coffee and food runs; with her co-workers pushing more secretarial work, like filing, to her; with sexual harassment; and with questions about how she even became an agent. But Carter meets all these tasks and accusations with witty retorts and a straight face. When asked to cover the phones while everyone else attends a briefing, she calmly picks up the phone and says, "Rose, forward all calls to the briefing room," while looking at the chief. She follows with "Covered. Shall we?" while walking into the briefing room.[27] When Agent Sousa tries to stick up for Carter with the other agents, she asks him not to, explaining "I'm also more than capable of handling whatever these adolescents throw at me."[28] The tropes of being the token woman in the SSR office are introduced in the first episode and carried throughout the show. Ratcliffe notes in her review of *Agent Carter* that Carter spends "most of the first season educating her

25. Turner and Dunn, "'I'm Your Person.'"
26. *Marvel's Agent Carter*, "Now."
27. *Marvel's Agent Carter*, "Now."
28. *Marvel's Agent Carter*, "Now."

co-workers . . . on her skillset."[29] She also saves the city and the country several times in the process of proving her worth. By the end of the season, the chief looks to Carter, asking her to catch the man responsible right before he throws himself out the window to save the SSR from a bomb strapped to his chest.

Throughout the television show, Carter is a strong, capable woman and an accomplished agent in espionage and combat. In season 2, the focus shifts to Carter's development of her standpoint through flashbacks to her childhood and young adulthood before joining the SOE. In a flashback to Carter as a young girl, she is shown playing outside in a game where she is saving a princess and slaying a dragon. Her mother admonishes her for playing and getting dirty, telling her, "One of these days, you're going to have to start behaving like a lady."[30] Later in this episode's flashbacks, Carter is talking to her older brother, Michael, at her engagement party, and as he questions her about turning down the job at the SOE, she uses "we" to talk about the plans for "our" life,[31] meaning herself, her fiancé, and even society at large. Carter winds up leaving home and placing her engagement ring on a dresser on her way out, a visual of leaving society's gendered expectations of her. The end of season 1 demonstrates that Peggy Carter has already developed her feminist standpoint of understanding her own worth when, in the season finale, Thompson takes all the credit for her work and Sousa begins to stand up for her again. But Carter tells Sousa, "I don't need a congressional honor. I don't need Agent Thompson's approval or the president's. I know my value. Anyone else's opinion doesn't really matter."[32] But season 2 adds to our understanding of how she developed this standpoint. This is a personal standpoint, wherein Carter mostly sees herself in relation to the patriarchy but defies this system by knowing her value and finding ways to use her talents to help society.

In season 1, there is only a glimmer of Carter moving her standpoint against the patriarchal system into a growing consciousness of the political realm for other women. This is when she defends Angie, a waitress at the local diner, from a regular male customer who torments and sexually harasses her. At the end of episode 1, Carter holds a fork to his chest, explaining that she could kill him with it, and insisting that he find another establishment in which to dine.[33] But it is in season 2 that she moves her

29. Ratcliffe, "'Agent Carter.'"
30. *Marvel's Agent Carter*, "Smoke."
31. *Marvel's Agent Carter*, "Smoke."
32. *Marvel's Agent Carter*, "Valediction."
33. *Marvel's Agent Carter*, "Now."

standpoint into action for others' benefit; she moves from the personal to the political. She does this first with Dr. Jason Wilkes, a Black male scientist at Isodyne. In this season, Carter commiserates with Wilkes over the oppression they face, like Carter does with her love interest Jones in the comics; she also actively works to help him find opportunities and improve his position, even when he has lost his corporeal body. She knows Wilkes is an incredibly intelligent scientist who deserves more than the only job offered to him upon completing his PhD. She extends her privilege with Rose at the SSR as well when she convinces Chief Sousa to have Rose join them on a mission to steal uranium from atomic bombs before the villainous Whitney Frost can. Sousa keeps saying they can't take Rose because he's afraid she will get hurt. Peggy points out, "She's passed all the same training as the men upstairs and she protects all of you. . . . She's smart, she's resourceful; and I trust her with my life."[34] Carter extends her standpoint in season 2 to help others. This shift exemplifies Moya's "realist theory of identity," which emphasizes the extent to which "identities are subject to multiple determinations and to a continual process of verification. . . . It is in this process of verification that identities can be (and often are) contested, and that they can (and often do) change."[35] Through convincing Sousa and others of Rose's value and worth in the field and as an agent, equal to "the men upstairs," Carter has begun to expand her standpoint, moving from the personal to the political, from within to outside herself, and challenging the biases of others in the racist and patriarchal society.

Throughout, the Carter of the MCU is a strong and capable woman, a founder of S.H.I.E.L.D., and a tough leader when women were often not in those roles. In *Civil War* (2016), as her niece Sharon Carter eulogizes Peggy Carter, she talks about how much she looked up to her aunt:

> I asked her once how she managed to master diplomacy and espionage in a time when no one wanted to see a woman succeed at either. She said, compromise where you can. But where you can't, don't. Even if everyone is telling you that something wrong is something right. Even if the whole world is telling you to move, it is your duty to plant yourself like a tree, look them in the eye, and say, "No, you move."[36]

Clearly, in this eulogy Peggy Carter was a role model for her niece and the way in which she developed her own standpoint of what it means to be

---

34. *Marvel's Agent Carter*, "The Atomic Job."
35. Moya, "Postmodernism," 139.
36. *Captain America: Civil War.*

a woman in a patriarchal society. This speech is a variation on one Captain America gives in an issue of *Amazing Spider-Man,* which is based on a Mark Twain speech. The fact that these words are then revised to be a feminist call that Peggy shares with the next generation of women agents demonstrates Carter passing down her standpoint. Carter plays an important role in the MCU, paving the way in the chronological story narrative for women in S.H.I.E.L.D., and in the Marvel studios as the first female to have her own production.

Mahoney argues that Carter is postfeminist in part because of Captain America's "implicit presence" in the series, which renders Carter's acts as small additions to his narrative, and that "her heroism is therefore construed as an extension or imitation of his acceptable male protectionism rather than anything uniquely or dangerously feminine."[37] Agent Carter as a character, while set historically in an early stage of second-wave feminism, also brings to mind ideas from third-wave and even fourth-wave feminism through-out her comic, film, and television narratives. Through an analysis of Agent Carter in the comics, in film, and in television, fans have seen a character that resonates with not just historic but also current political feminist arguments. Other critics of Carter as a feminist heroine have criticized her for her love affair with Captain America. Agent Carter reappears in the *Captain America* and *Avengers* movies because she plays an important role in his life and in the founding of S.H.I.E.L.D. Captain America calls Carter "the love of his life" in *Endgame.* And eventually, he gives up being Captain America to return to the 1940s and live a life with Carter at the end of the film. Scholars and media critics sometimes criticize Carter's character for not letting go of Captain America and her love for him, but in both MCU and the comics, Peggy Carter does move on from Captain America to have a fulfilling professional life and romantic relationships with other men. Stunningly, these same critics use a double standard for Captain America himself, never criticizing him for not moving on from his love for Peggy Carter. In the MCU, Captain America gives up his career to go back in time and have another chance with Carter, which I believe is more a testament to Carter than to him.

Scholars have cited several problems with narratives of feminist waves being disparate, including that they do not always encompass all voices;[38] chronological ordering glosses over or loses whole time periods;[39] and while making heroines of specific activists, it can ignore grassroots efforts.[40] Chamberlain argues, "In rejecting waves as generational difference, or the new

37. Mahoney, "Marvel's *Agent Carter,*" 76.
38. Springer, "Third Wave Black Feminism."
39. Laughlin et al., "Is It Time to Jump Ship?"
40. Laughlin et al., "Is It Time to Jump Ship?"

replacing the old, affect allows for a narrative in which each new incarnation contributes to an energized period of action to an ongoing feminist ocean."[41] Chamberlain insists on analyzing feminist waves through the use of "affective temporality," wherein each past generation feeds into the new generations and some of the fights do not change, while others evolve given the historical specificity of the moment. Therefore, I argue that MCU Agent Carter speaks to the fourth wave, in which her character was reborn. She uses the latest technology, combats sexism in everyday life and the workplace, is brilliant in science knowledge, and uplifts others, all while expanding her own consciousness. I do not believe that all readers and viewers see her through a postfeminist lens, thinking that "feminism's work is done." Instead, I see an echo of the movement that brought forth female scientists posting "distractingly sexy" photos on social media, the Everyday Sexism project, and grassroots groups working to uplift each other as they fight their own battles. Standpoint theory furthers an analysis of Carter because it recognizes the fluidity of developing a feminist consciousness: "Particularly important in this conversation is a constant recognition of the fluid and dynamic nature of standpoints, whose temporary stabilization facilitates an engagement with the social and political concerns of the moment, but whose continuous negotiation simultaneously allows for open and progressive communication."[42] Therefore, we can see the fluidity of watching an early second-wave feminist battle forces of evil and forces of patriarchy simultaneously while also considering how it relates to present-day struggles, which still affect the everyday lives of women in the workplace, especially women in male-dominated workplaces.

However, as feminist critics, we also have to recognize not only that standpoints are ever-evolving but also that when we use them in literary and media criticism, they might reflect the standpoint of the critic. As Lenz argues, "A more salient question, then, is to what extent any given literary analysis represents the standpoint of the *critic*, rather than the character or author."[43] Therefore, my reading of Agent Carter as a transmedia feminist, crossing generational times and media platforms, may very well be because I work in a male-dominated workplace where I have had to deal with sexual harassment, not too different from what Carter experienced. I view Agent Carter as a feminist character in the ways she connects audiences to second-wave, third-wave, and fourth-wave feminism, and thus her character reasserts the need for feminism across generations.

---

41. Chamberlain, *Feminist Fourth Wave*, 9.
42. Lenz, "Postcolonial," 117.
43. Lenz, "Postcolonial," 116.

Bibliography

Ahmed, Saladin (w), Javier Rodriquez (p), and Alvaro Lopez (i). *Exiles*, no. 3. Marvel, May 2018.

Buxton, Marc. "Agent Carter Comics: A Readers Guide." *Den of Geek*, January 5, 2016. https://www.denofgeek.com/us/books-comics/agent-carter/242441/agent-carter-comics-a-readers-guide.

Captain America: Civil War. Directed by Joe Russo and Anthony Russo. Walt Disney Pictures, 2016.

Captain America: The First Avenger. Directed by J. Johnson. Walt Disney Pictures, 2011.

Captain America: The Winter Soldier. Directed by Joe Russo and Anthony Russo. Walt Disney Pictures, 2014.

Chamberlain, Prudence. *The Feminist Fourth Wave: Affective Temporality.* New York: Palgrave Macmillan, 2017.

Chapman, Matt. "Agent Carter Season 3 Cast, Release Date, Trailer, Plot, Spoilers and Everything You Need to Know." *Digital Spy*, August 28, 2018. https://www.digitalspy.com/tv/ustv/a864970/agent-carter-season-3-hayley-atwell-cast-cancelled-trailer-release-date-renewal/.

"Character Close Up: Agent Peggy Carter." Marvel, n.d. https://www.marvel.com/comics/discover/442/agent-carter.

Damore, Meagan. "Goodbye, 'Agent Carter,' We Still Know Your Value." *CBR*, May 14, 2016. https://www.cbr.com/goodbye-agent-carter-we-still-know-your-value/.

Englehart, Steve (w), Sal Buscema (p), Frank Robbins (p), and Frank Giacola (i). "Scream the Scarlet Skull." *Captain America #185* (May 1975). [Marvel Comics Group].

Englehart, Steve (w), Sal Buscema (p), and Vince Colletta (i). "Slings and Arrows," *Captain America*, no. 179. Marvel Comics Group, November 1974.

Englehart, Steve (w), Sal Buscema (p), and John Verpoorten (i). "Cap Goes Mad!" *Captain America*, no. 162. Marvel Comics Group, June 1973.

Englehart, Steve (w), Herb Trimpe (p), Frank Giacola (i), and Mike Esposito (i). "Cap's Back!" *Captain America*, no. 184. Marvel Comics Group, April 1975.

Harding, Sandra. *Is Science Multicultural?: Postcolonialisms, Feminisms, and Epistemologies.* Bloomington: Indiana University Press, 1998.

Laughlin, Kathleen A. et al. "Is It Time to Jump Ship? Historians Rethink the Waves' Metaphor." *Feminist Formations* 22, no.1 (Spring 2010): 76–135.

Lee, Stan (w), Gene Colan (a), Adam Austin (p), and Gary Michaels (i). "If a Hostage Should Die!" *Tales of Suspense*, no. 77. Marvel Comics Group, May 1966.

Lenz, Brooke. "Postcolonial Fiction and the Outsider Within: Toward a Literary Practice of Feminist Standpoint Theory." *NWSA Journal* 16, no. 2 (Summer 2004): 98–120.

Mahoney, Cat. "Marvel's *Agent Carter*: [Peggy Punches Him in the Face]." *Women in Neoliberal Postfeminist Television Drama Representing Gendered Experiences of the Second World War.* Cham, Switzerland: Palgrave Pivot, 2019.

Marvel's Agent Carter. "The Atomic Job." *ABC*, 42:00. February 9, 2016.

———. "Now Is Not the End." *ABC*, 43:00. January 6, 2015.

———. "Smoke and Mirrors." *ABC*, 43:00. February 2, 2016.

——. "Valediction." *ABC*, 42:00. February 24, 2015.

Moya, Paula M. L. "Postmodernism, 'Realism,' and the Politics of Identity: Cherrie Moraga and Chicana Feminism." In *Feminist Genealogies, Colonial Legacies, Democratic Futures*, edited by M. Jacqui Alexander and Chandra Talpade Mohanty, 125–50. New York: Routledge, 1996.

Ratcliffe, Amy. "'Agent Carter' Showrunners Explain Peggy's Friendship with Jarvis, Madame Masque's Role." *CBR*, January 12, 2016. https://www.cbr.com/agent-carter-showrunners-explain-peggys-friendship-with-jarvis-madame-masques-role/.

Riesman, Abraham. "Who Is Agent Carter? A Brief History of the Marvel Heroine." *Vulture*, January 19, 2016. https://www.vulture.com/2015/01/agent-carter-hayley-atwell.html.

Ryan, Maureen. "Why 'Marvel's Agent Carter' Should Battle On." *Variety*, March 1, 2016. https://variety.com/2016/tv/columns/marvels-agent-carter-1201718887/.

Springer, Kimberly. "Third Wave Black Feminism." *Signs* 25, no. 4 (Summer 2002): 1059–82.

Turner, Kathleen M., and Jennifer C. Dunn. "'I'm Your Person': Television Narrates Female Friendships in the Workplace from *Cagney and Lacey* to *Grey's Anatomy*." In *Transgressing Feminist Theory and Discourse: Advancing Conversations Across Disciplines*, edited by Jennifer C. Dunn and Jimmie Manning, 165–78. New York: Routledge, 2018.

CHAPTER 6

Jessica Jones

A Superhero, Unadorned

Amanda K. Kehrberg

A dark night in Hell's Kitchen: Jessica Jones saunters down the sidewalk, framed by neon lights and billowing smoke from a nearby steam stack. She stops and heaves a sigh, glancing back at a bright-green sign advertising her beverage of choice: Fine Whiskies (or, at least, whiskies). Her green canvas camera bag swings at her side as she enters the bodega: she's tall and lanky, dressed in her staple boots, distressed boyfriend jeans, and black-leather moto jacket, her wavy black hair swaying freely with the light tinkling of the doorbell.

Jessica has barely had time to browse the liquor shelves before a man enters and raises a gun, shouting at the shop owner, "Just give me the cash, man!" She echoes the cashier's reaction: "Shit." The would-be robber cocks his gun—and then he's down, gripping his bleeding head in pain, hit by an expertly thrown whiskey bottle.[1] But before Jessica can apprehend him, she has to take the dropped gun away from the shop owner, who has already grabbed it and threatened the thief with increasing aggression. She holds him by the scruff of his shirt: "Get your goddamn phone and call the god-

---

1. In the original version of this scene in the comics, *Alias: Vol. 3*, Jessica first throws a can of soup—and misses. But using an icon of domestic Americana as a would-be weapon is very representative of a character who eschews normative gender roles.

damn police," she says. "Now." As she heads for the door, holding another bottle of whiskey, he calls her back to pay. She rolls her eyes, shoulders collapsing in incredulous submission, and returns to the counter.

This scene from the final episode of the second season of Netflix's *Jessica Jones* (2015–19) captures the subversion of the classic superhero that defines Jessica as a character. It is both a visual and a narrative subversion: she neither looks nor acts the part of a traditional, normative hero. There is no flashy, bombastic valor here—only a sort of begrudging willingness to help from someone who is clearly struggling with her own inner villains. There is no colorful spandex—only comfortable, casual, distressed layers. But more than this, there is a fluidity and breakdown of stable roles that is essential to understanding Jessica Jones. It takes only seconds for the shop owner to go from victim to aggressor, the thief from criminal to desperate victim, and Jessica herself from hero to—in the shop owner's eyes—would-be thief.

Both Jessica Jones the comic book heroine and the Netflix lead (as played by former model Krysten Ritter) have been celebrated by popular and academic sources as distinctly feminist characters, praised for the narrative centering of women, diminished sexual objectification of women's bodies, and behind-the-scenes championing of women creators. But reading Jessica Jones specifically through the lens of postmodern feminism, with its rebellion against binary gender, reveals what makes this character uniquely revolutionary: through her refusal of the traditional superhero costume, she refuses to *do* gender as a necessary part of *doing* heroism. By directly problematizing the superhero costume as a source of gendered control, Jessica presents a subjective challenge to binary gender performativity *and* to gendered, binary morality. If superheroes are champions of goodness, Jessica challenges the audience, then why is goodness normatively gendered?

Importantly, this postmodern feminist reading of the superhero costume is done most successfully through the transmedia expansion of the character into the Netflix streaming universe. As theorized by Henry Jenkins, transmedia storytelling is an act of "world making," spreading a story across multiple media platforms and encouraging active participation and interaction from fans.[2] As comics and media fandom become an increasingly diverse space, women still face issues with sexual harassment and body shaming. For these fans, Jessica's treatment of a traditional superhero costume acts as a metaphor for objectification, while her easily recognizable outfit invites inclusive cosplay.

---

2. Jenkins, *Convergence Culture*, 21.

"Not trim. And definitely not nice"

The character of Jessica Jones first launched in 2001 in the comic book series *Alias*, written by Brian Michael Bendis and illustrated by Michael Gaydos. It was published under Marvel Comics' brand-new MAX label, launched for adult readers only, and distinguished itself immediately as the "first time the F-bomb was used repeatedly."[3] As the hero Thor says to a young Jessica, "Young maiden of Midgard, thy language leaves something to be desired."[4] Indeed, for a character immediately defined by her "give-no-fucks attitude about what is expected of her as a woman by men and other women," Jessica was given quite a few to dole out.[5] Jessica's superpowers include superhuman strength and resistance to injury, as well as an ability to jump extremely high and control her fall in a way that might, possibly, be defined as flying. In the comics, Jessica's powers are the result of exposure to radioactive chemicals following a car accident that kills the rest of her family; in the Netflix series, her powers are instead the result of secret experiments that save her life following the crash.

As Nicholas William Moll explains, "While Jessica is a protagonist, the character is not presented within *Alias* as a superheroine in outlook or activity."[6] She lacks everything that would traditionally define the superhero in comics: the secret identity, the costume, the superhero moniker, the membership in famed superhero teams, and, for female heroes in particular, the male counterpart. The gritty spectrum of grays that distinguished the comics visually were echoed in Jessica's shapeless, baggy clothes and unwillingness to intervene, often leaving matters of justice to existing institutions. In fact, when we meet Jessica in both the comics and the series, she is a *former* superhero turned hard-boiled, world-weary private eye. Jessica's negotiation with the trauma and containment of the superhero identity is where she most distinguishes herself as a uniquely feminist character.

Jessica Jones, from her portrayal in the original comics, to the Netflix series, to the recent audiobook,[7] is a character overcoming trauma and dealing daily with the effects of posttraumatic stress disorder (PTSD). In this she follows a long line of Marvel superheroes who owe their complex character-

---

3. Weiner, "Super Jessica Jones," Kindle loc. 42.
4. Bendis (w), Gaydos (a), *Jessica Jones: Alias Volume 4*.
5. Johnson, "Jessica Jones's Feminism," Kindle loc. 3066.
6. Moll, "Elite and Famous," Kindle loc. 651.
7. *Jessica Jones: Playing with Fire* was still airing as of the writing of this chapter but already featured our hero going straight from beating up ice-cream-truck villains to a therapy appointment.

izations to the genius of Stan Lee. But Jessica's world is one in which "the wrongs to be righted, those that official justice cannot and will not address, are specifically gendered."[8] Her story is one of challenging and surviving toxic masculinity, patriarchy, gendered violence and shame, the fight for choice and control over one's own body, and the failures of systems to support and believe women. These issues are best embodied in the supervillain Kilgrave (dubbed the Purple Man in the comics), played by David Tennant in the Netflix series.[9] Kilgrave's superpower is mind control, and for months he held Jessica under his power. This dichotomy is, itself, subversive: Jessica's power, her super strength, is normatively masculine, while Kilgrave's, expressed through communication, is normatively feminine—he needs Jessica, literally, to do the heavy lifting. In both the comics and the series, Kilgrave's abduction of Jessica begins when he sees her in an act of heroism; thus, being a hero for the Jessica we meet is tainted by its subsequent containment by toxic masculinity. Ultimately, Jessica reclaims the mantle of hero to protect other vulnerable women from Kilgrave's powers, and through facing him reclaims her own empowered sense of self.[10]

"I threaten your masculinity, or whatever"

To borrow the language of internet memes, Jessica Jones the comic book character walked so that Jessica Jones the Netflix lead could run. Though premiering just under two years before the MeToo hashtag launched a national movement, *Jessica Jones* seems in direct conversation with the forthcoming push for increased gender parity both behind and in front of the camera. The series showed an early commitment to empowering women creators, helmed by creator-showrunner Melissa Rosenberg, a writing staff of at least 50 percent women, and a slate of all-female directors in the final season.[11] Widely praised as a feminist triumph, the show demonstrated third-wave feminism's value of change via participation and action. Rosenberg had identified a gap in the rise of prestige television: the antiheroine,

---

8. Nadkarni, "Feminism and Resistance," 75.

9. In the Marvel comics, the villain's full name is Zebediah Killgrave; in the Netflix series, he chooses to go by the single name Kilgrave. For the purposes of this chapter, he is referred to by the Netflix spelling.

10. In the series, Kilgrave threatens an innocent college student, Hope Schlottman, as well as Jessica's best friend and adopted sister, Trish Walker. In the comics, Kilgrave's final threat comes against Jessica's daughter, Danielle.

11. Green, "Fantasy, Gender and Power."

a female protagonist whose flaws could match those of Tony Soprano.[12] And while Rosenberg distanced herself from feminist progress as the goal,[13] instead focusing on the show as a deep character study, her vision for Jessica moved subtextual themes from the comics to explicit text.

Most importantly, the series names Kilgrave's abuse of Jessica rape, parting dramatically from the comic source. It is brutally honest in its look at the aftermath of rape; as Melissa C. Johnson notes, the comic "gives Jones a fuller, richer life than the first season of the television series, but it may only do so because it refuses to recognize the full impact of rape on the lives of women."[14] While comic Jessica goes on to marry and have a child with superhero Luke Cage, and receives support from the broader hero community, Netflix Jessica is largely isolated. She treats her PTSD with a combination of a severe alcohol addiction[15] and a mantra taught to her by one of many failed therapists, the repeated street names of her idyllic childhood. As Netflix's Marvel universe gives a street-level grounding to the broader Marvel Cinematic Universe, so Rosenberg's *Jessica Jones* uses the disbelief Jessica faces in naming Kilgrave's powers as a metaphor for systemic rape culture, turning the fantastical supervillain into a personification of patriarchy.[16] Even Kilgrave's hurried defense when Jessica confronts him—that he didn't know what he was doing, that he has to choose his words *so* carefully—has the echo of pushback to a post-MeToo human resources training. As adopted sister Trish Walker says to Jessica in a moment of support and solidarity, "Men and power, it's seriously a disease."[17]

Netflix's *Jessica Jones* is also progressive in pushing past patterns of women's representation in media, particularly in male-dominated-and-consumed genres. Over the past decades, scholars have noted an increase in women detectives and action heroes, particularly on television, as well as complex female characters in neo- and feminist noir. And yet, while these characters may transgress many tropes of feminine characters—disrupting the passivity associated with femininity and taking hold of an active gaze traditionally coded as masculine—their transgressions are nevertheless generally recontained via the sexualizing, objectifying gaze of both male characters

---

12. Fuller and Edwards, "Integrity, Family and Consent."

13. Kiley and Roman, "Mirrored Archetypes."

14. Johnson, "Jessica Jones's Feminism," Kindle loc. 3070.

15. One calculation suggests that she spent about $665 on on-camera liquor in the first season. See Canal, "Jones Spends on Booze."

16. For more on this, see also Binns, "Femme Fatale"; Devereaux, "Cycles of Abuse"; Wigard, "Chronotopal Representation."

17. *Jessica Jones*, "AKA 99 Friends."

and the camera itself. Although the world of the mediated superhero has seen increased female inclusion both narratively and creatively,[18] it remains a genre with much room for improvement. Despite the fantastical nature of superheroes, writes Carol A. Stabile, creators apparently "cannot imagine women who can protect or who need no more protection than men," exemplifying an American culture "unable to imagine femininity absent vulnerability."[19] In a study of decades of comics' representation of female characters, Carolyn Cocca finds rampant sexual objectification and a consistent underrepresentation of female characters even in female-led comics, though these trends decreased in the 2010s.[20] The Marvel Cinematic Universe reveals many of the same issues, with few female-titled films, and only thirteen of twenty-three films passing the Bechdel test.[21]

Arriving in this environment as a female-lead superhero series centered on women's issues, *Jessica Jones* is understandably read as a feminist success. But it is in the character's subversion of the gender binary through the metaphor of the superhero costume that it pushes and extends both postmodern feminist theory *and* the norms of the superhero genre.

"Keep telling me who I am, I dare you"

Postmodern feminist theory draws on postmodernism's breakdown of heretofore stable, separate categories (like low art vs. high art) to tear apart the traditional gender binary juxtaposing normative femininity and masculinity so that "one cannot be played against the other as normal and deviant, valued and stigmatized."[22] Heralding a multiplicity of gender and sexual identities, postmodern feminist scholars analyze how mass media and pop culture support structures of heteronormativity and binary hegemony. Foremost among these scholars is Judith Butler, whose conceptualization of "performativity" deconstructs gender as not a "stable identity" but one that must be continuously reconstituted through both "a stylized repetition of acts" and the "stylization of the body."[23] According to Butler, gender is not some-

---

18. Curtis and Cardo, "Third-Wave Feminism."
19. Stabile, "Sexism and Superheroes," 91.
20. Cocca, "Portrayals of Women."
21. Temuzion, "Sex Equality." Named for author Alison Bechdel, the Bechdel test requires that at least two female characters speak to each other about something other than a man.
22. Lorber, *Gender Inequality*, 285.
23. Butler, "Performative Acts," 419.

thing that *is* but rather something that is *done*—and something that, if done wrong in the context of a heteronormative society, may endanger the doer.

Like the performance of a role on the stage, the performance of gender is marked by inauthenticity and the presence of an audience. Sandra Lee Bartky draws on Foucault's concept of panopticism in contending that this "audience" is understood to be ever present in consuming the gendered spectacle of women's bodies.[24] It is an audience both external, regardless of gender identity, and internalized, exemplified in *Jessica Jones* by the chauvinistic language and actions of both male and female characters.[25] In one of the early scenes of the series, it seems even Jessica herself has taken on the role of gender-binary panopticon. She perches on a fire escape, pointing her zoom lens at the lit-up windows of unsuspecting residents. Through one window frame, she watches an overweight woman leaving her cardio machine for a juicy burger; through another, a man steals a moment to sniff his female companion's high-heeled shoes. Jessica's reaction to these gender transgressions is swift and judgmental: she mocks the exerciser and says "ew" to the sniffer. But there are complicated layers to this scene. On the one hand, it is the camera's judgment that speaks through Jessica, acting stereotypically to punish nonnormative gender, expressed here through the purported failed femininity of the overweight woman or the failed masculinity of the man obsessed with women's shoes. But this doesn't quite make sense with what we know of Jessica; instead, Jessica's displeasure can be read as disapproval of structures of heteronormativity that force the woman into uncomfortable cardio and force the man to hide his fetish. Throughout her stories, Jessica is fearsome in protecting her individuality and subjectivity, which makes her an especially interesting character within the construct of performativity. As theorized by Butler, performativity has been critiqued for suggesting that there is no subject behind the performance who wields agency,[26] while others argue that it is definitively an act of subjectivity, renegotiating and reconstituting the gendered self dependent on shifting contexts.[27] For Jessica, because the performance of gender is critiqued through the metaphor of costume, there is clearly an active agent (if you will, a secret identity).

---

24. Bartky, "Modernization of Patriarchal Power."

25. Kilgrave is not the only chauvinist in Hell's Kitchen, as third-wave feminism critic Ariel Levy would recognize. It is Trish who seeks to squeeze Jessica into a pink-and-white spandex costume, and it is Jeri Hogarth (the ball-breaking lesbian lawyer played by Carrie-Anne Moss) who both disbelieves Jessica and Hope's claims about Kilgrave's power and mocks her former assistant and lover's lawsuit, asking: "Did you not see the way she dressed?" (season 2, episode 1). Also see Levy, *Female Chauvinist Pigs.*

26. Salih, "On Judith Butler."

27. Jackson, "Performativity Identified."

"Shut up and sit shot-gun"

If DC Comics' Clark Kent is the definitive superhero alter ego, then his true female counterpart is the Hot Librarian.[28] Both remove glasses to reveal an ideal of heteronormative gender expression: Kent reveals Superman, a paragon of masculine strength and heroism; the Librarian reveals a paragon of femininity, the hypersexualized, voluptuous woman. As Aleah Kiley and Zak Roman explain, "Traditionally, male superheroes imbued with normative masculine codes have defined the comic book hero archetype . . . when strong women do appear, they are frequently represented in a sexualized manner, thereby taming female empowerment."[29] Comic books have a long history of championing heteronormativity as one of many traditional American values, celebrating strong, masculine heroes and relegating women to secondary roles, emphasizing their sexuality and weakness and their need, therefore, of rescue.[30] Indeed, one study of superhero content aimed at children found both that gender stereotypes were consistently present and that exposure to the content produced "greater adherence to gender stereotypes for boys . . . both in the short- and long-term."[31] Superheroes' representation of gendered, sexual ideals goes hand in hand with the traditional narrative thrust to uphold and maintain the status quo.[32]

In Netflix's *Jessica Jones*, these gender norms are problematized, vilified, and rejected. Even the car crash that led to her family's deaths is tied to heteronormative gender roles. In season 2, Jessica learns that her mother survived the crash, too, subject to the same extreme experiments that turned her into a powered person. Her reconnection with her mom is dangerous for Jessica on multiple levels, not least because it destroys the illusion she had of her idyllic family life in the suburbs. Jessica's mother, Alisa, paints a different picture: of a brilliant mathematician whose ambition was stymied by a resentful husband, a dynamic that comes to a head when Alisa consents, once again, to let Jessica's father drive the family. Calling Jessica's father a terrible driver, Alisa contends that if she hadn't agreed to "shut up and sit

---

28. "Hot Librarian."

29. Kiley and Roman, "AKA Occasionally," Kindle loc. 908.

30. See also D'Amore, "Accidental Supermom"; Lavin, "Women in Comic Books"; Moll, "Elite and Famous"; Robinson, *Feminisms and Superheroes*; Schubart, "Bulk, Breast, and Beauty."

31. Coyne et al., "Gender Stereotyped Play," 427. For more on gender stereotypes and superhero multimedia for youth, see Baker and Raney, "Equally Super?"; Dallacqua and Low, "Cupcakes and Beefcakes."

32. Brown, "Maternity and the Monstrous-Feminine."

shot-gun" that day (as in life), the whole family would be alive.[33] The great supervillain of Jessica's life is not just the patriarchal metaphor made manifest in Kilgrave but the actual, daily, mundane adherence to heteronormative gender roles.

"Jewel is a stripper's name"

As Maggie Humm explains, "The core of feminist theory is a struggle with representations . . . [and taking action to] deconstruct these false selves."[34] Jessica's confrontation of her trauma from her time with Kilgrave, as well as her rejection of others' expectations of her, is likewise a deconstruction of false selves. But the false self that she spends the most time combatting is the hero, as represented by a costume. Consider the scene in which Trish approaches her with a superhero costume: the more normatively feminine Trish holds the bright white-and-purple costume aloft, with its low neckline and tight, spandex fabric. Jessica immediately dismisses the outfit as fit only for "trick or treating" or "some kinky role-play scenario." When Trish suggests Jewel as a superhero name, Jessica is typically incredulous: "Jewel is a stripper's name. A really slutty stripper. And if I wear that thing you're gonna have to call me Camel Toe."[35] Putting aside how Jessica's language problematically undermines third-wave feminism's reclamation of terms like *slut*, it's clear that what she objects to is the reduction of herself to a gendered body, and a normatively gendered identity. She cannot separate the heroic identity from the gender performance it entails; thus, what Jessica makes clear is that other superheroes are performing gender. *Doing* heroism, as Jessica understands it, cannot be separated from *doing* gender; and when she does attempt heroics without the costume is when she is narratively punished through the patriarchal villain of Kilgrave.

Jessica's rejection of the secret identity as Jewel and the costume itself are the starkest departures the Netflix series makes in its first season from the character's comic book origins. In the comics, when we first meet Jessica-the-former-superhero, it is after she has shed the identity of Jewel and its accompanying pink hair and shiny, skintight costume. When Kilgrave first sees her, it is in this costume; thus, she associates the costume and Jewel per-

---

33. *Jessica Jones*, "AKA Shark in the Bathtub."

34. Humm, *Feminism and Film*, 193.

35. *Jessica Jones*, "AKA The Sandwich Saved Me." Funnily, Jessica's first act of heroism occurs in the series when she is dressed as a sandwich.

manently with her sexualization, objectification, and gendered violence and abuse at the hands of Kilgrave. In the comics, this understanding is reflected through stylistic choices that further reinforce the metaphor of superhero costume for heteronormative gender performance. While Jessica's daily life is presented in the spectrum of dull grays and hard, heavy shadows, "recollections of her time as a superheroine, however, are presented in the four color style emblematic of superhero comic books with defined, thin, lines and a limited but bright color pallet [*sic*]."[36] In other words, her time as Jewel looks visually like most comic books. Indeed, Bendis and Gaydos push to the point of parody in their distinction between the new Jessica Jones and twentieth-century superheroes. The color palette is not the only difference; Jessica is also drawn differently in these sequences, with fuller, pouty lips, wide eyes, and a voluptuous figure that threatens to burst from the top of her costume.[37] In one panel in *Alias: Volume 3*, she even produces two pink orbs of energy from her red-clenched fists, filling the frame like a pair of breasts. It's all a direct nod to the traditional sexualization, objectification, and fragmentation of women's bodies in superhero comics. In the costume, Jessica Jones becomes the heteronormative Jewel, whose gender performance is defined by this hypersexualization; her arc is about negotiating a way to be the heroic body without the gendered body.

There is one other representation of Jessica Jones as Jewel, however: *Lego Marvel's Avengers*, the video game.[38] The player meets her on a street corner in downtown New York, in a strange, contorted pose, wondering aloud what is keeping her four nanny applicants.[39] The would-be nannies for her daughter, Danielle, include fellow superheroines Squirrel Girl, Mantis, Echo, and She-Hulk. Interestingly, this same story does take place in the comics, but it includes a much wider variety of applicants (including, of course, Deadpool). In the comics, Squirrel Girl gets the job, something that makes perfect sense given Squirrel Girl's unique construction as a feminist, pacifist, caring superhero.[40] Even this scene can be read as subversively calling attention to both past representations of superheroines as maternal ideals[41] and the rhetoric around working supermoms in modern America. In the

---

36. Moll, "Elite and Famous," Kindle loc. 686.

37. Bendis (w) and Gaydos (a), *The Underneath*.

38. Traveller's Tales, *Lego Marvel's Avengers*.

39. Though in the comics, Jessica does not reclaim the Jewel persona, she does have a child with fellow superhero Luke Cage. In fact, she goes on later to adopt a gendered version of his superhero identity, becoming Power Woman to his Power Man.

40. Goodrum, Prescott, and Smith, *Superhero Narrative*.

41. D'Amore, "Accidental Supermom"; Brown, "Supermoms?"

bright, colorful universe of Lego Marvel, Jessica Jones's superhero identity *is*, in effect, working mom, and to reach a supermom ideal in the twenty-first century requires the labor of not just two superhero parents but a superheroine nanny.

In the comics, Jessica's rejection of normative gender performance as represented through superheroism finds a voice in her disgust at female heroes based on existing male heroes. Asked what a fleeing new superheroine looked like, she vulgarly remarks: "Like Spider-Man with little tits."[42] Again, this could be read as potentially regressive; the way she dismisses She-Hulk, too, is concerning given She-Hulk's transgression of normative superheroine tropes through both her career as a successful lawyer and her oversized green muscles (which feature prominently in the comics as she plays with Jessica's baby). But with Jessica it is likely more of a reach for authenticity and individuality independent of gender binaries. This argument is reflected in season 3 of the series, in which a serial killer criticizes her standard outfit: "Take your intentionally indifferent rebel-rock garb, for example. They are your cape, your mask, and your armor."[43] It isn't the first time someone has described her look as knowingly constructed enough to qualify as artifice; in season 1, she sits uncomfortably as a neighbor refers to her childhood self as "the strangest tomboy."[44] But to Jessica, the idea of the authentic subject beneath the labels, performance, and binaries is essential.

In the Netflix series, the four-color palette of normative superheroes exists in the broader transmedia Marvel universe, so Jessica's rejection of the Jewel costume is as much a critique of the MCU itself and its representations of gender. And though her experience with Netflix Kilgrave lacks the Jewel outfit, it is still represented through gendered costumes. When she first meets Kilgrave, her attire is one of the first things he comments on. We see later in flashbacks how he has dressed her to emphasize her femininity and sexuality: she appears in violet gowns and sparkling chandelier earrings, in layers of light yellow chiffon blowing in the terrace breeze, and in tight, fur-trimmed coats. When he jokes, "Really, I can't get her to wear a dress for the life of me," what he means is, I can only do it because *I* can *make* her.[45] While Jessica doesn't change costume to trick Kilgrave in later scenes in the show, when she either pretends she is under control or seeks

---

42. Bendis (w) and Gaydos (a), *The Underneath*.

43. *Jessica Jones*, "AKA A Lotta Worms."

44. *Jessica Jones*, "AKA WWJD."

45. *Jessica Jones*, "AKA WWJD." Jessica's response to this is masterful: "I'll wear one to your funeral."

to bait him into using his powers by playing to his fantasies, it is still a performance: one of heightened, stylized femininity and sexuality.

"The burden we have to carry"

Throughout the Netflix series, Jessica rejects binaries and labels, particularly as they relate to gender and heroism. As much as she is defined as a hero by other characters, she is also defined by her gender: she is called a "lovely young woman," a "mess of a woman," a "small woman," an "unusual woman," to name a few. She mockingly pre-empts the label given to her by one man: "A bitch?" But the only label she adopts is when Luke Cage refers to her as "a piece of shit." We see her next in a pile of trash in an alley, where she contends she belongs. Thus, she is as likely to reject—though not as directly—gendered constructs as she is to reject heroic constructs. The entire arc of the series follows her journey to accepting that she can be a hero, but there is little progress made: Jessica ends the series finale exactly where she began, just about to run away before deciding, at the last moment, to stay.

One of the ways to read her rejection of the "hero" label is how it is applied through binary moral constructs. As noted, superhero actions and ethics tend to be rooted in normative masculine ideologies, focused on strength and violence. Multiple scholars have undertaken analyses of how female heroes act in feminist ethical paradigms.[46] In *Jessica Jones*, the spectrum of femininity represented by Jessica and Trish is reflected in each character's morality. As Trish's mother, Dorothy, says of the two from the time they were children, "You were her protector. She was your conscience."[47] This is a dynamic that Trish seeks to maintain throughout the series; that is, Trish, defined by more normative femininity, is also defined as more normatively moral. But what does normatively feminine morality look like, in the context of superheroes?

One possibility is Nel Noddings's ethics of care, developed from a feminist standpoint and "based on a relational ontology; that is, it takes as a basic assumption that all human beings—not just women—are defined in relation."[48] To a certain extent, this relational nature is founded in how women have traditionally been defined by society through their relations to others (again, with a connection to the grammar of object vs. subject): pos-

---

46. See Goodrum, Prescott, and Smith, *Superhero Narrative*; Greven, *Bionic Woman*.
47. *Jessica Jones*, "AKA The Perfect Burger."
48. Noddings, *Ethics & Moral Education*, 236–37.

sessed—in practice and syntax—as another's wife, mother, or sister. Embracing the positive nature of relational values, Noddings defines care ethics by virtues like friendship and empathy. Feminist scholars critiquing Noddings's ethic of relational-prioritizing care problematize its use of traditional gender roles, emphasize the need for a dual ethic of justice and self-care, and contend that, in practice, women who support and care for dangerous and violent relations may act ultimately only to support systems of cruelty.[49] While Noddings emphasizes that her theory calls everyone, not just women, to be carers, she nonetheless suggests the possibility of exacerbating cruelty in severing relational ties unless necessary for personal safety.

Jessica is faced three times with the exact dilemma contained in Noddings's care ethics. The first happens both in the comics and at the end of season 1, when a desperate Kilgrave seeks to keep Jessica by offering himself to her command. "I can't be a hero without you," says the Netflix Kilgrave, whom even Jessica admits was never taught the difference between right and wrong. While Netflix Jessica quickly dismisses the offer, comics Jessica is more torn: "I considered it. Of course I considered it . . . How easy it would be to put Kilgrave and his power over all people in a position to stop the assholes . . . For my daughter. . . . I could save the world."[50] In season 2, it is Jessica's mother who asks Jessica to watch over and contain her dangerous, violent spells in exchange for a continued relationship; we never quite know whether Jessica would have accepted, as it is Trish who deems Jessica's mother too dangerous and kills her. Finally, in season 3 (and in every season, this moral dilemma occurs in episode 9 exactly), it is a serial killer who threatens to out Trish as a murdering vigilante unless Jessica ignores his crimes. Here, again, she chooses what she views as right over her care for and relationship with her adopted sister.

If anything, Jessica's feminist ethic is one defined only by obligation, one that must be negotiated consistently, based on context and situation, as changeable and fluid as gender. It is complicated by power differentials and systemic oppression. For example, Jessica emphasizes to Hope (a young victim of Kilgrave's) that neither of them is responsible for what they each did while under Kilgrave's control. And yet, the guilt remains. When Trish expresses the anger that ultimately overwhelms her at the moral failings of the world, it is Jessica whose usual cynicism manifests as a kind of quiet acceptance: that anger, she says, "is the burden we have to carry."

---

49. See Card, "Caring and Evil"; Hassan, "Care Critique"; Hoagland, "Nel Noddings"; Kaplan, "Woman as Caretaker."

50. Bendis et al., *Return of the Purple Man.*

"I love that I wasn't wearing tight jeans, I was wearing comfortable, practical things"

Jessica Jones premiered on Netflix in 2015 to a much-changed, increasingly diverse world of geek culture and fandom. Though the increasing influx of female fans to conventions—as creators, stars, and consumers—was widely celebrated, it was not without tension. Women fans appearing in cosplay express enthusiasm for how attending conventions in costumes is an act of sexual empowerment and triumph over traditional objectification, but they still face alarming amounts of body shaming and sexual harassment.[51] Other fangirls may seek to make their presence in these still male-dominated spaces invisible to avoid stigmatization.[52] Responding to trends of sexual harassment and abuse of women fans in particular, New York Comic Con introduced a new campaign in 2014: "Cosplay Is Not Consent."[53] Placed prominently throughout the convention center, these signs reminded patrons that costumes did not give anyone the right to touch another's body. The slogan directly reflects the arc of Jessica Jones as a character; she fights to prove that neither heroism, nor costuming, nor caring, constitute consent, against a villain who believes he has a right to her body.

This message from the character is especially amplified, and poignant, in the Netflix series—the evolution of a medium (television) long engaged in conversation with feminism before film, ensconced as it was in the domestic space of the home.[54] In this transmedia extension of the Marvel mothership, character supplants spectacle as audiences are invited to binge-watch and enmesh themselves in deep identification. As Stephanie Green explains, "Team Rosenberg's take on the MCU figure of Jessica Jones offers a key example of how the roles and representations of women in transmedia narratives can engage audiences in recognizing some of the inconsistences and tensions of social, cultural, and identity politics in compelling and accessible ways."[55] According to Lillian Cespédes González, it is precisely the community-fostering, interaction-encouraging nature of transmedia worldbuilding that ultimately engages fans in challenging patterns of sexism and producing industry change.[56] But the message was not meant to deny fans

---

51. McKinney, "How Cosplay Empowers Women."
52. Orme, "Femininity and Fandom."
53. Mulkerin, "'Cosplay Is Not Consent.'"
54. Johnson, "Rhetoric of Pleasure."
55. Green, "Fantasy, Gender and Power," 182.
56. Cespédes González, "Gender and the Marvel Phenomenon."

the joys and play of costumes. Cosplay is in fact an important way that women participate in transmedia narratives as creators and active consumers, building both faithful adaptations of characters or mixing them up, including participating in gender swapping.[57] Rather, from the beginning, Rosenberg set out to design Jessica Jones as a "Halloween costume."[58] The outfit she wears—boots, distressed boyfriend jeans, black moto jacket, and gray scarf—was crafted to be both easily recognizable in its repetition and inclusive, accessible, and welcoming to a growing cohort of diverse comics fans. A quick Google search demonstrates the success of these efforts; there are endless pages with guides to recreating Jessica's "costume," from Pinterest boards to YouTube tutorials, and even handmade scarves sold on Etsy. The new look had such an impact that it retroactively impacted the original comics character, as Bendis shifted Jessica's look to better reflect the Netflix character.

"It's all personal, Mel"

One would be forgiven for thinking the Marvel Cinematic Universe's representation of female characters looked rather like the old sexism in a new package. Using the case studies of Black Widow, Scarlet Witch, and Mystique, Robyn Joffe contends that the MCU continues postfeminist patterns of undermining strong female characters through double standards, sexualization, and objectification.[59] But in the transmedia extensions of the Marvel world, different modes of representation were given room to flourish—in particular, on Netflix, Melissa Rosenberg's adaptation of the deeply flawed former-superhero Jessica Jones. Through the lens of postmodern feminism as constructed by scholars like Judith Butler, Jessica Jones functions uniquely within both Marvel and the history of comics more broadly to make visible how superheroes *do* gender at the same time they *do* heroism, exemplified through the metaphor of the costume for gender performance. Jessica's denial of the costume, then, allows her to negotiate her own gender as she does her own heroism—with difficulty, and cynicism, and a few rolls of the eyes, but still with a stubborn sense of integrity.

It is not surprising that Netflix's *Jessica Jones* was particularly popular among millennials, for whom "intentionality and self-definition" are "among

57. Nichols, "Feminine Agency in Cosplay."
58. Rosenberg and Ritter, "Marvel's Jessica Jones."
59. Joffe, "Treatment of Female Superheroes."

the most treasured character traits."[60] As Louisa Ellen Stein explains, millennials as television audiences are particularly receptive to themes of ambiguity and "gender negotiation."[61] This trend has continued into the next generation, as youth increasingly reject labels and stable gender categorization. According to research by the Trevor Project in 2019, for example, 25 percent of LGBTQ youth ages thirteen to twenty-four did not identify with the gender binary, including many who chose to write in their own personal experience with gender-identity negotiation.[62]

But perhaps the resonance of Jessica Jones with today's younger fans is best exemplified through the nineteen-year-old singer-songwriter Billie Eilish, who in 2020 became the youngest artist ever (and only the second artist) to sweep all four major Grammy Award categories. Long known for her baggy, non-form-fitting clothing, making her unique among sexualized young female artists, Eilish explained that she chose her outfits specifically to obscure the body underneath and to ward off gendered criticism: "Nobody can have an opinion because they haven't seen what's underneath."[63] There is a clear reflection in Eilish's choice of nonforming (and thus nonconforming) clothes to the oversized, casual outfits worn by Jessica Jones. If Jessica's fight is against a presumption of consent contained in her costumed, gendered performance, or in merely her heroic performance, then is Eilish's against a presumption of consent to her gendered, sexed body contained in her fame? Is the patriarchal threat to each woman activated specifically by their supposed courting of attention and audience through their acts as hero (as superhero) or hero (as celebrity)? In discussing how transgressive gender performance is published by heteronormative society, Butler argues that we must question whether "the category of woman is socially constructed in such a way that to be a woman is, by definition, to be in an oppressed situation."[64] If so, both Jessica and Eilish can be read as acting to avoid systemic, gendered oppression by hiding the sexed subject/body.[65] This self, this body, is the secret identity.

---

60. Fuller and Edwards, "Integrity, Family and Consent."
61. Stein, *Millennial Fandom*, Kindle loc. 996.
62. "Research Brief."
63. De Elizabeth, "Billie Eilish."
64. Butler, "Performative Acts," 423.
65. Indeed, since the original draft of this chapter, Eilish has faced fan backlash for symbolically revealing her gendered body. After appearing in a corset in a cover shoot for British *Vogue*, Eilish commented in an interview that she had "lost 100,000 [Instagram] followers, just because of the boobs." See Nolan, "Billie Eilish."

Bibliography

Baker, Kaysee, and Arthur A. Raney. "Equally Super?: Gender-Role Stereotyping of Superheroes in Children's Animated Programs." *Mass Communication and Society* 10, no. 1 (May 2007): 25–41. https://doi.org/10.1080/15205430709337003.

Bartky, Sandra Lee. "Foucault, Femininity, and the Modernization of Patriarchal Power." In *Feminist Theory Reader: Local and Global Perspectives,* edited by Carole R. McCann and Seung-kyung Kim, 404–18. New York: Routledge, 2010.

Bendis, Brian Michael (w), and Michael Gaydos (a). *Jessica Jones, Alias Vol. 3: The Underneath.* New York: Marvel Comics, 2003.

———. *Jessica Jones, Alias Vol. 4: The Secret Origins of Jessica Jones.* New York: Marvel Comics, 2016.

Bendis, Brian Michael (w), Michael Gaydos (a), Matt Hollingsworth (c), and Cory Petit (l). *Jessica Jones, Vol. 3: Return of the Purple Man.* New York: Marvel Worldwide, 2018.

Beukes, Lauren, Vita Ayala, Sam Beckbessinger, Zoe Quinn, and Elsa Sjunneson. *Jessica Jones: Playing with Fire.* Serial Box, 2020. https://www.serialbox.com/serials/jessica-jones?season=1.

Binns, Daniel. "'Even You Can Break': Jessica Jones as Femme Fatale." In Rayborn and Keyes, *Jessica Jones.*

Breckenridge, Janis. "Sobriety Blows: Whiskey, Trauma and Coping in Netflix's *Jessica Jones.*" In Rayborn and Keyes, *Jessica Jones.*

Brown, Jeffrey A. *Beyond Bombshells: The New Action Heroine in Popular Culture.* Jackson: University Press of Mississippi, 2015.

———. "Supermoms? Maternity and the Monstrous-Feminine in Superhero Comics." *Journal of Graphic Novels & Comics* 2, no. 1 (June 2011): 77–87. https://doi.org/10.1080/21504857.2011.576885.

Butler, Judith. "Performative Acts and Gender Constitution: An Essay in Phenomenology and Feminist Theory." In *Feminist Theory Reader: Local and Global Perspectives,* edited by Carole R. McCann and Seung-kyung Kim, 419–30. New York: Routledge, 2010.

———. "Performativity, Precarity and Sexual Politics." *AIBR. Revista de Antropología Iberoamericana* 4, no. 3 (2009): i–xiii. https://doi.org/10.11156/aibr.040303e.

Canal, Emily. "Forbes Calculated How Much Jessica Jones Spends on Booze." *Forbes,* November 25, 2015. https://www.forbes.com/sites/emilycanal/2015/11/25/netflix-jessica-jones-whiskey-drinking/#4a7ff12c4c58.

Card, Claudia. "Caring and Evil." *Hypatia* 5, no. 1 (March 1990): 101–8. https://doi.org/10.1111/j.1527-2001.1990.tb00393.x.

Cespédes González, Lillian. "*Jessica Jones*: Gender and the Marvel Phenomenon." In Rayborn and Keyes, *Jessica Jones.*

Cocca, Carolyn. "The 'Broke Back Test': A Quantitative and Qualitative Analysis of Portrayals of Women in Mainstream Superhero Comics, 1993–2013." *Journal of Graphic Novels and Comics* 5, no. 4 (2014): 411–28. https://doi.org/10.1080/21504857.2014.916327.

Coyne, Sarah M., Jennifer Ruh Linder, Eric E. Rasmussen, David A. Nelson, and Kevin M. Collier. "It's a Bird! It's a Plane! It's a Gender Stereotype!: Longitudinal Associations Between Superhero Viewing and Gender Stereotyped Play." *Sex Roles* 70, nos. 9–10 (2014): 416–30. https://doi.org/10.1007/s11199-014-0374-8.

Curtis, Neal, and Valentina Cardo. "Superheroes and Third-Wave Feminism." *Feminist Media Studies* 18, no. 3 (2018): 381–96. https://doi.org/10.1080/14680777.2017.135 1387.

Dallacqua, Ashley K., and David E. Low. "Cupcakes and Beefcakes: Students' Readings of Gender in Superhero Texts." *Gender and Education* 33, no. 1 (2021): 68–85. https://doi.org/10.1080/09540253.2019.1633460.

D'Amore, Laura Mattoon. "The Accidental Supermom: Superheroines and Maternal Performativity, 1963–1980." *The Journal of Popular Culture* 45, no. 6 (2012): 1226–48. https://doi.org/10.1111/jpcu.12006.

De Elizabeth, "Billie Eilish Reveals the Reason for Her Baggy Clothes in New Calvin Klein Ad," *Teen Vogue*, May 11, 2019. https://www.teenvogue.com/story/billie-eilish-baggy-clothes-calvin-klein.

Devereaux, Shaadi. "Netflix, Uncovering Cycles of Abuse and Chill: Jessica Jones and Domestic Violence." *Model View Culture*, November 25, 2015. https://modelviewculture.com/pieces/netflix-uncovering-cycles-of-abuse-and-chill-jessica-jones-and-domestic-violence.

Doane, Mary Ann. *Femmes Fatale: Feminism, Film Studies and Psychoanalysis.* New York: Routledge, 1992.

Donnelly, Matt. "Women Creators, Fans at Comic-Con Rise Up Against Culture of Misogyny." *Variety*, July 23, 2019. https://variety.com/2019/film/features/women-at-comic-con-fan-culture-1203276161/.

Fuller, Brian, and Emily D. Edwards. "Integrity, Family and Consent: The Ontological Angst of *Jessica Jones*." In Rayborn and Keyes, *Jessica Jones*.

Gilligan, Carol. *In a Different Voice: Psychological Theory and Women's Development.* Cambridge; London: Harvard University Press, 2006.

Goodrum, Michael D., Tara Prescott, and Philip Smith. *Gender and the Superhero Narrative.* Jackson: University Press of Mississippi, 2018.

Green, Stephanie. "Fantasy, Gender and Power in *Jessica Jones*." *Continuum* 33, no. 2 (2019): 173–84. https://doi.org/10.1080/10304312.2019.1569383.

Greven, David. *The Bionic Woman and Feminist Ethics: An Analysis of the 1970s Television Series.* Jefferson, NC: McFarland, 2020.

Hassan, Thea. "An Ethic of Care Critique." *Sociology* (2008): 159–62.

Hoagland, Sarah Lucia. "Some Concerns about Nel Noddings' *Caring*." *Hypatia* 5, no. 1 (1990): 109–14. https://doi.org/10.1111/j.1527-2001.1990.tb00394.x.

Horbury, Alison. "Post-Feminist Impasses in Popular Heroine Television." *Continuum* 28, no. 2 (2014): 213–25. https://doi.org/10.1080/10304312.2014.888043.

"Hot Librarian." *TV Tropes.* Accessed August 3, 2020. https://tvtropes.org/pmwiki/pmwiki.php/Main/HotLibrarian.

Humm, Maggie. *Feminism and Film.* Edinburgh: Edinburgh University Press, 2008.

Jackson, Alecia Youngblood. "Performativity Identified." *Qualitative Inquiry* 10, no. 5 (2004): 673–90. https://doi.org/10.1177/1077800403257673.

Jenkins, Henry. *Convergence Culture: Where Old and New Media Collide.* New York; London: NYU Press, 2006.

Jessica Jones. Season 1, episode 4, "AKA 99 Friends." Directed by David Petrarca. Netflix. Aired November 20, 2015.

———. Season 1, episode 5, "AKA The Sandwich Saved Me." Directed by Stephen Surjik. Netflix. Aired November 20, 2015.

———. Season 1, episode 8, "AKA WWJD." Directed by Simon Cellan Jones. Netflix. Aired November 20, 2015.

———. Season 2, episode 1, "AKA Start at the Beginning." Directed by Anna Foerster. Netflix. Aired March 8, 2018.

———. Season 2, episode 2, "AKA Freak Accident." Directed by Minkie Spiro. Netflix. Aired March 8, 2018.

———. Season 2, episode 7, "AKA I Want Your Cray Cray." Directed by Jennifer Getzinger. Netflix. Aired March 8, 2018.

———. Season 2, episode 9, "AKA Shark in the Bathtub, Monster in the Bed." Directed by Rosemary Rodriguez. Netflix. Aired March 8, 2018.

———. Season 3, episode 1, "AKA The Perfect Burger." Directed by Michael Lehmann. Netflix. Aired June 14, 2019.

———. Season 3, episode 11, "AKA A Lotta Worms." Directed by Sarah Boyd. Netflix. Aired June 14, 2019.

Joffe, Robyn. "Holding Out for a Hero(ine): An Examination of the Presentation and Treatment of Female Superheroes in Marvel Movies." *Panic at the Discourse: An Interdisciplinary Journal* 1, no. 1 (2019): 5–19.

Johnson, Melissa C. "*Jessica Jones*'s Feminism: AKA *Alias* Gets a Fixed-It." In Rayborn and Keyes, *Jessica Jones.*

Johnson, Merri Lisa. "Ladies Love Your Box: The Rhetoric of Pleasure and Danger in Feminist Television Studies." In *Media and Cultural Studies: Critical Approaches,* edited by Rhonda Hammer and Douglas Kellner, 374–91. New York: Peter Lang, 2010.

Kaplan, Laura Duhan. "Woman as Caretaker: An Archetype That Supports Patriarchal Militarism." *Hypatia* 9, no. 2 (May 1994): 123–33. https://doi.org/10.1111/j.1527-2001.1994.tb00436.x.

Kiley, Aleah, and Zak Roman. "'AKA Occasionally I Give a Damn': Mirrored Archetypes and Gender Power in *Jessica Jones.*" In Rayborn and Keyes, *Jessica Jones.*

"Krysten Ritter & the Cast of Marvel's Jessica Jones Drop by Marvel LIVE!" [Video]. *Marvel Entertainment,* October 10, 2015. https://www.youtube.com/watch?v=2zYJRyo2U3M.

Lavin, Michael R. "Women in Comic Books." *Serials Review* 24, no. 2 (1998): 93–100. https://doi.org/10.1080/00987913.1998.10764448.

Levy, Ariel. *Female Chauvinist Pigs: Women and the Rise of Raunch Culture.* Collingwood, Victoria, Canada: Black Inc., 2010.

Lorber, Judith. *Gender Inequality: Feminist Theories and Politics,* 5th ed. New York: Oxford University Press, 2012.

McKinney, Kelsey. "'I Feel like a Force No One Can Stop': How Cosplay Empowers Women." *Vox,* October 29, 2014. https://www.vox.com/2014/10/29/7014057/cosplay-women-self-empowerment.

Moll, Nicholas William. "Elite and Famous: Subverting Gender in the Marvel Universe with *Jessica Jones.*" In Rayborn and Keyes, *Jessica Jones.*

Mulkerin, Tim. "How the 'Cosplay Is Not Consent' Movement Changed New York Comic Con." *Mic,* October 9, 2017. https://www.mic.com/articles/185079/how-the-cosplay-is-not-consent-movement-changed-new-york-comic-con.

Nadkarni, Samira. "'I Was Never the Hero That You Wanted Me to Be': Feminism and Resistance to Militarism in Marvel's Jessica Jones." In *Gender and the Superhero Narrative,* edited by Michael Goodrum, Tara Prescott, and Philip Smith, 74–100. Jackson: University Press of Mississippi, 2018.

Noddings, Nel. *Caring: A Feminine Approach to Ethics & Moral Education.* Berkeley: University of California Press, 2013.

———. "A Response." *Hypatia* 5, no. 1 (1990): 120–26.

———. *Women and Evil.* Berkeley: University of California Press, 1991.

Nolan, Emma. "Billie Eilish Reveals She Lost 100,000 Followers After Posting Corset Pic." *Newsweek,* September 27, 2021. https://www.newsweek.com/billie-eilish-lost-100000-followers-corset-pic-boobs-1632957.

Nichols, Elizabeth Gackstetter. "Playing with Identity: Gender, Performance and Feminine Agency in Cosplay." *Continuum* 33, no. 2 (2019): 270–82. https://doi.org/10.1080/10304312.2019.1569410.

Orme, Stephanie. "Femininity and Fandom: The Dual-Stigmatisation of Female Comic Book Fans." *Journal of Graphic Novels and Comics* 7, no. 4 (2016): 403–16. https://doi.org/10.1080/21504857.2016.1219958.

Rayborn, Tim, and Abigail Keyes, eds. *Jessica Jones, Scarred Superhero: Essays on Gender, Trauma and Addiction in the Netflix Series.* Jefferson, NC: McFarland, 2018. Kindle.

"Research Brief: Diversity of Youth Gender Identity—The Trevor Project." *The Trevor Project,* October 29, 2019. https://www.thetrevorproject.org/2019/10/29/research-brief-diversity-of-youth-gender-identity/.

Robinson, Lillian S. *Wonder Women: Feminisms and Superheroes.* New York: Routledge, 2004.

Rosenberg, Michelle, and Krysten Ritter. "Marvel's Jessica Jones: Krysten Ritter & Melissa Rosenberg Talk Jessica's Hallway Moment." Interview by ComicBook Staff. *ComicBook,* September 6, 2017. https://comicbook.com/news/marvels-jessica-jones-krysten-ritter-and-melissa-rosenberg-on-ed/.

Salih, Sarah. "On Judith Butler and Performativity." In *Sexualities and Communication in Everyday Life: A Reader,* edited by Karen E. Lovaas and Mercilee M. Jenkins, 55–68. Los Angeles: Sage Publications, 2006.

Schubart, Rikke. "Bulk, Breast, and Beauty: Negotiating the Superhero Body in Gal Gadot's Wonder Woman." *Continuum* 33, no. 2 (2019): 160–72. https://doi.org/10.1080/10304312.2019.1569382.

Shugart, Helene. "Supermarginal." *Communication and Critical/Cultural Studies* 6, no. 1 (2009): 98–102. https://doi.org/10.1080/14791420802663702.

Stabile, Carol A. "'Sweetheart, This Ain't Gender Studies': Sexism and Superheroes." *Communication and Critical/Cultural Studies* 6, no. 1 (2009): 86–92. https://doi.org/10.1080/14791420802663686.

Stein, Louisa Ellen. *Millennial Fandom: Television Audiences in the Transmedia Age.* Iowa City: University of Iowa Press, 2015.

Temuzion, K. V. "Sex Equality in Marvel Movies." *International Journal of English Literature and Social Sciences* 4, no. 6 (2019): 1738–39. https://doi.org/10.22161/ijels.46.17.

Traveller's Tales. *Lego Marvel's Avengers.* Warner Brothers Interactive Entertainment, 2016. Playstation 4.

Voelker-Morris, Robert, and Julie Voelker-Morris. "Stuck in Tights: Mainstream Super-hero Comics' Habitual Limitations on Social Constructions of Male Superheroes." *Journal of Graphic Novels and Comics* 5, no. 1 (2014): 101–17. https://doi.org/10.1080/21504857.2014.889732.

Weiner, Robert G. "Foreword: The Not Quite Super Jessica Jones." In Rayborn and Keyes, *Jessica Jones.*

Wigard, Justin. "'Is That Real or Is It Just in My Head?' 'Both'; Chronotopal Representation of Patriarchal Villainy and the Feminist Antihero in Marvel's Jessica Jones." In Rayborn and Keyes, *Jessica Jones.*

PART 3

Embodied Power

Otherness, the Body, and the Superheroine

CHAPTER 7

"Don't Scare Me Like That, Colonizer!"

Black Panther's Shuri through a Postcolonial Feminist Lens

Rachel Grant

Before T'Challa can ascend to the throne of Wakanda as its king, he must challenge the other tribes in a ceremonial battle. When spiritual advisor Zuri asks if there's anyone of royal blood who wishes to challenge for the throne, Wakanda princess Shuri slyly raises her hand. Gasps fill the crowd as they anticipate her response. As T'Challa's younger sister, she says, "This corset is really uncomfortable, so can we all wrap this up and go home?"

As a Black female Marvel character, Shuri is a unique version of a super-heroine because she is able to strip away the damsel-in-distress role associated with princesses; also, her aptitude for science demonstrates the vitality of Afrofuturism. The first Marvel film nominated for a Best Picture Oscar, *Black Panther* was groundbreaking to the Black community. The film gave hope to many in the African-diasporic lineage that media representations had evolved to show Black characters in power and free from oppression.

While the film centers on the Black Panther, Wakanda's King T'Challa, it is the Black female supporting characters, like Shuri, that truly break down stereotypes and misconceptions of Black womanhood. The film's news coverage and responses to the film on social media merge the narrative of Black women as key to preserving Wakanda by promoting Black women's complexity. This chapter explores Wakanda's Black womanhood through a postcolonial feminist lens as a means to challenge oppression through media representations. Specifically, Shuri, a Wakandan princess and sister to T'Challa, showcases the potential in this representation. While she exhibits superpowers in the comic series, she manifests her extraordinary abilities in the film through her demonstrated intelligence and superb scientific abilities. The main research questions are these: How is the character Shuri situated with Afrofuturist society (art, fashion, and comics)? How do news coverage and Black Twitter merge with this narrative outside the film?

Colonized Black Bodies

Since the nineteenth century, public displays of "other" societies were common forms of entertainment.[1] The spectacle of the colonized Black female subject included Sarah Bartman, also known as "Hottentot Venus" in 1810 Europe. After her death, her sexual parts were preserved and displayed for many years in Paris.[2] Thus, it is hard for Black female bodies to escape the fantasies of the Western imagination. In the film *Black Panther*, Black womanhood is transported beyond the colonial understanding of desire. Throughout the film, Black female characters poke fun at their Westernized sexualization as well as dismantle it.

Scholar Evelynn Hammonds describes the Black woman being "rendered simultaneously invisible, visible (exposed), hypervisible and pathologized in dominant discourses."[3] Black women contend with the controlling media images that reaffirm ideology of domination. Black feminist scholar Patricia Hill Collins stated that Black women have been exploited by racism, sexism, poverty, and other forms of social injustice that transmuted into norms and became inevitable parts of their lives.[4] Drawing on the work of Kimberlé Crenshaw, this chapter applies intersectional theory to practice by highlighting "lived experiences" through the means of reclaiming the narrative of Black women.[5] From this perspective, *Black Panther* is key in challenging the control images of Black women. Female characters resist mainstream notions of domination by holding key positions of power with the Wakandan empire.

---

1. Simmonds, "My Body, Myself."
2. Gilman, "Black Bodies, White Bodies."
3. Hammonds, "Black Female Sexuality," 93.
4. Hill Collins, *Black Feminist Thought*.
5. Crenshaw, "Demarginalizing," 139.

Postcolonial Theory

Postcolonial scholars argue that feminism suppresses a broad understanding of gendered experiences. Scholars Vanaja Dhuruvarajan and Jill Vickers argued that the one-world framework of women's movements supports the notion that women share the same experiences and needs in a presumed "global sisterhood."[6] The emergence of diverse women's movements and approaches challenges the idea that Western women's solutions can be applied everywhere. The Western category of *woman* is no longer sustainable because women share insights from multiple contexts and become translators of difference.[7] Globalization has made lives more interconnected, but its processes result in polarizing consequences.[8] Local cultures are being swamped by Western culture and colonialism. The Indian feminist Gayatri Spivak argues for the rejection of all histories written by or from the perspective of the colonizer.[9] She stated that we should write histories and other discourses that value difference in totally new spaces. The goal of postcolonial theory is to redefine identities; cultures must be put in the context of power and knowledge. Arif Dirlik stated that postcolonial theory is intended "to achieve an authentic globalization of cultural discourses by the extension globally of the intellectual concerns and orientations originating at the central sites of Euro-American cultural criticism."[10] In terms of postcolonial feminism, this is the breakdown of "binarisms"—to show how policies and practices on economic and political levels are informed by the concern of maintaining the hegemony of white people and their culture.[11] The Western colonizer privileges race and constructed deficiencies, including biology and culture.[12] The notions of superiority become the colonizer's mission to institutionalize practices and policies. As practices are naturalized, inequalities take on character. Chandra Mohanty indicates that the construction of the unproblematic "third world woman" and her positionality as a "victim" supports imperialistic-power knowledge networks.[13] This dual existence reinforces human/nature relations of the subordinated other. "By

---

6. Dhuruvarajan and Vickers, *Gender, Race and Nation*, 9.
7. Dhuruvarajan and Vickers, *Gender, Race and Nation*, 26.
8. Dhuruvarajan and Vickers, *Gender, Race and Nation*.
9. Spivak, *Confessing Excess*.
10. Dirlik, "Postcolonial Aura," 329.
11. Dirlik, "Postcolonial Aura."
12. Fanon, *The Wretched*.
13. Mohanty, "Feminist Scholarship."

the means of dualism, the colonized are appropriated, incorporated into the selfhood and culture of the master, which forms their identity."[14] The deconstruction of the colonial identity calls for the altering of Western societies. Scholar Himani Bannerji states that being on the margin does not automatically mean that one is aware of one's subordination.[15] She argues, "It is only when marginalized people have access to knowledge that they are able to raise their critical consciousness to articulate their concerns. Knowledge is power. Without it, marginalized people are a muted group and subjected to interpretations of their experiences by those who have power."[16] To destroy the residue of colonialism requires marginalized people to create authentic work and redefine their experiences.

African Diasporic Tradition and Pan-Africanism

While the film *Black Panther* adds to the notions of Blackness, Western themes are featured throughout. For example, combining Pan-African languages, symbols, design, and iconography is an effort to rescue the past from potential erasure or loss and can therefore most fittingly be described as a "variant of Third Cinema."[17] It overlooks the complex diversity of African cultures and experiences, providing an African aesthetic for white audiences to consume and a return to the African dream for Black audiences.

Black Panther focuses on African-diaspora counterdiscourses, but not all discourses have the same power. Black nationalism has taken the lead in resurrecting and inventing African models in the US.[18] Negative representations of Africa justified Black enslavement, segregation, and continuing poverty. Black nationalists have always argued that African Americans deny their connections to Africa at the peril of allowing racist subtext to circulate without serious challenge.[19] At the same time, nationalists have recognized that counterattacks on negative portrayals of Africa stimulate political mobilization against racism in the US. Afrocentric construction of a political memory attempts to set standards of social relations that can be both liberating and confining.

14. Plumwood, "Logic of Colonization."
15. Bannerji, *Thinking Through.*
16. Bannerji, *Thinking Through,* 38.
17. White, "I Dream a World."
18. White, *Dark Continent,* 119.
19. White, *Dark Continent,* 119.

Throughout social media and news coverage, the film added to the excitement about and interest in African culture. At a time when Hollywood's representational politics are relevant, *Black Panther* featured an all-Black cast in Marvel's genre of predominantly white characters. The film's social media presence is significant in combatting the resurgence of racist politics. *Black Panther* offered Black communities another form of resistance to tackle.

Afrofuturism

Black Panther reverses racial dynamics and erases the invisibility of the "other." Edward Said stated that the power to create your narratives is imperative to the unfolding of your destiny.[20] The narrative of Afrofuturism offers directions for how Black people can imagine a future in a world not dominated by white people. The expert use of Vibranium through science and technology embodies a type of agency that challenges the current Black racial identity.[21] According to scholar Ytasha Womack, Afrofuturism is an intersection of imagination, technology, the future, and liberation.[22] As a critical theory framework and artistic aesthetic, Afrofuturism blends science fiction, fantasy, Afrocentricity, and non-Western beliefs. Afrofuturist narratives, which are entrenched in futurism inspired by the science fiction genre, position Black communities within futurist imaginaries to address present and any future prospects of their marginalization and erasure.[23] Based in the Black Arts movement and the Black Power movement, cultural arenas serve as the primary site of political action.[24] Afrofuturism as an expression of suppressed and marginalized imaginaries represents a dynamic alternative to the dominant, mainstream of Black reality. The hope of future personal growth, social advancement, and community is expressed through creative agency. Womack argues that there's a power in breaking the past's rigid identity parameters.[25]

The feminine aspect of humanity reigns freely in Afrofuturism. The subconscious and intuition, which metaphysical studies dub the feminine side

---

20. Said, *Orientalism*.
21. Khan, "Viewing Black Panther."
22. Womack, *Afrofuturism*.
23. Womack, *Afrofuturism*.
24. Ongiri, *Spectacular Blackness*.
25. Womack, *Afrofuturism*, 24–25.

of us all, are prioritized in the genre. The feminine side is neither guided by Western mythology nor limited by popular takes on history. Women have decision-making power over their creative voice. They make their own standards and sculpt their own lens through which to view the world and for the world to view them.[26]

Thus, Afrofuturism transcends the formulation of identity. It provides a feminist space for women to feel empowered because it allows a critique for the ways that people associate science and technology. In a white, hypermale sci-fi space, this artistic expression sets the stage for the multidimensional Black female character.[27] Technology positions Black women as central figures. This genre influences Black women audiences because it shows them how to operate within "complex worlds both past and present, women who are vulnerable in their victories and valiant in their risky charge to enlighten humanity."[28] Afrofuturism's endorsement of the vision of science makes it complicit in erasures of other knowledge systems that have shaped the histories and experiences of non-Western civilizations, an erasure antithetical to postcolonial and postcolonial feminist perspectives.

As a transmedia form, Afrofuturism wields its power through various fields and industries, including African futuristic fashion, music, and video games.[29] The film's expression of Black womanhood identity is reflected in social media and news coverage of Black audiences.

Methods

I conducted an analysis of Marvel films (*Black Panther, Infinity War,* and *Endgame*) and Nnedi Okorafor's contemporary *Shuri* comic book series (2018–19). Okorafor's Shuri series presents the character based on the film adaptation, but with several new storylines and Pan-African influences. Born in the US to Nigerian immigrant parents, Okorafor is known for weaving African cultures into creative settings and memorable characters. She stated that in her storyline arc she "wanted to reintroduce Wakanda to Africa and plant some seeds for that budding relationship with Shuri at the helm."[30] I examined news coverage and Twitter posts from January 2018 to 2020 using critical technocultural discourse analysis to consider the form, the user, and

---

26. Womack, *Afrofuturism,* 104.
27. Womack, *Afrofuturism,* 24–25, 109–10.
28. Womack. *Afrofuturism,* 110.
29. Womack. *Afrofuturism.*
30. Okorafor (w) and Stott (i), "Living Memory."

the interface with the underlying digital ideologies.[31] In order to gather news coverage and Twitter posts, I searched for the following words: "Black Panther," "Wakanda," and "Shuri." For the Twitter search, I used the same words, but as hashtags.

Discourse produces knowledge through language, and since all social practices entail meaning, both our language and our conduct have discursive aspects.[32] Discourse is recognized as social interaction, as power and domination, as communication, as contextually situated, as social semiosis, and as a complex, layered construct.[33] In Foucault's view, discourse defines and dictates the way something can be talked and reasoned about and used to regulate the conduct of others through power.[34] One such way that discourse reproduces itself is through its mass media channels. More specifically, Gitlin states that ideology is not manufactured by commercial culture; instead, it relays, reproduces, processes, packages, and focuses ideology arising from social elites, from social movements, and throughout society.[35] A critical discourse analysis identifies causes of social wrongs and produces knowledge that could mitigate them.[36]

Technocultural analysis explores how cultural differences can be discussed via the internet. It is the analysis of popular culture forms in the use of daily technology.[37] "Internet studies needs to meld close interface analysis with issues of identity and pay attention to the ideologies that underlie them."[38] According to Brock, technology serves as a cultural tool to influence and mediate racial identity.[39] Internet users, content providers, and designers filter their digital experiences through frames as they redistribute online resources along racial lines.[40] Analyzing Twitter as an information source captures the influence of marginalized communities on online discourse. Through direct action, oppressed communities voice demands for change in their daily lives. Stories and social media posts serve the dual purpose of illustrating how culture shapes online media. This chapter adds to understanding of how Westernized media discuss race and gender through the creating of Afrofuturist counternarratives.

31. Nakamura, "Cultural Difference."
32. Hall, "The West and the Rest."
33. Van Dijk, *Discourse Studies.*
34. Hall, "Power, Knowledge and Discourse."
35. Gitlin, "Prime Time Ideology."
36. Fairclough. *Language and Power.*
37. Nakamura, "Cultural Difference," 34.
38. Nakamura, "Cultural Difference," 35.
39. Brock, "From the Blackhand Side."
40. Brock, "From the Blackhand Side."

"I have developed an update": Technological Leadership

Shuri is the head of the Wakandan empire's technology and science. While Wakanda is perceived as among the poorest and most underdeveloped countries, its thriving infrastructure is hidden from the outside world. This is a key component of Afrofuturism's ability to redefine hegemonic Western culture's representations of the Third World. The concept of technological prowess is reserved for developed, civilized countries. Even more, Wakanda's tech industry is under the leadership of a youthful Black woman. Her youth is key to her goal of taking Wakanda into the future, and her story line presents her age as an inspiration to young audiences. At the age of eighteen, Shuri maintains a lab where she controls the mining of Vibranium, one of the most powerful substances in the world. In the film we see her using technology to alter systems of power. Instead of exploiting laborers' bodies to gather and collect the Vibranium, she uses technology to do the work. This is a resistance to colonial subversion and inferiority. Her leadership promotes a more advanced understanding of science, replacing underclass labor and marginalized labor.

Shuri embodies this notion of future thinking as she invents weaponry and tools for the Black Panther. She discusses technological upgrades with T'Challa after he returns from his mission to rescue Nakia. He thinks she is there to see him off before his royal ceremony. Shuri tells him, "You wish! I am here for the EMP beads. I have developed an update." He tells her they worked fine. She responds, "How many times do I have to teach you? Just because something works doesn't mean that it cannot be improved." As he hands her the beads, T'Challa says to her, "You are teaching me? What do you know?" She responds, "More than you." This exchange in the film reflects reformation of leadership as Shuri positions herself as the educator despite her age. In another example, when T'Challa comes to Shuri's lab, she shows him his new uniform. "Old tech. Functional, but old," she says. "People are shooting at me—wait, let me put my helmet on!" Rooted in youth, Shuri's use of technology is a push for reimagining who can be creators outside a Western framework. Scholar Elana Levine argues that discourses of empowerment celebrate action heroines as strong and intelligent women capable of undermining threats against themselves, their families, and their communities, and even humanity more broadly.[41]

In Okorafor's series, we still see Shuri's genius side, but the series delves into the princess's inner life. The story begins with Shuri's designing

---

41. Levine, "Remaking Charlie's Angels."

of advanced spaceships that would carry T'Challa to explore a wormhole in space for what was supposed to be a few days.[42] The series focuses on Shuri rescuing her brother. Another similarity to the films is the alliances with other Marvel Universe characters, Storm, Groot, and Rocket. In issue 5, Shuri calls on the help of Iron Man / Tony Stark to help reverse a black hole in Mali.[43] A key feminist aspect of these alliances is how Shuri situates herself as a collective.[44] For example, she and Tony Stark hold a press conference at which she states, "I did call Mr. Stark for help. Is the world really ever saved by one person?"[45]

The feminist narrative comic series centers on resisting hegemonic norms of superheroism. For most of the comic series, Shuri doesn't wear the Black Panther costume, even in combat with villains.[46] She's authentically herself and separates her identity from her brother's. So, at the end of issue 5, she creates a new Black Panther costume, incorporating the wings she designed in issue 1.[47] Shuri's Black Panther is ready to spread her wings and take on alien invaders in her own way.

After the film's 2018 release, throughout social media, Shuri's technology leadership role is praised and often applauded by fans. One fan tweeted, "If you would not die for Shuri, daughter of Ramonda, princess of Wakanda, heir to the throne and to the mantle of Black Panther, then you're in the sunken place and should stay there."[48] News coverage of the film often also featured Shuri's intelligence or leadership. For example, W magazine interviewed the actress Letitia Wright and described her in the headline as "Wakanda's Brainy Princess."[49]

Although Shuri is praised for her youthful ambition, the film does navigate the pushback against technology. Within Wakanda, rituals and traditions are based in ancient understandings and hierarchies. For example, in the first ritual ceremony, the leader of the Jabari tribe, M'Baku, decides to challenge for the throne. He rebukes the technology advancements made in Wakanda: "We have watched and listened from the mountains. We have watched with disgust as your technological advancements have been overseen by a child who scoffs at tradition." This is criticism of youth, advance-

---

42. Okorafor (w) and Romero (i), "Gone."
43. Okorafor (w) and Romero (i), "The End of the Earth."
44. Hill Collins, Black Feminist Thought, 228.
45. Okorafor (w) and Romero (i), "End of the Earth."
46. Okorafor and Ayala et al., Shuri 1, nos. 1–10.
47. Okorafor (w) and Romero (i), "End of the Earth."
48. Depressed Happy Nightmare Woman, "If you would not."
49. Pechman, "Black Panther."

ment, and technology, but it is a gendered response to female roles in STEM fields. In increasing representation of Black female voices in technology, Afrofuturism provides leverage in engendering more active engagement of underrepresented voices. As scholar Woodrow Winchester stated, the film, "through its Afrofuturistic imagery, plotline, and premise, could inspire black/African-American young people to explore STEM and STEM careers, mirroring many of the discussions and outcomes of the STEM-engagement efforts spurred by the release of the movie *Hidden Figures*."[50]

Superhero Powers

With an aptitude for STEM, Shuri also embodies the drive and ability to fight crime and to stand for justice. In the Marvel films, she doesn't engage in direct combat except for the final battle scene. In the *Black Panther* film, Black female characters Nakia and Okoye fight alongside T'Challa, while Shuri is more behind the scenes in the combat. For example, in South Korea after Nakia and Okoye chase after Klaue, Shuri and T'Challa join forces using virtual reality. Shuri drives the car from the lab and assists him in the chase. Her warrior role is intertwined with science, but her distance from the battle reinforces her privilege as royalty. In 2018 her princess status was further cemented when she became an official Disney princess.[51] She was crowned the second Black Disney princess after Princess Tiana from *Princess and the Frog*. Most Disney princesses are criticized for reinforcing submissive gender roles, specifically the damsel-in-distress stereotype. Their story lines focus on being rescued and living "happily ever after" with a man. Also, they are characterized as weak. While a few current Disney princesses have broken this mold, like Mulan, Tiana, and Moana, the addition of Shuri creates more complexity.[52] Her personality shows a lack of interest in everything having to do with royal duties and practices. Her resistance to these traditions is featured in the *Black Panther* film. Before she expresses her hatred of wearing a corset, T'Challa jokes with her: "I can't wait to see what kind of update you make to your ceremonial outfit." In response, Shuri gives him the finger as she walks away and quickly apologizes to her mother. Her defiance counteracts her royal position.

The comic books paint a very different picture of this Disney princess. As next in line to the Wakandan throne, Shuri undergoes training to become

50. Winchester, "Afrofuturism."
51. Pockross, "Letitia Wright"; "'Black Panther's' Shuri."
52. Daley, "Every Disney Princess."

the Black Panther. After T'Challa is wounded in battle and comatose, she assumes the Black Panther mantle. Inside the comic book series, she possesses all the abilities given to the Black Panther after accessing the heart-shaped herb.[53] Shuri manages to both save Wakanda and resurrect her comatose brother. She is also capable of animorphism, which allows her to transform herself and whoever she is in direct contact with into a flock of black birds or a singular large bird.[54]

The *Shuri* solo volume highlights Shuri's superpowers through Wakandan/Pan-African spirituality. Throughout the series, Shuri is accompanied by ancestors, who guide her journey. In issue 8, Shuri ventures to the Djalia plane of the Wakandan memory before her official ceremony as the Black Panther.[55] In this plane, they address her as Aja-Adanna, keeper of the Wakandan memory. There she learns that her ancestor-given abilities have disappeared. Later, in issue 10, it is the ancient future memories of her ancestors that help her defeat the Space Lubber, a giant grasshopper.[56] Thus, her superpower exists through the ancestral lived experience.[57]

Overall, Shuri's superheroine power profile doesn't fit the typical female model. Fans of the film could not agree more with the shift of Black women portrayals. A Twitter user in 2018 stated, "Black Panther was just beyond words amazing & I'm in love with the women of Wakanda. Shuri, Okoye, Nakia & Ramonda were such strong, intelligent & badass women."[58] Media culture emphasizes a hegemonic feminine ideal by promoting thinness, whiteness, and hyperfemininity that compel women of varying body sizes, races, and performances of femininity to meet standards of attractiveness.[59] Another tweet reflected this: "Rewatched Black Panther tonight. The women of Wakanda (Okoye, Nakia, Shuri) really stand out among the MCU women. Black Widow is out there . . . just changing her hair color."[60] While this tweet pokes fun at white femininity, it addresses the complexity of heroines. Viewers are drawn to story lines with diverse experiences.

According to Lise Shapiro Sanders, one of the distinguishing features of third-wave feminism is the privileging of the "diversity of women's experience over the similarities amongst women."[61] In this way, women of color

53. Coates et al., *Black Panther* 6, nos. 3–6.
54. Coates (w) and Stelfreeze (i), "A Nation Under Our Feet: Part 9."
55. Okorafor (w) and Stott (i), "24/7 Vibranium."
56. Okorafor (w) and Stott (i), "Living Memory."
57. Crenshaw, "Demarginalizing."
58. Just Trish, "Black Panther."
59. McRobbie, "Postfeminism"; McRobbie, *Aftermath of Feminism*.
60. David, "Rewatched Black Panther."
61. Shapiro Sanders, "'Utopia' Collaboration," 7.

were recruited into the fight for equality, while at the same time a recla-mation of the symbols associated with traditional femininity was initiated. "Girl Power" became the central message of third-wave feminism, the idea that women could be powerful while still being "girly."[62]

In this case, Shuri challenges those stereotypes. Her complexity, allowing her to fight in both physical and intellectual ways, reflects different modes of female empowerment. Once Shuri officially becomes the Black Panther in the Nnedi Okorafor series, readers see this similar rooting of power by asserting her authority.[63] In her ceremony speech, Shuri states, "T'Challa isn't dead, I know this. But I also know that it is time for me to lead in his place. Spider-Man and Ms. Marvel reminded me how important it is for someone like me to stand up and be strong and unafraid of the weight of responsibility."[64] She acknowledges her own lived experiences when she emphasizes "someone like me," which elevates Black women's positionality and standpoint.

"Another broken white boy": Anti-imperialist Values

In the beginning of the Black Panther film, the legend goes that Wakanda has been hidden from outsiders. The fact that the nation has not been colonized adds to the appeal of a postcolonial lens. The film celebrates the diversity and complexities of indigenous people without the effects of oppression. While this is a cinematic interpretation of Afrofuturism, the reality of the African continent and its diasporic traditions are entrenched in colonial lega-cies. News coverage around the film sought to bring attention to the dynam-ics of colonialism. For example, Medium.com published an article about Haiti being "the real life" Wakanda with "badass women."[65] Scholars Childs and Williams assert that "colonial preoccupation" exists in the mind.[66] Shuri reflects and resists Western influences despite never living under impe-rialism. In the Black Panther film, she presents these moments as comedic relief. For example, Agent Ross wakes up in Shuri's lab and asks, "Is this Wakanda?" She replies, "No, it's Kansas," a US pop culture reference to the film The Wizard of Oz. In one of the movie's final scenes, T'Challa takes Shuri to Oakland. She states, "When you said you'd bring me to California when

62. Kendal, "Perfect Girl."
63. Okorafor (w) and Stott (i), "24/7 Vibranium."
64. Okorafor (w) and Stott (i), "24/7 Vibranium."
65. Bettinna, "Haiti."
66. Childs and Williams, Post-Colonial Theory.

I was a kid, I thought you meant Coachella, or Disneyland. Where are we?" These are subtle nods to the Western popular culture that Shuri has been exposed to which reflects the expansion of globalization. Also, these Western cultural references are used to connect with audiences in terms of humor.

Shuri's resistance to colonialism in the movie features some of the more humorous moments. She is very critical of the inadequacies of white characters. In the film when Agent Ross is brought to the lab by T'Challa, Nakia, and Okoye, Shuri states, "Great! Another broken white boy for us to fix," referring to Wakanda's growing reputation of recovering white men. After the events in the film *Civil War*, Captain America went to Wakanda to assume his nomad persona. He struggled to figure out where to go from here and his identity as a hero. His brother, Bucky, went to Wakanda to recover from his brainwashing and get his psyche back. The arrival of Ross is another instance of Wakanda saving white men from the tolls of Western society. Shuri's statement is sarcastically embedded with power. She notes her nation's superiority without colonialism. In another scene with Agent Ross, she tells him, "Don't scare me like that, colonizer!" He questions her about the period between his being shot and being healed. He says, "I don't think bullet wounds magically heal overnight." Shuri responds, "They do here, but not by magic, by technology." Then she asserts her authority and tells him not to touch anything. In her interactions with white men, she asserts her intellect and dominance against Western hegemonic forces. In the *Infinity War* film, Shuri explains to Bruce Banner how they might stop Thanos by extracting the Mind Stone from Vision. When she devises a solution, she says, "I'm sure you did your best." Again, Shuri challenges the "othering" of non-Western civilizations.

In the comic book series, pan-African alliances emphasize a postcolonial framework where Western influences are challenged. For example, Shuri is summoned by her mother, Queen Ramonda, to attend a meeting called the Elephant's Trunk, composed of Wakandan women who meet secretly to discuss the nation's future.[67] They inform Shuri that she is to take up the mantle of Black Panther in the absence of her brother. The members of Elephant Trunk fill in the gendered gaps as they comprise a single mother, a professor, a high school student, and an academy director. This reflects their intersectional experiences, as all types of women have voice in the Wakandan community. In addition to this group, readers are introduced to the Egungun, a pan-African alliance that T'Challa had been working with for over two years in secret. This group represents "a two way flow of informa-

---

67. Okorafor (w) and Romero (i), "Gone."

102 • RACHEL GRANT

tion and resources between Wakanda and the rest of Africa."[68] The alliance's name infuses Yoruba language into the series with a masking tradition of the "Yoruba collective ancestral spirits."[69] The volume centers on postcolonial unity as it addresses Wakandan/pan-African politics. This is significant in Shuri's leadership role in Afrofuturism because she is breaking down barriers rooted in identity.

Fans also understood the importance of the Wakanda anticolonial community as it sought to redefine gender roles. A tweet read, "You call it Black Panther, I call it Shuri, Nakia and Ramonda saved Wakanda from running into the ground. Alternative titles: The Americans are at it again with their colonialization bullshit, Don't take the vibranium bad things will happen."[70] The film educated audiences in postcolonial theory by recognizing Black women's stories. Shuri doesn't fit the stereotype of the Third World "victim" because she becomes the knowledge base for the Avengers. As a superhero, she exudes a vast range of intelligence including Westernized culture, but instead of embracing those ideals she challenges them and asserts her own experiences.

Conclusion

As a superheroine, Shuri defies gender stereotypes of Black women. She embraces the space for Black women to be themselves. She expresses "a deeper identity and then uses this discovery to define Blackness, womanhood or any other identifier in whatever form their imagination allows."[71] Within the Marvel films, comic books, and Twitter, she represents the future of tech-savvy culture. For African diasporic communities, she establishes Black personhood in oppression. As a young woman, she's a role model that empowers women to be smart and innovative in fields dominated by the patriarchy. The complexity of Shuri's character demonstrates how sci-fi narratives can reconstruct dominant notions of inequality and oppression, especially through a postcolonial lens of Afrofuturism.

The impact of the technoculture through multiple platforms creates social change for marginalized communities. Leading up to the film's February 2018 release in the US, Twitter users were stressing the importance of social change in the film industry. As one fan tweeted, "It's Black Panther

---

68. Okorafor (w) and Romero (i), "Timbuktu."
69. Okorafor and Romero, "Timbuktu."
70. Jenny#blm, "You call it."
71. Womack. *Afrofuturism*, 100–101.

Week. I am ready. Yes it's week long I'm celebrating this Black excellence all week Like Kwanzaa but for Wakandans. Wakwanzaa!,"[72] followed by hashtags featuring all the main Black characters' names. The film's popularity was fueled by an audience ready to see "Black excellence" on the screen—in other words, a cinematic experience where Black communities were redefined beyond oppression. Shuri represents a new level of visibility and media representation because of her range of acceptance: by followers of Disney princesses and by STEM professionals. As Marvel films have launched spaces for white femininity, the lack of race and gender has generated buzz. The Black womanhood of Wakanda has created new story lines within the Marvel Universe that don't encompass Westernized norms. Shuri's popularity is based on her resistance to those norms. Her intelligence is praised as an innovator of the future. As an Afrofuturist woman, Shuri emerges from limitless spaces and into the reimagination of feminized, racialized identity.

Bibliography

Ayala, Vita (w), and Paul Davidson (i). "A Friend in Need: Part Two." *Shuri* 1, no. 7. Marvel Comics, 2019.

Ayala, Vita (w), Paul Davidson (i), and Leonardo Romero (i). "A Friend in Need: Part One." *Shuri* 1, no. 6. Marvel Comics, 2019.

Bannerji, Himani. *Thinking Through.* Toronto: Women's Press, 1995.

Bettinna. "Haiti: The Real Life Black Panther's Wakanda with Badass Women Warriors Too." *Bettymedia*, February 18, 2018. https://medium.com/bettymedia/haiti-the-real-life-black-panthers-wakanda-with-badass-women-warriors-too-2118426a3fd9.

"'Black Panther's' Shuri Is the Newest Disney Princess." *Yahoo News*, February 20, 2018. https://www.yahoo.com/entertainment/black-panthers-shuri-newest-disney-185406136.html.

Brock, Andre. "From the Blackhand Side: Twitter as a Cultural Conversation." *Journal of Broadcasting & Electronic Media* 56, no. 4 (2012): 529–49.

Childs, Peter, and Patrick Williams. *An Introduction to Post-Colonial Theory.* New York: Routledge, 2014.

Coates, Ta-Nehisi (w), and Chris Sprouse (i). "A Nation Under Our Feet: Part 5." *Black Panther* 6, no. 5. New York: Marvel Comics, 2016.

———. "A Nation Under Our Feet: Part 6." *Black Panther* 6, no. 6. New York: Marvel Comics, 2016.

Coates, Ta-Nehisi (w), and Brian Stelfreeze (i). "A Nation Under Our Feet: Part 3." *Black Panther* 6, no. 3. New York: Marvel Comics, 2016.

---

72. Smith, "Black Panther Week."

———. "A Nation Under Our Feet: Part 4." *Black Panther* 6, no. 4. New York: Marvel Comics, 2016.

———. "A Nation Under Our Feet: Part 9." *Black Panther* 6, no. 9. New York: Marvel Comics, 2017.

Crenshaw, Kimberlé. "Demarginalizing the Intersection of Race and Sex: A Black Feminist Critique of Antidiscrimination Doctrine, Feminist Theory and Antiracist Politics." *University of Chicago Legal Forum* (1989): 139–68.

Daley, Katerina. "Every Disney Princess Movie Ranked." *ScreenRant*, February 28, 2019. https://screenrant.com/every-disney-princess-movie-ranked/.

David (@davidprevails). "Rewatched Black Panther tonight. The woman of Wakanda (Okoye, Nakia, Shuri) really stand out among the MCU women. Black Widow is out there . . . just changing her hair color." Twitter, May 6, 2018.

Depressed Happy Nightmare Woman (@GlitterNGoth). "If you would not die for Shuri, daughter of Ramonda, princess of Wakanda, heir to the throne and to the mantle of Black Panther, then you're in the sunken place and should stay there." Twitter, February 17, 2018.

Dhuruvarajan, Vanaja, and Jill Vickers. *Gender, Race and Nation: A Global Perspective.* Toronto: University of Toronto Press, 2002.

Dirlik, Arif. "The Postcolonial Aura: Third World Criticism in the Age of Global Capitalism." *Critical Inquiry* 20, no. 2 (1994): 328–56.

Fairclough, Norman. *Language and Power.* London: Routledge, 2015.

Fanon, Frantz. *The Wretched of the Earth.* New York: Grove Press, 1963.

Gilman, Sander. "Black Bodies, White Bodies: Towards Iconography of Female Sexuality in Late Nineteenth Century Art, Medicine and Literature." In *"Race," Culture and Difference,* edited by James Donald and Ali Rattansi, 171–97. London: Sage, 1992.

Gitlin, Todd. "Prime Time Ideology: The Hegemonic Process in Television Entertainment." *Social Problems* 26, no. 3 (1979): 251–66.

Hall, Stuart. "Foucault: Power, Knowledge and Discourse." In *Discourse Theory and Practice: A Reader,* edited by Margaret Wetherell, Stephanie Taylor, and Simeon J. Yates, 72–81. London: Sage, 2001.

———. "The West and the Rest." In *Formations of Modernity,* edited by Stuart Hall and Bram Gieben, 185–227. Cambridge: Polity Press, 1992.

Hammonds, Evelynn. "Toward a Genealogy of Black Female Sexuality: The Problematic of Silence." In *Feminist Genealogies, Colonial Legacies, Democratic Futures,* edited by M. Jacqui Alexander and Chandra Talpade Mohanty, 93–104. New York: Routledge, 1997.

Hill Collins, Patricia. *Black Feminist Thought: Knowledge, Consciousness and the Politics of Empowerment.* New York: Routledge, 2000.

Jenny#blm (@myrmintofu). "You call it Black Panther, I call it Shuri, Nakia and Ramonda saved Wakanda from running into the ground. Alternative titles: The Americans are at it again with their colonialization bullshit, Don't take the vibranium bad things will happen." Twitter, September 12, 2018.

Just Trish (@TrishLaver). "Black Panther was just beyond words amazing & I'm in love with the women of Wakanda. Shuri, Okoye, Nakia & Ramonda were such strong, intelligent & badass women. I love them for myself but more so for the young girls who will watch them & embrace them as their role models." Twitter, February 18, 2018.

Kendal, Evie. There's No One Perfect Girl: Third Wave Feminism and the Powerpuff Girls. *Colloquy* no. 24 (2012): 234–52.

Khan, Tabassum "Ruhi." "Viewing Black Panther through a Postcolonial Feminist Lens." *Women and Language* 56, no. 1 (2019): 97–104.

Levine, Elana. "Remaking Charlie's Angels: The Construction of Post-Feminist Hegemony." *Feminist Media Studies* 8, no. 4 (2008): 375–89.

McRobbie, Angela. *The Aftermath of Feminism: Gender, Culture, and Social Change.* London: Sage, 2008.

———. "Postfeminism and Popular Culture: Bridget Jones and the New Gender Regime." In *Interrogating Postfeminism*, edited by Yvonne Tasker and Diane Negra, 27–39. Durham, NC: Duke University Press.

Mohanty, Chandra. "Under the Western Eyes: Feminist Scholarship and Colonial Discourses." In *Media and Cultural Studies: Keyworks*, edited by M. Gigi Durham and Douglas MacKay Kellner, 347–64. Malden, MA: Wiley-Blackwell, 2012.

Nakamura, Lisa. "Cultural Difference, Theory, and Cyberculture Studies: A Case of Mutual Repulsion." In *Critical Cyberculture Studies*, edited by David Silver and Adrienne Massanari, 29–36. New York: NYU Press, 2006.

Okorafor, Nnedi (w), and Leonardo Romero (i). "Gone." *Shuri* 1, no. 1. New York: Marvel Comics, 2018.

———. "The Baobab Tree." *Shuri* 1, no. 2. New York: Marvel Comics, 2019.

———. "Groot Boom." *Shuri* 1, no. 3. New York: Marvel Comics, 2019.

———. "Timbuktu." *Shuri* 1, no. 4. New York: Marvel Comics, 2019.

———. "The End of the Earth." *Shuri* 1, no. 5. New York: Marvel Comics, 2019.

Okorafor, Nnedi (w), and Rachael Stott (i). "24/7 Vibranium." *Shuri* 1, no. 8. New York: Marvel Comics, 2019.

———. "Godhead." *Shuri* 1, no. 9. New York: Marvel Comics, 2019.

———. "Living Memory." *Shuri* 1, no. 10. New York: Marvel Comics, 2019.

Ongiri, Amy Abugo. *Spectacular Blackness: The Cultural Politics of the Black Power Movement and the Search for a Black Aesthetic.* Charlottesville: University of Virginia Press, 2009.

Pechman, Alexandra. "Black Panther Breakthrough Star Letitia Wright on How She Became Shuri, Wakanda's Brainy Princess." *W*, February 16, 2018. https://www.wmagazine.com/story/who-is-letitia-wright-shuri-black-panther/.

Plumwood, Val. "Dualism: The Logic of Colonization." In *Feminism and the Mastery of Nature*, 41–68. New York: Routledge, 1993.

Pockross, Adam. "Letitia Wright Weighs In on Shuri Officially Being a Disney Princess." *SyFy*, May 29, 2018. https://web.archive.org/web/20210115160606/https://www.syfy.com/syfywire/letitia-wright-shuri-officially-being-a-disney-princess.

Said, Edward. *Orientalism*. New York: Vintage Books, 1978.

Shapiro Sanders, Lise. "'Feminists Love a Utopia': Collaboration, Conflict, and the Futures of Feminism." In *Third Wave Feminism: A Critical Exploration*, edited by Stacy Gillis, Gillian Howie, and Rebecca Munford, 3–15. Hampshire: Palgrave Macmillan, 2007.

Simmonds, Felly Nkweto. "My Body, Myself: How Does a Black Woman Do Sociology?" In *Feminist Theory and the Body: A Reader*, edited by Janet Prince and Margrit Shildrick, 50–63. New York: Routledge, 1997.

Smith, Alanna (@AlannaMode). "It's Black Panther Week. I am ready. Yes it's week long I'm celebrating this Black excellence all week Like Kwanzaa but for Wakandans. Wakwanzaa!" Twitter, February 12, 2018.

Spivak, Gayatri. *Confessing Excess: Women and the Politics of Body Reduction.* Albany: State University of New York Press, 1990.

Van Dijk, T. A. *Discourse Studies: A Multidisciplinary Introduction.* London: Sage, 2009.

White, E. Frances. *Dark Continent of Our Bodies: Black Feminism and the Politics of Respectability.* Philadelphia: Temple University, 2001.

White, R. T. "I Dream a World: Black Panther and the Re-Making of Blackness." *New Political Science* 40, no. 2 (2018): 421–27.

Winchester, Woodrow W. III. "Afrofuturism, Inclusion, and the Design Imagination." *Interactions* 25, no. 2 (2018): 41–45.

Womack, Ytasha. *Afrofuturism: The World of Black Sci-Fi and Fantasy Culture.* Chicago: Chicago Review Press, 2013.

CHAPTER 8

Kamala Khan / Ms. Marvel, Islamic Feminism, and a Global Dialogue

Maryanne A. Rhett

In the "Mecca" storyline of *Ms. Marvel* (nos. 19–22), Ms. Marvel discovers that Josh, "former captain of the football team, Zoe's ex-boyfriend," and someone she has known since elementary school, is the villain Discord. Forced to see what she calls the "real Discord" and the "real Josh," she, in turn, reveals her true identity—the real Ms. Marvel, the real Kamala Khan—by taking off her mask. The revelation breaks down some of the difficulties Ms. Marvel has struggled with in proving her "good guy" qualities in the wake of a smear campaign against her and all superpowered humans in Jersey City.[1] She and Josh are both faced with realities that are easily obscured by emotions and perceptions. Josh admits that he had always wondered, as he says; the mask is not really all that concealing, but he never believed it because Kamala never gave off a Ms. Marvel vibe. As Josh and Kamala learn to see each other under their masks, Nakia (another school friend) and Tyesha (Kamala's sister-in-law) march to the building where superhumans have been gathered for "deportation back to New York City." While united in their desire to have the superhumans released, Nakia and Tyesha are at odds over the place of the hijab in everyday society. All four characters, in the same temporal space, struggle with questions of identity tied up in outward appearances and inward self-identities.

---

1. Wilson, "Mecca: Part 3 of 4."

Tyesha objects to Nakia's attempts to make the hijab "a secular symbol" because she feels that it robs the garment "of its intended meaning." Tyesha sees commodity creep in the modern interpretation of the hijab, especially in the US. She thinks it loses its meaning when companies like Nike mass-produce them and they can be casually worn by anyone. Nakia challenges Tyesha: "Who's to say what the original intended meaning is? All the Quran says is that believing women should draw their outer garments around themselves, 'so they may be identified,' i.e., identified as Muslim. Boom."[2] For Tyesha and Nakia, the hijab is a powerful symbol of self-identity, choice, and outward recognition. This fits with what Elizabeth Warnock Fernea found in 1998 when she asked Islamic women around the world about the place of the hijab in feminist discourse. Fernea says that, at the time, the "*hijab* [was] an important *new* development in Muslim countries where it [was] equated with piety and belief."[3] While it is not always a choice afforded women, where it is, it is made "based on [a woman's] reading of religious texts. . . . Thus we have diversity in attitude, strategy, and dress, which might be said to characterize the entire" Islamic world.[4] Miriam Cooke has similarly argued that rather than rejecting Islam, the Qur'an, or the hadith, Islamic feminists work "within the systems that are trying to marginalize them" and thus fight the patriarchy, not the faith.[5] Islamic "feminism" is a complicated theoretical concept, not only tied up in questions of women's rights, equality, and patriarchy but overlaid with cultural mores and neocolonial perceptions. Even linking the two words *Islamic* and *feminism* is hotly contested among scholars and activists the world over.

As with the very few other Islamic superheroes in the Marvel (and DC) Universe, the question of alter-ego concealment is intrinsically tied to their marked and unmarked identities as Muslims. Often Islamic superheroes apply conservative Islamic dress choices as part of their superhero costuming.[6] In this way the hijab (in the case of the X-Men's Dust, an abaya) becomes both a tool of concealment of identity and a tool of identification as Islamic. Ms. Marvel's costume choices are no different. Early iterations of the Ms. Marvel costume are founded on a burkini that Kamala's mother bought her, the one her mother pointed out that Kamala would never wear.[7] Later,

---

2. Wilson, "Mecca: Conclusion."

3. Fernea, *Islamic Feminism,* 421.

4. Fernea, *Islamic Feminism,* 421.

5. See Cooke, "Multiple Critique."

6. See Pakistani pop star Aaron Haroon Rashid's *Burka Avenger* (television) and Egyptian art student Deena Mohamed's *Qahera—The Superhero* (webcomic).

7. Wilson, "No Normal."

when Kamala must become Ms. Marvel traveling in Pakistan, she relies on the traditional Pakistani outfit, the chudi daar, and shawl to conceal her identity. Both garments act to conceal her identity and simultaneously signal her religious orientation.

Feminism is far more than a question of clothing choices, though a large number of the movement's most pivotal moments rest on the question of clothing (i.e., the right to wear pants or the proverbial burning of the bra). Islamic feminism, specifically, is like global feminism more generally, and is more than clothing, but it also not too far removed from clothing questions. The hijab has long been a central feature of Islamic feminists' agendas, whether as something to be removed or as something to be donned. As Miriam Khan's 2019 edited volume notes, *It's Not About the Burqa*. During the G. Willow Wilson *Ms. Marvel* era (April 2014–April 2019) the creative team behind the book, especially editor Sana Amanat, introduced the non-Muslim world, and reintroduced the Muslim world, to the complexity of not only feminism in a classic superhero narrative but also, more critically, to the concept of Islamic feminism.

So much of what happens in G. Willow Wilson's *Ms. Marvel* series touches on themes of feminism, especially Islamic feminism, but does so on the edges of Kamala Khan's narrative. The bridges between Kamala as a young, female, Muslim American and Ms. Marvel, a feminist superhero exhibiting hints of her Islamic alter ego, are delicate, often openly expressed by those around Kamala / Ms. Marvel, but not overtly tackled by herself.

Kamala Khan / Ms. Marvel is the complex embodiment of the history of Islamic women, a teenager from Jersey City, New Jersey, and a bendable, healable, and powerful superhero allied with the Avengers. She, too, is the inheritor of her maternal ancestor's bravery. These women have a "secret [they] carry, a strength that is waiting to appear."[8] As Ms. Marvel, Kamala wears women's Islamic dress to help hide her non-super self. Still, the Islam that Kamala participates in is more than clothing deep. G. Willow Wilson, the longtime writer for the series, wove together a cosmopolitan sense of Islam for Kamala to inhabit, one drawing directly on feminist tropes equally identifiable as "Western" and as "Islamic."[9]

---

8. Wilson, "Civil War II, No. 9."

9. Wilson's autobiography *The Butterfly Mosque* explores her life being raised in an upper-middle-class white American setting and her eventual conversion to Islam. Traveling extensively throughout the Islamic world, and having lived in a variety of US cities, Wilson has long studied the cultural norms and tropes of both US, or "Western," societies and Islamic communities. This background is evidently drawn from as she plays with images that speak to both "typical American" high schoolers and specifically to the woman's Islamic experience.

Introductions

In 2014 Marvel Comics resurrected the *Ms. Marvel* title, evolving her and her storyline into a thoroughly contemporary character, personifying an increasingly globalized world. The cover of issue 1 of *Ms. Marvel* graphically introduces the world to a new superhero, born of many cultures and syncretic backgrounds: Kamala Khan, wearing a black T-shirt and blue jeans with a colorful scarf (one that can be understood as both fashionable in a US setting and potentially useful as a hijab, what Margot Badran has called "traditional camouflage"[10]) around her neck. We do not see Kamala's eyes, only her mouth, set in determination, and the lower part of her face from the tip of her nose down. Her left hand is raised to just above her waist, clenched in a fist, and displaying three bracelets, and two, maybe three, rings. The largest bracelet Kamala is wearing is a silver, stylized Arabic rendition of her name.[11] At her right, Kamala is holding three textbooks, from top to bottom: *Illustration and Design*, *Hadith to Live By*, and *US History*. The three books, chosen by cover artist Sara Pichelli, are a snapshot of our hero before her transition to superhero. A student at Coles Academic High School in Jersey City, New Jersey, Khan would certainly be expected to be taking a US history class. *Illustration and Design* reflects Khan's propensity for art, particularly comic art, and allied field popular arts (i.e., computer games). The last book, *Hadith to Live By*, suggests the centrality of faith to her life, but as a component, not the all-encompassing-ness of religion that US popular media tends to lend to non-Christian, nonwhite characters. There is complexity in Khan, and this first cover gives us a glimpse into that complexity.

As Ms. Marvel, Kamala Khan embodies the superhuman nature of all post-Golden-Age-era superheroes as well as the conflict of being superhuman and living among non-super friends and family. Kamala must navigate the complexities of being a teenager with amazing abilities and powers, on the one hand, and typical hormonal and emotional challenges of any teenager, on the other. To all of this, she has added dimensions that Peter Parker never faced. She is cisfemale, with Subcontinent ancestry, and Muslim. *Ms. Marvel* reflects what Adrienne Resha has termed the Blue Age of Comics, representative of an expansion in the comics industry of character qualities, audience inclusivity, and material delivery.[12] Superheroes of the Golden through Bronze Ages often struggled only with placing themselves in the

---

10. Badran, *Feminism in Islam*, 118.

11. Later in the series, a new bracelet is introduced and becomes an integral part of the Ms. Marvel costume. That bracelet is discussed in more detail later in this chapter.

12. Resha, "Blue Age."

realities of being a superhero among non-super humans. While Superman did embody the very essence of the alien, he was nevertheless identified as a white cismale, which negated most of the challenges he could have faced as Clark Kent. Later heroes, like Peter Parker / Spider-Man, did have to navigate the dynamic of adolescence alongside their superness, but again they were often cismale, white, and otherwise associated with the dominate normative cultures surrounding them. Even women (really, until Storm) added only the complexity of being female to their list of challenges. Kamala was not the first nonwhite, female, Muslim superhero, but she was the first to top sales charts in any appreciable way and as such offers us a robust lens through which we can come to understand feminism in both a modern US setting and Islamic feminism in a modern global setting.

The complexity we glimpse on the cover of issue 1 reflects more than the complexity that modern comics are seeking to achieve, advocating for voices often forgotten in the superhero universes. *Ms. Marvel* issue 1 begins a conversation with readers about the ideological complexity of feminism. Too often couched in terms of Occidentalist rhetoric, feminism is scalable. Communally and regionally defined, feminism can reflect personal and community-based norms, but it is also nationally and religiously informed, and even above that, it is defined by temporality and geopolitical trends. Feminism is, like Kamala, complex and multifaceted. Understanding Kamala / Ms. Marvel helps us understand the nature of global dialogues between and among Western-style feminism and what emerged as Islamic feminism. Feminism in Egypt, for example, has a long history dating back to the early twentieth century. Margot Badran contends that despite the conventional narrative to the contrary, early Egyptian feminism was not Western in its influence, nor was it restricted to largely upper- and upper-middle-class women. Badran notes that it was (and is) indigenous, cross-class, and grounded in Islam and nationalism, but always challenging the patriarchy.[13]

Western Feminism and Islamic Feminism

Elizabeth Warnock Fernea, the well-regarded and well-traveled anthropologist, went *In Search of Islamic Feminism* in 1998. She found a colorful array of perspectives that mirrors, across the Islamic world, the variety and intensity of feminism as it is found in "the West." Feminism has evolved tremendously since the turn of the twentieth century, when women in New York,

---

13. See Badran, *Feminism in Islam*, ch. 5.

London, and Cairo took to the streets advocating for political, educational, and biological freedom. That history tends to segregate the suffragists of Egypt and Turkey from their sisters in the US and Great Britain, and this has made the advent of Marvel's Kamala Khan so seemingly novel. Feminism is too often couched in overtly Orientalist "West versus the Rest" rhetoric, and thus it is hard to see the rich global dialogue taking place, both historically and contemporarily. This dialogue is played out in the family history of Kamala's material ancestors. Their stories, which reflect at least some of personal narratives of G. Willow Wilson and Sana Amanat, tell a story less of divergence, more of convergence.

As a theme of comics analysis, feminism has largely been confined to the Western-centric traditions of third-wave (and previous waves) feminism. Comics, while a global phenomenon, tend to elucidate critique in nationalistic or perhaps regionalized settings. It is less surprising, therefore, that the feminist analysis and discussion applied to these works tends to be nationalistic or regional in scope as well. Like the medium, however, feminism is a global phenomenon, and while it is shaped by local and regional pressures, it, like comics, is in a global dialogue about its very nature. The *Ms. Marvel* series, as resurrected first under Sana Amanat (editor), G. Willow Wilson (writer), and Adrian Alphona (artist), is an excellent lens through which we may explore the global and local natures and complexities of comics and feminism.

Feminism has not had a long, obvious history in the genre of comics; Islamic feminism, even less so, yet in the comics market of the 2010s it was *Ms. Marvel* who achieved the designation as highest-selling digital title for the Marvel publishers.[14] What is more, Khan's successes as a comic *book* hero (even if that book was digital) propelled her at lightning speed onto, as Joe Quesada has dubbed them, the spokes of the wheel: that is, the other media in which we see Marvel characters reaching out to audiences. In September 2016 Quesada put into words the uniqueness of characters like Khan to transcend the page with such rapidity. Noting that it was not so long ago that women and characters of color struggled to gain traction, Marvel made the right decisions in editor and creative team, and "now we have a character that's very recognizable—very, very quickly. That doesn't happen a lot."[15] As a result, Quesada foretold Kamala's future in the array of Marvel media beyond the printed page. Since 2016 Ms. Marvel has made her cinematic debut in the 2018 animated film *Marvel Rising: Secret Warriors*, several tele-

14. "Ms. Marvel."
15. Couto.

vision appearances including *Avengers Assemble* and *Marvel Rising,* and to much acclaim in a variety of video games, for example *Lego Marvel's Avengers* and as the main character in the 2020 *Marvel's Avengers* game.

Comic books are themselves easily transported across national boundaries and become global phenomena, and when produced digitally this is done with even more ease, but in the case of Kamala Khan, her place in a multitude of media platforms has had an even more profound impact in exporting to the world Amanat's, Wilson's, Alphona's, as well as subsequent creators' expressions of Islamic feminism through the story arc(s) of Kamala's life. For example, Ms. Marvel appears in the Japanese anime *Marvel Future Avengers* and befriends one of the main characters, Chloe. In the series, Chloe is the only female character, a nod to traditional tropes which tend to demand that there be only one female per team. Her friendship with Ms. Marvel and other female "walk-ons" is the only outlet she has for understanding what a female superhero is. In much the same way that Ms. Marvel became a realized icon to look up to in real-life communities of female fandom, Chloe and Kamala's relationship suggests the importance of having role models even among superheroes. While described as a "do-gooder," Chloe is also part of the "action women" superhero class. Like Kamala's, Chloe's early story line is one of self-discovery, as she and her team realize that Hydra, not the Avengers, are the bad guys and they must learn to undo their training.

Even in *Marvel's Avengers* the story of finding oneself and one's cultural identity transcends the Khan narrative. Sandra Saad, the first-generation Egyptian American voice-personality of the video game Kamala, recounted how she had long been told that the only parts she was ever likely to be offered were "wife of terrorist." Such harmful tropes, which place her heritage firmly in the "bad guy" category, negate her nature as a woman by making her "only a wife," not an individual with a story of her own. Kamala Khan is the lead in *Marvel's Avengers,* itself an astounding feat for a character only a few years old, but the cohesiveness with which game designers presented Khan is perhaps even more remarkable. As Saad notes, "Kamala is Pakistani, Kamala is Muslim. But the game isn't about her religion because that's not what life is."[16] The game is certainly a video game, with all the glory and explosions one could ask for, but it is also a subtle narrative about family and identity. Khan's relationship with her father remains a thread in the narrative and includes "touches, which nod to the tension of wanting to embrace American ideals but not lose one's heritage."[17] Across the

---

16. Martens, "Star of Marvel's Avengers."
17. Martens, "Star of Marvel's Avengers."

platforms, Kamala Khan reaches out to audiences in deeply personal ways, weaving a seemingly new understanding of what being a woman can mean, maybe even a woman of Islamic heritage.

Like Chloe, Khan spends a great deal of time grappling with who and what she is. A sixteen-year-old from Jersey City, New Jersey, she comes from a Pakistani immigrant family who are, to greater and lesser degrees, devout Muslims. Sana Amanat is the editor who realized that the reborn Ms. Marvel can be easily taken as a real-life Kamala Khan. Growing up in pre-dominantly white New Jersey suburbs, Amanat is the daughter of Pakistani immigrants and spent much of her childhood struggling to fit in. Amanat is the foundation on which Ms. Marvel was built, but the structure above this was led in large part by Khan's first author, G. Willow Wilson, her-self an important piece of the evolving landscape of feminism, even Islamic feminism, in mainstream popular culture. Wilson, a practicing Muslim, has lived extensively in Egypt and the US and navigates the complexities of those cultures in all her work. In terms of sequential art, before writing *Ms. Marvel*, Wilson authored *Cairo*, a surrealist story blending modern tropes and concerns with images of Middle Eastern lore (e.g., jinn). Wilson, unlike Khan, is of European ancestry, but the feminism she exudes in her work is a blend not only of the efforts of 1960s radicals and eighteenth-century French revolutionaries but of turn-of-the-twentieth-century suffragists and women's rights activists from Egypt, England, and the US.

The complexity of feminism, in both Western and non-Western set-tings, has taken center stage among a variety of modern comics, including Egyptian web comics, Iranian and Syrian graphic novels, and Anglo-British superhero comic books.[18] In July 2013 Deena, a self-styled "generally unre-markable muslim egyptian [sic] female who resides within the land of many protests and pyramids," and a graphic design student,[19] concisely expressed this complexity in her web comic, *Qahera*. In "Part 2: On Femen," Deena's Muslim superhero Qahera questioned the militant (topless) feminists of the West who, she declared, "have constantly undermined and ignored women. [Who] seem unable to understand that we do not need [their] help."[20] The dichotomy between a Western feminism and non-Western feminism is noth-ing new. Malak Hifni Nassef (1886–1918) and Huda Sha'rawi (1879–1947) embodied such dichotomies even as neighbors in the Egyptian state. As

18. See Mohamed, *Qahera*; Satrapi, *Persepolis*; Cornell, *Captain Britain and MI: 13*, no. 1; Satrapi, *Embroideries*; Abirached, *A Game for Swallows*; *New X-Men*, 2002, in particular "Dust."

19. Mohamed, "About Me."

20. Mohamed, "On Femen."

Lelia Ahmed has noted, "Where Sha'rawi espoused a Westward-looking feminism, already in the 1900s and 1910s, Malak Hifni Nassef was articulating the basis of a feminism that did not automatically affiliate itself with westernization."[21] As we have already seen, even the idea that Egyptian feminism bubbled up from indigenous sentiment or was an import from outside is a point of contention among scholars. In any event, feminism was, and continues to be, larger than the demand for political equality; it is embedded in the nature of colonial history and with the coinciding racism.

Kamala Khan / Ms. Marvel embodies the fusion of ideas, a fusion made visual in how her power appears to have been passed down through the decades from mother to daughter. While her maternal ancestors do not appear to have been able to use the Inhuman abilities that become realized in Kamala, they always seem to be aware of them.

Voyages

In *Ms. Marvel* "Civil War II" (nos. 8–10), the story of four generations of women in Kamala Khan's family is traced from Bombay to Karachi and eventually to Jersey City, New Jersey. The arc, which follows the history of Kamala's great-grandmother (Aisha), grandmother, and mother (Muneeba) from India through Pakistan and ultimately to the US, is embedded with subtle clues about the nature of Islam and Islamic feminism as well as hints at the origins of Kamala / Ms. Marvel's superpowers. Initially this subplot begins in Bombay, 1947, as sectarian violence increases in the wake of the Partition of India.[22] Aisha, pregnant with Kamala's grandmother, is trying to leave India and migrate to Pakistan, where Muslims have been promised their own country. Kamala's great-great-grandfather says, "but we're Indians," to which her paternal grandfather responds, "not anymore." As the three set out on the arduous journey, the audience is told that the "wedding bangles" Aisha wears hold the money she gathered by selling off her other jewelry, to be used in their new life. In this broken narrative we hear that "even in the midst of civil war, life can begin again. Sometimes there is little hope. But there is never no hope. Something, however small, remains."[23] As the audience, we see in Aisha's life the seeds of Kamala's inhuman heritage.

---

21. Ahmed, *Women and Gender.*

22. In 1947 the UK gave up control of the Indian Subcontinent, setting the stage for the creation of the modern states of India and Pakistan (Pakistan, at the time being East Pakistan, now Bangladesh, and West Pakistan, now the Republic of Pakistan).

23. Wilson, "Civil War II, No. 8."

A shooting star / comet passes overhead as Aisha askes the gods for a sign of safety for her child to come.

Sometime around 1999 the story picks up again as Kamala's grandmother and Muneeba talk about the impending move to New Jersey. Muneeba does not want to leave Pakistan; she does not want her children to not know "home." Kamala's grandmother gives Muneeba the bracelets that secreted the money during Partition, saying, "Give them to your own daughter when she is old enough. She will be born on another continent, but her history will be our history. Remember that."[24] Again, the audience, if they do the math on this story line, cannot help but notice that the narrative of Kamala's maternal ancestry is tied to close contact with significant global events that have some connection to the *umma* (the global community of Muslims). The first portion is tied to the Partition of India and Pakistan. Muneeba and Yusuf journey to the US not long before the September 11 attacks. Both events have threads reaching across the umma. Partition is a linchpin in Salman Rushdie's *Midnight's Children,* and of course Rushdie goes on to incur the wrath of many Muslims with the publication of his work *Satanic Verses.* For many people in the non-Muslim world, Partition, the Islamic Revolution in Iran, or the fatwa issued against Rushdie are moments that punctuate and highlight their understanding of the Islamic world. For the generations born after 1979, the events of 2001 act in much the same way.

Several years later, around 2007, we meet a young Kamala who herself meets a young Bruno. The two bond over *Tween Mutant Samurai Turtles* and how beautiful he thinks her bracelets are.[25] This moment much more clearly fuses the past and the present through the conversation of American popular culture and family heirlooms. Nearly a decade later, Kamala returns to Karachi, in part running from her feelings about Bruno and in part to find what she feels is missing. In the end, however, she realizes that "the missing pieces aren't part of a place. They're part of me. They're things only I can figure out."[26] As the audience, of course, we know that those things she is seeking are what her maternal ancestors have always been aware of, only just as vaguely knowledgeable of what they mean as Kamala herself.

The backstory of the bracelets seems minor, if interesting, to the general arc of the series; however, their place linking Partition and the Civil War now being waged in the Marvel Universe is significant. On the surface, they highlight the reality that people, non-super or super, never can seem to get

24. Wilson, "Civil War II, No. 9."
25. Wilson, "Civil War II, No. 10."
26. Wilson, "Ms. Marvel No. 1 / No. 12."

along; more subtly, they create a thread linking four generations of women across the globe in powerful ways. The women, each in their own sense, sacrifice for their family's comfort and "home" in order to protect and prosper. These are not unusual depictions of women's stories, tying the female narrative to one of nurturing and caregiving. Beyond this, though, the intertwined trope of migration and protection brings the larger history of Islam more directly into the Marvel Universe. Wilson weaves together the legacy of the hijra[27] and of the population transfer that took place in the wake of the Partition of India, in her vignette about Kamala's family, all the while foreshadowing the greatness Kamala would come to inherit, by distinguishing the strength of the women in Kamala's ancestry.

Travel and Identity

Stories with Islamic elements very often come with travel and migration elements; likely this is because the faith began with a significant migratory moment and that moment is mirrored every year in the pilgrimage, hajj. The performance of hajj is obligatory for all Muslims, and while not all Muslims are able to meet the financial, physical, or emotional precepts that the pilgrimage demands, millions, even billions, over the centuries, have carried out the obligation. Both of these examples, the hijra and hajj, suggest a necessity, not just leisure, which "travel" tends to connote.

Kamala / Ms. Marvel looks at the place of hajj in her own experiences. She recognizes that as pilgrims return home from performing the ritual, from completing it, as she says, "The struggle, the journey, is over, and everyone is returning to the place where they feel safe," but she also recognizes that "you can't go through a pilgrimage and not come out changed. Sometimes the places and people you thought were safe look different once you've seen them from another perspective."[28] With enlightenment comes knowledge, yes, but too there is the pain of seeing the world in a new way.

---

27. The hijra took place between about the year 620 and 622 CE in the Hejaz, the western region of the Arabian Peninsula which today includes the cities of Mecca and Medina. While the hijra is often erroneously described as "flight," it is better understood as a migration. Western scholars of Islamic history have often described this period as one of "flight," although the timeline itself belies that term. During this period, the nascent population of Muslims in Mecca were being persecuted and harassed by the polytheistic Meccans, who held sociopolitical power. The prophet Muhammed was presented with the opportunity to alleviate the sufferings of his followers by having them move with him to the city of Yathrib (later Medina), about two hundred miles to the north.

28. Wilson, "Mecca: Conclusion."

For Kamala / Ms. Marvel the experiences that coincide with hajj bring into sharp relief her concern that she does not belong anywhere, that she has no "place where she can feel safe."

The space of safety that Kamala / Ms. Marvel craves can be seen as the physicality of the *haramiyya*—women's quarters, which for many Islamic feminists has been the space they have most advocated escape from. The harem, these female and private places in upper- and upper-middle-class Islamic homes, have in Western imagination come to connote sexual exoticism but are far more mundane and functional in the real world. While it is unlikely that Kamala would ever be happy confined to one portion of a building simply because she is a woman, the notion of a safe, inviolable space has appeal and is echoed across the superhero universes. Superman, after all, has his Fortress of Solitude; Batman, the Batcave.

In other ways, Wilson presents Islamic feminist motifs in "Army of One," when Kamala's brother, Aamir, gets engaged to Tyesha, a Black woman who converted to Islam of her own volition, before she met Aamir. Tyesha dresses modestly and has chosen a conservative path in her practice of Islam. Like Aamir she exhibits a reflective and thoughtful approach to faith, one developed as a young adult and through free will. Unlike Kamala and her friend Nakia, who were raised Muslim, Tyesha is a convert and gives the audience still another example of how Islamic feminism may play out. Her parents tell us that she was raised in the church and that her conversion has been difficult for them to come to grips with. This, coupled with Tyesha and Aamir being of different ethnic backgrounds, promises to cause more problems than not between the families. Tyesha's commitment to move in with Kamala's family until Aamir is done with his studies ingratiates her with Kamala's parents, who recognize this act as one esteeming "proper traditional" roles.[29]

Final Thoughts

Kamala, despite how she may feel in looking for her own space, reflects a very cosmopolitan sense of feminism, in the ease with which she can travel the world and participate in its very survival. Likewise, she does not face the struggles other feminists have faced. No one questions her place as a superhero because of her femaleness. Josh is vaguely surprised when Kamala reveals her identity to him, not because she is a woman but because she was a nerd. The equity that Kamala / Ms. Marvel struggles for is racial (couched

29. Wilson, "Army of One."

in superhuman vs. human rhetoric) and ageist. She is young, and new to her powers, when we first meet her. Her superhuman colleagues doubt her because of these qualities, not because of her female identity. It is age that again mirrors the local and global strains of feminism that Kamala interacts with. Among the various forms of Islamic feminism, or even Western feminism, there are shifts that represent generational change. Scholars who have studied Islamic communities across the world for significant periods of time (several decades) have noted that there is a tension between women who came of age in a more secular and less hijabi period and women coming of age in more recent years as practice (e.g., prayer) and covering have become more commonplace. Kamala is not only a woman of the US system, where women are, at least, politically equal with their male counterparts; she is also embedded in a community of believers who include all these strains of Islamic feminism. Even within her own generation the tensions are apparent, as Nakia rebukes Kamala for not wearing a hijab, and Tyesha rebukes Nakia for being too secular in her understanding of the hijab.

One distinction Fernea found in her global search for Islamic feminism was made by a Muslim from Portland, Oregon. There, the director of the Muslim Educational Trust claimed that for Islam, "women were very important. Aisha, particularly, was very influential. But cultural influences where Muslims live have discouraged women from claiming their full rights under Islam. If by feminism you mean the Western definition—men and women in conflict, then I would say we differ. We would say *complementary,* not equal."[30] Margot Badran and Ibtissam Bouachrine, among many other scholars, have struggled to contextualize where Islamic feminism intersects with and diverges from other forms of feminist thinking. Badran, looking back over a century of feminist thinking in Egypt, notes that women there have maintained an "independent feminist tradition. . . . They have rejected attempts of their opponents to impose restrictions on women in the name of Islam. . . . Women have not allowed their feminism and Islam to be polarized."[31] In the end, Ms. Marvel is the embodiment of intersectional feminism. She sits at the crossroads of several identities, all competing within her for dominance but always remaining in parity.

---

30. Fernea, *Islamic Feminism,* 369.
31. Badran, *Feminism in Islam.*

Bibliography

Abirached, Zeina. *A Game for Swallows: To Die, to Leave, to Return.* Minneapolis: Graphic Universe, 2012.

Ahmed, Lelia. *Women and Gender in Islam: Historical Roots of a Modern Debate.* New Haven, CT: Yale University Press, 1992.

Badran, Margot. *Feminism in Islam: Secular and Religious Convergences.* London: Oneworld, 2013.

Cooke, Miriam. "Multiple Critique: Islamic Feminist Rhetorical Strategies." *Nepantla: Views from South* 1, no. 1 (2020): 91–110.

Cornell, Paul. *Captain Britain and MI-13* 1, no. 1. Marvel Comics, July 2008.

Couto, Anthony. "Quesada on Marvel's Diverse Audience, Ms. Marvel's Future in TV & Film." *CBR*, September 6, 2016. Accessed February 8, 2021. https://www.cbr.com/quesada-on-marvels-diverse-audience-ms-marvels-future-in-tv-film/.

Fernea, Elizabeth Warnock. *In Search of Islamic Feminism.* New York: Anchor Books, 1998.

Martens, Todd. "The Star of the 'Marvel's Avengers' Game Is a Muslim Pakistani Teenager; a.k.a. Ms. Marvel." *Los Angeles Times,* September 4, 2020. https://www.latimes.com/entertainment-arts/story/2020-09-04/star-marvel-avengers-game-muslim-pakistani-teenager-ms-marvel.

Morrison, Grant (w)., and Ethan Van Sciver (a). "Dust." *New X-Men* 1, no. 133. New York: Marvel Comics, 2002.

Mohamed, Deena. "About Me." *Blog Like an Egyptian*, Tumblr. Accessed 2020. http://bloglikeanegyptian.tumblr.com/about.

———. "Part Two: On Femen." *Qahera—The Superhero*, July 20, 2013. https://qaherathesuperhero.com/post/61173083361.

———. *Qahera—The Superhero.* http://qaherathesuperhero.com/.

"Ms. Marvel Is Marvel's '#1 Digital Seller.'" *The Beat: The Blog of Comics Culture,* November 4, 2014. Accessed February 8, 2021. https://www.comicsbeat.com/ms-marvel-is-marvels-1-digital-seller/.

Resha, Adrienne. "The Blue Age of Comic Books." Last accessed July 31, 2020. https://scalar.usc.edu/works/blue-age-of-comic-books/index.

Satrapi, Marjane. *Embroideries.* London: Pantheon, 2005.

———. *Persepolis.* New York: Pantheon Books, 2003.

Wilson, G. Willow. (w). "Army of One: Part 1 of 3, No. 4." *Ms. Marvel,* 2016.

———. *The Butterfly Mosque.* New York: Grove Atlantic, 2010.

———. "Civil War II, No. 8." *Ms. Marvel,* 2016.

———. "Civil War II, No. 9." *Ms. Marvel,* 2016.

———. "Civil War II, No. 10." *Ms. Marvel,* 2016.

———. "Mecca: Conclusion, No. 22." *Ms. Marvel,* 2017.

———. "Mecca: Part 3 of 4, No. 21." *Ms. Marvel,* 2017.

———. "Ms. Marvel No. 1 / No. 12." *Ms. Marvel,* 2016.

———. "No Normal." *Ms. Marvel* 1. Marvel, 2015.

CHAPTER 9

"Misty" Knight

Dialogue with a Black Pearl in the Ivory Tower

Stephanie L. Sanders

Mercedes Kelly "Misty" Knight is a former New York City Police Department Police Officer.[1] She earned a college degree in criminology and graduated as valedictorian from the Police Academy.[2] As a sworn officer, Misty took an oath to never betray the public trust and to maintain the highest ethical standards to serve the community and the agency. After serving as a police officer for a number of years, she joined the ranks of detective.[3] Misty excelled in a male-dominated career, was respected by her colleagues, and was known for her intellect, intuition, and interrogation methods.

During a routine police call and visit to a local bank, Misty encountered an explosive device that caused extensive damage to her right arm.[4] Subsequently, she received a prosthetic bionic steel arm. Unable to continue active field duty, Misty assumed a temporary light-duty desk assignment.[5] The amputation and rehabilitation that followed were insistent reminders of the police career that never would be. It was painfully obvious that Misty

1. "Misty Knight."
2. Andrivet, "Misty Knight."
3. "Misty Knight (Earth-616)."
4. "Misty Knight."
5. "Misty Knight (Earth-616)."

should search for another job in criminology or social justice. Even Misty's colleagues viewed her injury as a major hindrance both personally and professionally. This moment of commiseration, however, was short-lived.

To reduce postinjury recovery time, Misty relied on arm rehabilitation and strengthening. During rehabilitation she honed her martial arts skills and grew proficient in hand-to-hand combat and investigations. In the end, Misty's bionic arm was seventy-five times stronger and more durable than any human arm. Her new bionic arm has the capacity to crush steel-like objects and to produce concentrated blasts of cryogenic energy that protect Misty and other benefactors from harmful threats.

Conocimiento: The Portrait of a Sacred Shift

In her work, Gloria Anzaldúa uses spiritual activism as an anchor to bring about healing, social justice, and inclusive communities.[6] While the term *spiritual activism* appears to be self-contradictory, the wording itself is part of Anzaldúa's practice to achieve change. Specifically, *spiritual* focuses on self-change or inner works, and *activism* strongly suggests public acts. By centering Misty's social identities of race and gender in the context of higher education, the expression further suggests that knowledge, or *conocimiento*, is produced. "Now let us shift . . . the path of conocimiento . . . inner works, public acts."[7]

Although Misty has superpowers, her desire to champion justice is indisputable as she faces villains in the context of higher education. In the story arc that follows, Misty's villainous encounters capture periods of calm, tensions, conflict, and eventually resolution. The first encounter explores the outsider-within status. Here, Misty uses her dual positioning to gain and use knowledge to transcend limitations posed by institutional contexts. I review how her character maintains power and avoids Blaxploitation. In the next encounter, watching the watchmen, Misty discovers that whether one is human or superhuman, superheroine or villain, both have limitations that require mastery of an inner self. Here, a comparison of how Black female characters differ with regard to pursuing justice alone or with others is explored. The final theme, Black pearls in the ivory tower, highlights Misty's face-to-face encounter with a supervillain, who is simply a shadow

---

6. Keating, "Citizen."
7. Keating, "Citizen," 53.

of his former self. Through storytelling and symbolic representations, we see Misty's persistence, superhuman strength, and character development.

Competing Frames:
Superheroine and Antijustice Villains

LITERATURE REVIEW

Institutions have long demonstrated a commitment to the idea of diversity. Following the civil rights era, which focused on racial integration and equal opportunity, the idea of diversity was anchored in institutional missions to support the full inclusion of the human experience.[8] During early iterations of the diversity idea, institutions rallied around affirmative action, equal employment opportunity, and multiculturalism. To manage the shift from compliance and law toward a more inclusive learning environment, historically white institutions hired mid- or executive-level personnel to advance diversity, equity, and inclusion (DEI) initiatives.[9]

The experiences of these change agents remain an increasingly significant area of interest. Among a growing segment of public liberal arts institutions, this significance is evident in town halls and community forums, workshops and trainings, conference themes, student advocacy, and faculty research. In the fall of 2020, a quick Google search for "diversity officers in higher education" yielded approximately 102 million returns from professional organizations, regional and national accrediting organizations, discipline standards, conferences, books, scholarly journal articles, named centers and institutes, blogs, podcasts, and academic programs. Scholars who study leadership and organizational change have greatly extended our knowledge and theorizing of the benefits of the diversity ideal. However, the day-to-day interactions of leaders at the helm of these changes, namely Black women, is woefully underexplored.[10] In what follows, Misty's experiences more fully contextualize the existing research literature on the intersection of race, gender, power, and organizational change in higher education.

8. Williams, *Strategic Diversity Leadership*.
9. Page, *Diversity Bonus*.
10. Grim et al., "Academic Diversity Officers."

OUTSIDER-WITHIN

Gloria Anzaldúa challenges us to develop a set of knowledges and new theorizing methods that aid our understanding of those on the margins of society.[11] In response to Anzaldúa's challenge, through narrative storytelling, Misty's character demonstrates how Black women make meaning of their work in historically white spaces. If the methodology of storytelling is traditionally used to silence and marginalize people of color, the same methodology can be used to occupy and transform the margins into places of resistance.[12] Rooted in Black feminism and critical race theory, intersectionality is an analytic tool used to explore how Misty's race, gender, and position play a role in her display of agentic behaviors. This method offers a liberatory response from members of traditionally marginalized groups. While no single effort could fully capture intersectionality, this framework provides a useful window to understand how intersectionality engages a range of issues, social identities, power dynamics, and legal and education systems. This level of analysis, while building interdisciplinary bridges, prompts several debates by engaging readers in lines of thought, epistemology, and knowledge that might otherwise be silenced, dismissed, or distorted.[13] By using Anzaldúa's outsider-within framework, I argue that this status generates new knowledge, stimulates Misty's consciousness, and moves her to collective action.

BLACK WOMEN AS AGENTS OF KNOWLEDGE

With excitement, Misty prepares to interview for the open position of diversity officer with the New York Universe-city College of Liberal Arts (NY-UCLA). She dresses two levels above the appropriate attire for an interview. Black binder in hand, Misty arrives at a nearly empty front office and waits for the interview chair to arrive. At 8:30 a.m. the chair arrives, scans the room twice, and overlooks Misty as the invited job candidate. To make herself visible, Misty introduces herself: "Hi! I'm Misty." After a pregnant pause, the interview chair quips, "Oh, you're Misty. Sorry! I'm Chad." Disheartened but not surprised at Chad's reception of her, Misty completes the

---

11. Anzaldúa, "Making Faces."
12. Solorzano and Delgado, "Transformational Resistance."
13. Delgado, "Storytelling"; Delgado, "Farber and Sherry"; Denzin and Lincoln, "Qualitative Research"; Jenkins, "Transmedia."

interview process with ease. Two weeks after the campus interview, Misty is offered the job as NY-UCLA's new diversity officer.

Hopeful that she would meet new colleagues, Misty hangs out in the faculty lounge during her first week on the job. On one occasion, Sophie and Brett file into the lounge, microwave their lunches, and grab a seat. Unaware that Misty is a new colleague, they show no indication of having seen her. That is, until Sophie asks her to make copies of a course handout. With a smile on her face, Misty gathers her lunch and replies, "I'm Misty, the new diversity officer. Someone in the front office should be able to assist you with copies." Well acquainted with these seemingly innocuous encounters, Misty recalls depictions of erasure and servitude, and expressions of someone's ability to diminish or exterminate her humanity, or her physical existence. Patricia Hill Collins likens Misty's minuscule day-to-day acts of marginalization to an "outsider-within" status.[14] Howard-Hamilton suggests that Black women "have been invited into places where the dominant group has assembled, but they remain outsiders because they are still invisible and have no voice when dialogue commences."[15]

Since institutional priorities, including diversity and inclusion, are largely influenced by context,[16] this leaves women and people of color in mid-level administrative positions feeling isolated and alienated,[17] tethered to specific outreach and special initiatives, and assigned a significant portion of labor to advance diversity work.[18] Although research is not silent regarding the work experiences of women of color, strategies for withstanding the impacts of being an outsider-within should not be overlooked. The positioning of this status suggests that valuable insight and knowledge is accrued on the margins (outside) and at the center (within). Take, for instance, Misty's character and first appearance on Marvel's *Luke Cage*, season 1, episode 3, "Who's Gonna Take the Weight?" In this episode, Misty partners with Detective Scarfe. Though Misty is unaware that Scarfe is a corrupt cop working outside the law, she insists that the two work together to determine who's responsible for a string of murders.[19] As a sworn officer, Misty had taken an oath to never betray the public trust and to maintain the highest ethical

---

14. Hill Collins, "Black Feminist," S14.

15. Howard-Hamilton, "Theoretical Frameworks," 21.

16. Worthington, "Diversity Officers."

17. Jackson, "Test for Diversity"; Smith, "Black Girl Magic"; Thompson, "Examining Perceptions."

18. Glover, "Existing Pathways"; King and Gomez, "Pathway"; Williams, *Strategic Diversity Leadership*.

19. Tatiana, "Luke Cage."

standards to serve the community and the agency. While she works to serve and protect her community, she gains insight into Scarfe's corrupt dealings that involve solving crimes, taking bribes, and extorting criminals. She also gains knowledge (conocimiento) regarding Cage's connection to these acts and his vacillation between being a hero for hire, with super strength, and a villain.[20] This dynamic seems to be mounting evidence that Misty is working alongside colleagues in a criminal justice system that is broken, full of police misconduct and violence, and in need of deep systemic change. Here, the emerging violence that permeates these characters raises questions about the treatment of power within an intersectional context, specifically with regard to space and place, power, and gender.

This is a complex dynamic for Misty, as an insider, to work against, especially since she has an affinity for Cage but not his choice of method for navigating the broken system. A critical feature that separates Misty from Cage and Scarfe is power and Blaxploitation. Though all three wield power, in the Luke Cage episodes the writers do an exceptional job of removing Misty from the Blaxploitation narrative specifically involving violence. It is not surprising, then, that Misty relies on her knowledge (conocimiento) and intellect and is vigilant in navigating a broken system, as an insider and an outsider-within. What is truly remarkable about Misty's character in the Marvel University is that as a cop and detective, she only sought to serve. After her bionic arm and superpowers, she still sought the opportunity to serve the good of others. While Cage and Scarfe may be powerful in their own communities, their approaches to forging or corrupting justice, respectively, are not enough to survive the world and make large-scale changes.

WATCHING THE WATCHMEN

The phrase *Quis custodiet ipsos custodes*, or who will guard the guards themselves, is connected to the Roman poet Juvenal.[21] The satirical phrase highlights the villainy of law enforcement, draconian dictatorships, and tyrannical governments. The phrase interrogates why the law does not protect those it is sworn to serve and protect. And it questions the accountability of vigilantes in positions of power who follow their own rules.[22] Drawing on Misty's character, the phrase further suggests that whether one is human or superhuman, superheroine or villain, both have limitations that require

---

20. Tatiana, "Luke Cage."
21. Sheptycki, "Politics of Policing."
22. Sheptycki, "Politics of Policing."

mastery of an inner self. This awareness results in either a superheroine who uses superpowers to defend a just world or a villain who uses superpowers to achieve nefarious ends.

Despite her superheroine status, Misty experiences a reflection point exacerbated by a current sociopolitical context, deep social divides, student calls to action, and groundswells of hashtag activism (e.g., #icantbreathe, #blacklivesmatter, #sayhername, #bluelivesmatter, #socialjustice). Precipitating Misty's reflection point are two national events with very different outcomes, occurring almost twelve hours and more than twelve hundred miles apart. On Monday morning, in New York City's Central Park, a white woman, Amy Cooper, calls 911 and reports that an "African American" man in Ramble Park is "threatening her life." That man is Christian Cooper. On Monday evening, a store employee calls the police on George Floyd, in Minneapolis, Minnesota, on the speculation of his passing a counterfeit twenty-dollar bill. While Christian lives to tell his version of events, George does not. The murders of George Floyd, Ahmaud Arbery, Breonna Taylor, and countless others are vestiges of broken systems on display for the entire world to see.

Although Misty takes pride in protecting and serving the university community, it only deepens the narrative to have a former officer and detective grapple with the methods used by those on the side of the law. While society, writ large, is attentive to the most overt displays of injustice (i.e., George Floyd), reckoning with it requires watching those in positions of power and addressing injustice in all its forms. This includes addressing subtle, day-to-day slights and advocating on behalf of those who bear the weight of such insults and assaults. These indicators are critical as Misty develops a new set of knowledges and practices that aid her understanding of how to best mete out justice in a broken system.

Outsider Partners. In her second opportunity to forge justice, Misty comes face-to-face with a team of antijustice villains. It is worth mentioning that Misty has an uncanny ability to solve crimes and spot perpetrators of injustice simply by looking at the evidence. By her own estimation, she is "Sherlock Holmes New York" and applies the same methodology to her new job at NY-UCLA. Some injustices are so subtle that neither the injured party nor the perpetrator entirely understands what is occurring. This is not the case for Misty, who is hypervigilant about all things justice—on and off campus.

During an executive team meeting focused on student belonging and inclusion, Misty's colleague (let's call her Abby) refers to Black female students as "loud and aggressive." The subtext implies that Black female students do not belong in the university community or the discipline, perhaps because of different compartments of behavior. According to Robin DiAngelo, Abby's comment is rooted in power, privilege, and a grand narrative of whites to control the racial narrative.[23] By way of example, Misty's colleagues on the interview team and in the faculty lounge give a nod to the same grand narrative to preserve their place in the social pecking order, as did Amy Cooper, who called 911 to report an "African American" man who "came out of the bush," and the police officer who murdered George Floyd.

Misty thinks to herself, "If I don't address Abby, I am complicit in oppressing others who look like me and I allow the stereotypes of Black women to continue." In ways that perhaps are not the case for Abby, as the only woman of color at the table, Misty has the added responsibility of balancing her professional role and managing any outward reactions to backhanded comments. The inner work of spiritual activism and deep reflection leads Misty to shift and take "the path of conocimiento . . . inner works, public acts."[24] Rather than violently grab Abby with her bionic arm, and reinforce the angry Black woman trope, Misty releases a concentrated beam of cryogenic energy. She showcases an energy shield to stop incoming assaults. The shield freezes the team and compels them to actively listen without taking a defensive posture or trying to escape what Misty is about to say.

Misty addresses the executive team: "This is not a moment to simply raise awareness about students you perceive as angry and loud . . . over time, these and similar comments have a much larger impact that led to barriers and inequitable and unjust outcomes for women of color." Misty continues, "These gendered slights marginalize, silence, and objectify Black female students who, perhaps like me, struggle with the paradox of hypervisibility and invisibility." As the energy shield thins and the meeting ends, Misty's colleagues welcome the teachable moment and the invitation for the leadership team to "shift . . . the path of conocimiento . . . inner works, public acts."[25] Misty takes this opportunity to invite her colleagues to a deeper place of understanding and to moderate the intersectional role of context, social identity, and sense of belonging.

Here, we see an intriguing contrast between Misty's character and that of comparable female characters in the Blaxploitation genre, particularly in terms of their representation and the nature of their working partnerships. An obvious character who comes to mind is Pam Grier's character, Coffy.

---

23. DiAngelo, *White Fragility.*
24. Keating, "Citizen," 53.
25. Keating, "Citizen," 53.

Coffy debuted in 1973,[26] when women of color were practically invisible
and stereotyped. Yet Coffy's representation on film depicted Black women
as visibly powerful, independent, and beautiful. A nurse by day and lone
vigilante by night, Coffy seeks revenge against drug dealers who played
a role in her sister's addiction to drugs.[27] In Marvel's *Iron Fist*, after Misty
loses her arm, she finds a friend in Colleen Wing, a Japanese martial artist
who avenges her grandfather's death. Together, the duo become Daughters
of the Dragon, later known as Nightwing Restorations.[28]

Although both characters' pursuit of justice is born of trauma, their
approach to justice is noteworthy. As Coffy metes out justice, there is an
undue emphasis on self-reliance and acting *alone* that results in the death of
many. In some ways, this portrayal of violence marks a site of intersectionality where gender, sex, race, and power relations are intensified and visible in
Coffy's character. This portrayal flips the liberation of Black women in film
on its head and becomes a story of vengeance against individuals. Unlike
Coffy's approach to justice, Misty teams up with Colleen both professionally
and personally, to defend their community and dismantle corrupt systems.
Together they perform jobs like investigations, recovery, and bodyguarding.
Misty also partners with campus colleagues with similar goals in mind—
to defend the university community and dismantle a corrupt system from
the inside out. Despite resistance and corruption, Misty is committed to her
brand of justice and maintains hope that the system can work. This comparison exposes the lack of emphasis on the systemic nature of oppression and
injustice. Further, it deepens the narrative of whether liberation and justice
are predicated on individual or collective actions.

BLACK PEARLS IN THE IVORY TOWER

A Change Is Gonna Come. While issues related to DEI and social justice
are commonly part of universities' mission and vision, implementing these
concepts can present a challenge. Higher education, like many social institutions, historically is designed to absorb as little change as possible. While
higher education prides itself on being an intellectual community of ambi-
tious scholars, at best, it is a microcosm of society that reflects greater political, social, and economic issues. As leaders in liberal education, intellectual
communities with progressive scholars and students should not only lead

---

26. Obenson, "Shaft"; Terry, "Gendering."
27. Obenson, "Shaft."
28. Beard, "Great Daughters."

change in higher education; they should also influence local communities and make a positive impact on society in general.

In higher education, decision-makers in positions of power to make change are situated at the top of the hierarchy (e.g., board of trustees president and vice president, provost and vice provost, chief financial officer). Despite the gulf of power and influence between Misty and other high-level executives, she is hopeful that she can enact real systemic change at NY-UCLA. Of course, this depends on the right working partnerships. Up until this point, Misty continues to engage in small-scale personal activism with antijustice villains. While such engagement may address individual-level change in isolation, it does nothing to dismantle unjust patterns and the structures that intersect and cause them. Aware of this knowledge, Misty prepares to sojourn to the power nucleus where antijustice villains hold greater institutional power and the ability to make large-scale change.

Two Sides of the Same Coin. Aside from the difference in power, position, and influence, Misty's bionic arm, physical strength, and intellect place her on a much higher plane than the Provost. Before the meeting, Misty researches the Provost's record. What she learns informs how she frames her campus-wide social justice proposal. She is familiar with major decisions he has made over the last thirty years. At each juncture of his academic career, he accrued greater levels of success, power, and influence. Holding a number of executive-level positions, the Provost developed an entourage of supporters, understood his allies, and appeared to be comfortable moving the university in a direction that serves the status quo. At the beginning of his career and during early iterations of the diversity idea, the Provost championed civil rights, equity, and multiculturalism. Because of legal concerns and the amount of resistance from stakeholders like faculty, alumni, and legislators, he pursued a career path that did not require vast amounts of emotional energy, coalition building, or excess labor to persuade people about the value-add of DEI and issues related to social justice. When multiple opportunities for career advancement and increased job responsibilities presented themselves, he took advantage of these without hesitation. At this point in his career, the Provost is simply a shadow of his former self. Though he projects a different image as a supervillain, his true predilection to make the world a better place through the vehicle of advocacy and activism never blossomed as he had hoped.

In stark contrast to the Provost's career path, Misty left a position of power, authority, and influence in law enforcement to forge justice and build coalitions with the expectation of expending much emotional energy and labor. With a measure of humility and alarm, however, she recognizes within herself the potential for similar career blunders regarding power grabs. In Misty's final encounter, two tendencies and two mindsets from shared worlds collide.

The Epicenter. Dressed in all-black, the Provost exits his office and greets Misty. "Hi, I'm Robert. Please call me 'Bob.' I understand you're here to discuss a proposal. Something about social justice and hiring a cluster of diversity officers across academic units?" Misty returns the gesture, introduces herself, and confirms the nature of her visit. Immediately she picks up on the limp handshake and interprets it as a lack of interest in her proposal. After a simple exchange of niceties, Misty opens the binder, presents Bob with a copy of the proposal, and waits for the right time to release the energy shield. As part of her pitch, she highlights national trends, aligns the rationale with the institution's mission and priorities, and articulates the value-add of such a progressive model. Impressed with Misty's proposal, Bob agrees to share the content with executive-level cabinet members for broad support. During the meeting Misty never releases the energy shield.

After a series of meetings with Bob to talk through the proposal, Misty realizes why she never used the energy shield. The answer lies in her personal acts of spiritual activism. Through this practice and over time, Misty develops a stronger sense of compassion and a broader perspective. Instead of practicing absolute exclusion toward villains who resist justice and immersing herself in a narrow world of persistent problems, she extends olive branches indiscriminately. Through spiritual activism, Misty believes that justice and fairness should be universal principles that transcend laws and conventions. Totally unaware of this inward change, Misty's more expansive state of being made Bob weaker and weaker with each encounter. This is a solemn portrait of spiritual activism. "Now let us shift . . . the path of conocimiento . . . inner works, public acts."[29]

After gaining broad support, Misty chairs a formal committee to recruit a cluster of twenty-five elite diversity officers known as Stalwarts for Social Justice (SSJ-25). Together, Misty and another colleague mentor SSJ-25 on the importance of collaborative work, on how to navigate power dynamics, and on how to strategically advance a social justice agenda. The group meets each month to share best practices and lessons learned. More importantly, the group learns how to navigate the margins and the center well enough to make systemic change.

29. Keating, "Citizen," 53.

Conclusion

Building on the scholarship of Black women who lead change, this chapter takes up the challenge to reflect on Anzaldúa's framework of spiritual activism and Hill Collins's intersectionality. Through narrative storytelling, I use the superheroine character of Misty Knight to develop the idea of knowledge or conocimiento, which is central to spiritual activism and change. The frame offers us deep insights into the intricacies of Misty's inner struggle between her humanity and her superhuman strength. For readers of Anzaldúa's framework, a strong argument is made for the importance of Misty's inner work as necessary to produce outward change. First, the emphasis on gaining new knowledge is a starting point for a deeper analysis of why systems of oppression pervade institutional structures. Misty's commitment to spiritual activism broadens our knowledge and epistemologies as she demonstrates the complexities of a shared world, agentic behaviors, and a course of action for improving its conditions. Next, although other Black female characters could easily champion the fight for social justice in higher education, Misty Knight is destined to do so. Even as a fictional character, the totality of her symbolic representations is critical to unfolding the story and deepening the narrative of power, Blaxploitation, and the collective work needed to dismantle corrupt systems and advance social justice. As an outsider-within, watchman, and Black pearl within the ivory tower, Misty reminds us that forging a social justice agenda in historically white spaces requires deep reflection, personal agency, and a strategy of surgical precision. Finally, for consumers of media and film, this chapter deepens the narrative of Black female representation. While most criticisms of these films voice concern over character representation, the scholarly treatments of the same characters tend to dismiss this analysis. I argue that these symbolic characters represent sites of intersectionality where gender, race, and power relations are hypervisible. In media and film, this representation still fits a very rigid male notion of power, liberation, and empowerment.

While some may argue that her sharp detective skills bring Misty superpowers, Misty is already a hero before her catastrophic accident necessitates a bionic arm. She has a strong sense of justice—both criminal and social—and an immense power within her human and superhuman persona to determine what exactly drives villains and supervillains toward change. To that end, institutions should view Black women as producers of legitimate knowledge with an ability to share this knowledge with accuracy. Complicating the credibility of their experiences is the fact that historically Black women have occupied tenuous positions in society and in higher education. With this in mind, we should re-examine Black women in light of a more complex understanding of context and power. In doing so, we can engage in the analysis of our own storytelling and dismantle oppressive forces that give way to more just institutions.

Bibliography

Andrivet, Sébastien. "Misty Knight." Writeups.org, n.d. Accessed January 20, 2021. https://www.writeups.org/misty-knight-marvel-comics-heroes-hire.

Anzaldúa, Gloria. *Making Faces, Making Soul / Haciendo Caras: Creative and Critical Perspectives of Feminists of Color.* San Francisco: Aunt Lute Foundation Books, 1990.

Beard, Jim. "9 Great Daughters of the Dragon Series." *Marvel,* September 6, 2018. https://www.marvel.com/articles/comics/great-daughters-of-the-dragon-misty-knight-colleen-wing-stories.

Delgado, Richard. "On Telling Stories in School: A Reply to Farber and Sherry." *Vanderbilt Law Review* 46, no. 4 (1993): 665–76.

———. "Storytelling for Oppositionists and Others: A Plea for Narrative." *Michigan Law Review* 87, no. 8 (1989): 2411–41.

Denzin, Norman K., and Yvonna S. Lincoln, eds. "Introduction: Entering the Field of Qualitative Research." In *Handbook of Qualitative Research,* edited by Norman K. Denzin and Yvonna S. Lincoln, 1–17. Thousand Oaks, CA: Sage, 1994.

DiAngelo, Robin. *White Fragility: Why It's So Hard for White People to Talk about Racism.* Boston: Beacon, 2018.

Glover, Melanie H. "Existing Pathways: A Historical Overview of Black Women in Higher Education Administration." In *Pathways to Higher Education Administration for African American Women,* edited by Tamara Bertrand Jones, LeKita Scott Dawkins, Marguerite M. Clinton, and Melanie Hayden Glover, 4–17. Sterling, VA: Stylus, 2012.

Grim, Jeffrey K., Laura Sánchez-Parkinson, Marie Ting, and Tabbye Chavous. "The Experiences of Academic Diversity Officers at the University of Michigan." *Currents* 1, no. 1 (2019): 131–50.

Hill Collins, Patricia. "Learning from the Outsider Within: The Sociological Significance of Black Feminist Thought." *Social Problems* 33, no. 6 (1986): s14–s32.

Howard-Hamilton, Mary F. "Theoretical Frameworks for African American Women." *New Directions for Student Services,* no. 104 (2003): 19–27.

Jackson, Jerlando F. L. "A New Test for Diversity: Retaining African American Administrators at Predominantly White Institutions." In *Retaining African Americans in Higher Education: Challenging Paradigms for Remaining Students, Faculty, and Administrators,* edited by Lee Jones, 93–109. Sterling, VA: Stylus, 2001.

Jenkins, Henry. "Transmedia Storytelling 101. Confessions of an Aca-Fan." *Disponible el* 14, no. 2 (2007). http://henryjenkins.org/2007/03/transmedia_storytelling_101.html.

Keating, AnaLouise. "'I'm a Citizen of the Universe': Gloria Anzaldúa's Spiritual Activism as Catalyst for Social Change." *Feminist Studies* 34, nos. 1/2 (2008): 53–69.

King, Jacqueline Elizabeth, and Gigi G. Gomez. *On the Pathway to the Presidency: Characteristics of Higher Education's Senior Leadership.* Washington, DC: American Council on Education, 2008.

"Misty Knight (Earth-616)." *Marvel Fandom,* n.d. Accessed January 20, 2021. https://marvel.fandom.com/wiki/Mercedes_Knight_(Earth-616).

"Misty Knight." *Marvel Directory,* 2013. Accessed January 20, 2021. http://www.marveldirectory.com/individuals/k/knightmisty.htm.

Obenson, Tambay. "'Shaft' Had Company: 10 Films That Defined the Blaxploitation Era." *IndieWire,* June 14, 2019. https://www.indiewire.com/gallery/blaxploitation-films-ranked-shaft/dolemite-2/.

Page, Scott E. *The Diversity Bonus: How Great Teams Pay Off in the Knowledge Economy.* Princeton, NJ: Princeton University Press, 2019.

Sheptycki, James. "The Politics of Policing a Pandemic Panic." *Australian & New Zealand Journal of Criminology* 53, no. 2 (2020): 157–73.

Smith, Allison Michelle. "Black Girl Magic: How Black Women Administrators Navigate the Intersection of Race and Gender in Workspace Silos at Predominantly White Institutions." PhD diss., Louisiana State University, 2016.

Solorzano, Daniel G., and Dolores Delgado Bernal. "Examining Transformational Resistance through a Critical Race and Latcrit Theory Framework: Chicana and Chicano Students in an Urban Context." *Urban Education* 36, no. 3 (2001): 308–42.

Tatiana. "Luke Cage 1.03 Review: 'Who's Gonna Take the Weight?'" *The Marvel Report,* October 2, 2016. https://themarvelreport.com/2016/10/luke-cage-1-03-review-whos-gonna-take-the-weight/.

Terry, John Robert. "Towards the Gendering of Blaxploitation and Black Power." *Madison Historical Review* 9, no. 1 (2012): 78–105.

Thompson, Renita Taylor. "Examining Perceptions of Black Administrators in Higher Education Regarding Administrative Leadership Opportunities." PhD diss., University of North Florida, 2016.

Williams, Damon A. *Strategic Diversity Leadership: Activating Change and Transformation in Higher Education.* Sterling, VA: Stylus, 2013.

Worthington, Roger L., Christine A. Stanley, and William T. Lewis Sr. "National Association of Diversity Officers in Higher Education Standards of Professional Practice for Chief Diversity Officers." *Journal of Diversity in Higher Education* 7, no. 4 (2014): 227–34.

PART 4

Answering the Call

*Marvel Superheroines as Responses to
Cultural Change*

CHAPTER 10

Part of the Team yet Always Apart

Black Widow through Multiple Marvel Series

Julie A. Davis and Robert Westerfelhaus

In a speech delivered by Winston Churchill on March 5, 1946, at Westminster College in Fulton, Missouri, the former British prime minister famously observed that "an iron curtain has descended across the continent" of Europe. Historians see this curtain as a symbolic border separating what was then the Soviet and American spheres of interest; economists, as a line between countries once controlled by the communist economic system and those that favored some form of capitalism. The boundary identified by Churchill also seemingly distinguished that portion of the world that produces superheroes who enjoy fame and mass popularity from the portion that does not. Indeed, even the most casual comic book readers, television viewers, and film audiences can easily name several superheroes who hail from places outside the former Warsaw Pact nations, but they would be hard pressed to name more than a very few with ties to the Russian Federation or to any of the countries that were once satellites of the former Soviet Union. Of those few, the name most likely to be mentioned is probably Black Widow (Natasha Romanoff) of the Avengers, who is arguably the star of Slavic superheroes. Others, such DC's Red Star or Marvel's Colossus, are, at best, merely secondary characters within the fictional worlds they inhabit. They and their cohorts are certainly not luminaries occupying the same stratospheric level of fame and popularity as Black Widow.

The dearth of Slavic superheroes within American and global popular culture can be attributed to several factors. First, the contemporary costumed superhero genre originated in the US during the Great Depression. The comic books featuring Superman, Batman, Captain America, Wonder Woman, and other Golden-Age pop culture pioneers were marketed to a domestic and not an international audience, one whose tastes and interests were parochial rather than cosmopolitan. A second related factor is that commercial concerns dictated the development of costumed superhero characters that appealed to prospective purchasers of such garish pulp magazine anthologies as *Action Comics* and *Detective Comics*, in which Superman and Batman, respectively, debuted. The immediate and widespread popularity of these characters, and most especially their proven profitability, prompted publishers to create additional costumed superheroes. Like Harry Potter decades later, these characters were rendered similar enough to consumers of pulp comic books that they could identify with their heroes and yet different enough from them in terms of special powers, bravery, and resources so as to be aspirational and inspirational for those same consumers, for whom comic book narratives offered a form of wish fulfillment. It is worth noting that the first cohort of costumed superheroes were exclusively White and decidedly Anglo-Saxon, attributes that appealed to, or which at the very least did not offend, the profitable consumer group that were comic books' intended audience. Not only were there no Black or Brown superheroes, but ethnic Whites, such as Italians or Slavs, were also conspicuously absent. These and other demographic lacunae have been relegated to the past, although there is admittedly still much to be done in terms of diversifying the fictional worlds of costumed superheroes. A third reason for the lack of Slavic superheroes in American popular culture is the Cold War between the US and the Soviet Union, which dominated much of the post–World War II twentieth century, as well as the continued tensions between the US and the Russian Federation. Depicting an audience's putative "enemies" as heroes is neither customary nor commercially shrewd. For that reason, depictions of Russians in particular and Slavs in general—the latter tainted by their cultural, historical, linguistic, and political associations with Russia—generally take the form of villains such as Sabbac or spies like Black Baroness, as well as other prominent examples of such included in the list of the fifteen most dangerous Russians in comics found in CBR's punningly named "Ruskie Business" article.[1] Another member of the Marvel Cinematic Universe's (MCU) pantheon, Winter Soldier (a.k.a. Bucky Barnes), extended this

---

1. Stevens, "Ruskie Business."

trend, depicting an American World War II hero and childhood best friend of Captain America who was kidnapped by the Soviets, tortured, and brainwashed into becoming a mindless assassin. Black Widow, in contrast, is one of the relatively rare Russian heroes included in the pop culture superhero pantheon. Yet significantly, her popularity, and in fact her hero status, did not occur until she left the Soviet system to join the American-centered spy agency S.H.I.E.L.D.

Some readers might find it strange that we point out the general absence of Slavic superheroes within American—and, by extension, global—popular culture. And to be frank, few people in the US pay attention to or care about this lacuna. But this is not the case for the tens of millions of Slavs who live in Eastern Europe and around the world. One of the authors of this chapter spent an academic year in Poland as a Fulbright fellow, has returned to that country seven times, and has spent time in other Slavic countries as well. This author can tell you that, while most of us who are not Slavs might not notice, the general absence and specific maltreatment of Slavs in the media does not go unnoticed or uncommented on by his Polish, Czech, and other Slavic friends who view the world through a different lens.

Black Widow's mass popularity also contrasts sharply with the status of most other female superheroes within and outside the MCU, only a few of whom enjoy her high profile, most notably Wonder Woman and the current iteration of Captain Marvel. Initially, and for many years, the primary audience toward whom costumed superheroes were targeted was largely male.[2] Consequently, superhero characters were created that affirmed and appealed to what were then traditional masculine tastes, and the stories in which they were featured possessed the same appeal. With only a few notable exceptions, such as Wonder Woman, superheroes were therefore strong, brave, decisive males, and female characters served as damsels in distress in need of rescue, as doting admirers of male heroes, or as salacious eye candy, and were—and still are—often depicted as being all three. Because of the hegemonic influence of American popular culture, the generic themes and conventions noted above have been exported worldwide, first in the form of conventional comic books and then in such media as film, television, and video games. The Marvel franchise of which Black Widow is a part has proved to be a commercial and critical success throughout the world. The Avengers films alone have enjoyed blockbuster success, becoming the most profitable film franchise of all time, and in the process setting box office

---

2. Duncan and Smith, *Power of Comics.*

records. Not surprisingly, the franchise has consequently exercised much cultural influence.[3]

In this chapter, we critique how Black Widow conforms to, and deviates from, the conventions of the American monomyth that has shaped the stories told by American popular culture, and consequently consumed throughout the world via global popular culture, including stories featuring costumed superheroes. We also take a critical look at the gendered treatment and sexual objectification of Black Widow, which is emblematic of the treatment of female costumed superheroes past and present. In looking at Black Widow's Slavic ethnic identity and her gendered treatment and sexual objectification, we acknowledge the critical importance of intersectionality in shaping the development and depiction of her character and the various ways audiences perceive her. Admittedly, our focus is rather narrow, as it would take a dissertation-length study to tease out and interrogate the many intersectional elements and effects present within as complex, multitextual cultural artifacts as the character of Black Widow and the Marvel Cinematic Universe (MCU) she inhabits. Before moving on to our analysis, we introduce more fully the character of Black Widow by providing an abbreviated sketch of her history as a character and charting some of the highlights of her appearances in different media and across various narrative arcs of the MCU.

Natasha Romanoff, a.k.a. the Black Widow

Most American adults likely met Natasha Romanoff, a.k.a. the Black Widow, in 2010's *Iron Man* 2.[4] This iteration of the character entered the MCU as Natalie Rushman, a member of Stark Industries. Upon her appearance, two male characters, Tony Stark / Iron Man and Happy Hogan, stopped what they were doing and stared at her. Pepper Potts, Stark's girlfriend and CEO of Stark Industries, described her to Stark as "a potentially very expensive sexual harassment lawsuit if you keep ogling her like that." Rather than examining her resume, Stark looked her up online, finding a lingerie photo as well as a litany of language skills. The scene ends with Stark stating "I want one." Stark later learned that she was a shadow S.H.I.E.L.D. agent and attempted to fire her. This initial introduction was rife with sexual objectification and firmly fixes the Black Widow as an object of the male gaze. Younger children likely met the character in a 2009 episode of Car-

---

3. Coggan, "Black Widow."
4. Franich, "Black Widow."

toon Network's *Super Hero Squad Show* called "Deadly Is the Black Widow's Bite." IMBd describes this TV-Y7-rated series as featuring "action packed, yet somewhat satirical alternate universe-style adventures."[5] Although the series ran for only two seasons, it has been included in the Disney+ streaming service, making it available to millions of viewers. We say more about this episode in our discussion of Black Widow's depiction as an object of sexual desire.

Since her first appearance in 1962's *Tales of Suspense* issue 52, Black Widow has been an evolving, if not confusing, character. Unusual among superheroes, Black Widow entered the Marvel universe as a noncostumed villain. A Soviet spy tasked with seducing and destroying Tony Stark / Iron Man, she soon defected to the US and transitioned into a hero, and later a member of the Avengers. Also unique among the group, Black Widow lacks either innate or technological superpowers. Character profiles list her superpowers as "None" while crediting "a Russian serum that improves her healing and immune systems, and slows her aging process," and her combat prowess demonstrates impressive training and skills.[6] Yet, despite decades of Marvel's attempt at narrative continuity, Black Widow's story line contradicted itself, offering her multiple entrants into the world of espionage. This inconsistency led Corrina Lawson to note, "various writers weren't sure of what to do with the character from appearance to appearance. That's no doubt why her personality has seemed so jumbled over the years."[7]

Not until the 2009–10 comic miniseries *Black Widow: Deadly Origins* did these disparate threads weave into a coherent narrative, albeit one full of brainwashing and implanted memories. From her entrée into the world of Soviet government as an infant, through intense training, multiple romantic interests, one marriage, and a plethora of superhero teams, the character has been a part of the larger Marvel Multiverse for decades. The character made her television debut in 1966's animated *The Marvel Super Heroes* and then took a hiatus until a 2009 episode of *The Super Hero Squad Show*. After her 2010 introduction in *Iron Man 2*, Black Widow appeared in a variety of Avengers- and Spider-Man-themed animated series, including *Avengers Assemble* and several *LEGO Marvel Super Hero* specials. As Darren Franich notes, she "was a perpetual bit player in various Marvel cartoon shows."[8] After appearing as a nonplayable character in the 2001 *Punisher* video game, Black Widow became a playable character in the 2010 releases of the *Iron*

5. IMDb, "Superhero Squad."
6. Cink (a) and Zhang (i), *Marvel*, 31.
7. Lawson, "Comics," para. 10.
8. Franich, "Avenger," para. 5.

Man 2 and *Super Hero Squad Show* games. She has since appeared in a large variety of video games available in both console and mobile platforms.

BLACK WIDOW AS OXYMORON: A RUSSIAN SPY AS AN AMERICAN MONOMYTHIC HERO

The composition of the various permutations of the Avengers is mostly American, except for the extraterrestrial god Thor, Wakanda's Black Panther, and, of course, Slavic superhero Black Widow. It should not be surprising, then, that the story arc of which she is a part conforms to the conventions of the narrative formula of the American monomyth. Myths are narratives that create connections, helping bind people in the here and now and across time through a shared vision of who they are and their place in the world. According to Robert Jewett and John Shelton Lawrence, the US has developed its own distinctive mythos, a variation of the universal monomyth identified by the Jungian scholar Joseph Campbell, which they term the *American monomyth*.[9] This myth has shaped and is shaped by mainstream America's conception of itself, and it can be seen informing a wide range of generic narratives, including detective stories, fantasy, horror, science fiction, Westerns, and—relevant to this study—stories featuring costumed superheroes. Jewett and Lawrence describe the American monomythic formula thus: "A community in a harmonious paradise is threatened by evil; normal institutions fail to contend with this threat; a selfless superhero emerges to renounce temptations and carry out the redemptive task; aided by fate, his decisive victory restores the community to its paradisiacal condition; the superhero then recedes into obscurity."[10]

The outsider status of heroes, and their eventual exit—literal, figurative, or both—are central features of monomythic narratives. Like a strong medicine, the psychological and physical qualities required for heroic action are potent and necessary when facing a powerful threat, but they are potentially threatening in themselves if the heroes possessing them are permitted to remain within the very communities they saved. The iconic protagonists of traditional Westerns or classic film noir are illustrative examples, social outsiders who are never really accepted as members of the communities they enter and which they are later expected to leave. This same dynamic is also seen in conventional depictions of superheroes, who are never truly inte-

---

9. Jewett and Lawrence, *American Monomyth*.
10. Jewett and Lawrence, *American Monomyth*, 6

grated into the communities they serve. When their salvific work is done, they too leave, whether physically or, in many but not all cases, figuratively by means of secret identities.

As a Slav, and especially as a Russian, Black Widow is an outsider with respect to the mainstream American culture in which the MCU is embedded and of which it is an expression. And yet she employs her well-honed skills, ironically obtained through the training and physical and psychological enhancements provided to her through the auspices of the Soviet Union, which was at the time the US's primary adversary, in the service of Nick Fury's Avengers initiative. She is, therefore, a cultural and ethnic outsider. In this respect, she differs from the traditional monomyth outsider, who hails from outside a particular community but still shares much culturally with the members of that community. Clint Eastwood's Man with No Name and Humphry Bogart's noir detectives have essentially the same cultural DNA as the spaghetti Western townspeople and the urban denizens they encounter. The same is not true of Black Widow, whose background is radically different from that of her Avenger colleagues. She is thus doubly an outsider.

Being the sole female member of the Avengers team in the narrative arc that begins with 2012's *Marvel's the Avengers* and lasts until Scarlett Witch joins the team in 2015's *Avengers: Age of Ultron* also serves to distance her from her colleagues. Additionally, Black Widow's Russian roots render her alien to the American cultural milieu in which she primarily operates as an Avenger. And as a woman, she is treated differently from her male companions in ways we identify and discuss in the next section. While there are women protagonists in American monomythic narratives, notably Diana Prince's Wonder Woman and more recently the Carol Danvers version of Captain Marvel, they are rare. The mythic formula still favors males. Even so, Black Widow is a valued member of the Avengers team and a popular-enough character within the MCU that she has been featured in her own eponymous film. While this is the twenty-fourth film in the MCU, Black Widow is only the second female superhero, after Captain Marvel, to have a film named after her.

The heroes of American monomyth narratives possess special qualities that set them apart from others. They are far faster, stronger, braver, and have more endurance than the average person. Superheroes are endowed with even greater powers. Black Widow's special "super" powers, while impressive, pale in comparison to those of other members of the Avengers. She cannot fly like Thor or Iron Man. She lacks the strength of Hulk, the magical-mystical powers of Dr. Strange, the speed of Spider-Man, or the impressive array of powers possessed by Captain Marvel, including her super speed, super strength, capacity to absorb energy, and ability to shoot photon blasts from her hands. The list could go on and on. Superheroes typically acquire their powers in one of four ways: some are naturally endowed with them through no merit of their own, such as Thor; some have their powers given to them, as is the case with Captain America or Songbird (formerly known as Screaming Mimi); some, like The Hulk or Spider-Man, acquire powers as the result of an accident; and still others diligently develop themselves and enhance any natural gifts they may possess through training and technology, such as Hawkeye or Iron Man. These categories are not mutually exclusive. Black Widow is an example of a hero who obtained her powers through hybrid means. She acquired her martial arts skills through her rigorous KGB training; and thanks to Soviet science, she ages more slowly and heals more quickly than is natural. These traits enable Black Widow to function as a monomythic superhero. Note, however, that the superpowers possessed by females such as Black Widow are typically less impressive than those of their male counterparts, like The Hulk, Spider-Man, or Thor. This power disparity promotes and perpetuates the hierarchical privileging of male superheroes over their female counterparts. There are, of course, notable exceptions, such the current iteration of Captain Marvel or Wonder Woman in the DC universe, but these remain rare, although admittedly things are improving in that regard.

Although Black Widow is a member of the Avengers team, she still functions sometimes as a solo superhero who goes her own way, guided by her own moral compass. The flexible formula of the American monomyth can comfortably accommodate such tensions. There is precedent for monomythic heroes who join with others in pursuing a common objective, as can be seen with the Magnificent Seven film franchise and numerous superhero teams. Such teams are composed of heroes viewed collectively as outsiders from the communities they serve and save. Despite her position as an Avenger, Black Widow's loyalties remained unclear. For instance, in *Captain America: Winter Soldier* (2014), she carried out a parallel mission, gathering data from a ship that had been hijacked, rather than protecting hostages, which she told Captain America "was your mission, and you did it beautifully." Unlike Captain America, whose World War II–era scruples limited his willingness to accept some of the less savory elements of espionage and defense, "Agent Romanoff is comfortable with everything," as S.H.I.E.L.D. director Nick Fury pointedly notes. Later in the film, Black Widow discussed her alienation from Rogers: "When I first joined S.H.I.E.L.D. I thought I was going straight, but I guess I just traded in the KGB for Hydra. I thought I knew whose lies I was telling. But I guess I can't tell the difference anymore." Later, Black Widow and Captain America, with some help from other heroes, expose S.H.I.E.L.D.'s secrets to the world, effectively ending the spy agency. Black Widow's experience as part of a Soviet and Russian espionage agency allowed her to see the dangers in an American version, and perhaps prompted her to eliminate the agency that claimed to be protecting her adopted country.

American monomythic teams like the Magnificent Seven or the Avengers are often, although not always, populated by alpha loners who do not always play well together. Internecine tensions of this kind are frequently featured in the Avengers films and other offerings of the MCU. In 2015, during *Captain America: Civil War*'s apocalyptic battle scene between the Avengers and allies, Black Widow began the battle on the side of Iron Man / Tony Stark, attempting to capture Captain America and Bucky Barnes and bring them to justice for the murder of T'Chaka, the king of Wakanda. However, once Captain America and Barnes neared their escape vehicle, Black Widow stalled Black Panther, allowing them to escape. Later, Stark accused her: "You let them go, Nat . . . It must be hard to shake the double agent thing. It sticks in the DNA." And he warned her, "They're coming for you." In both instances, as a typical American monomythic hero, Black Widow followed her own code of right and wrong, without regard for team or societal expectations.

Black Widow also sees herself as separate from other costumed superheroes, and indeed from most members of the human race. Paul Cornell portrayed a conversation that Black Widow had with her former husband, another superpowered Russian.[11] She noted, "Those of us who took the serum . . . [the Russian variant of the super soldier serum, ellipses in original] our sheer age makes us see the world differently. The best we can hope for is to treat each other gently."[12] The multiple facets of her identity—age, nationality, occupation, training, to name a few—prevent her from joining in the zeitgeist of her erstwhile comrades, keeping her constantly on the outside looking in.

In keeping with the expectations of the American monomyth's narrative formula, Black Widow must eventually remove herself from the community on whose behalf she exerts herself. Some mythic heroes simply leave the communities they had protected and restored, like the stereotypical Western hero riding into the sunset, or the jaded noir detective slowly driving off along the neon-streaked, rain-slickened streets of his urban jungle. Other

---

11. Cornell (w), Raney (i), and Leon (i), *Black Widow*.
12. Cornell (w), Raney (i), and Leon (i), *Black Widow*, Kindle loc. 92.

American monomythic heroes exit symbolically, as when a costumed super-hero absents herself by removing her mask and resuming her secret iden-tity. Still others do so not only by leaving the community but by shuffling off their mortal coil, dramatically dying in one last heroic act. This latter method is the means by which Black Widow exits, sacrificing herself so that Hawkeye can live and recover the Soul Stone, even fighting Hawkeye so that she can make that sacrifice. This act not only eliminates Black Widow as an individual, it also erases any Russo-Slavic presence within the Avengers, removing the woman who is arguably the highest-profile Slav within the MCU. While this might not be filmmakers' intention, it is the effect, intended or not. Black Widow, as a double-outsider, is treated as expendable.

BLACK WIDOW AS OBJECTIFIED OTHER: GENDER IN COMICS

For most of its history, the genre of costumed superhero narratives tradition-ally treated females as supporting characters who did "not exist outside of their relationship with the [male] superhero."[13] Females were mostly foils for the genre's male protagonist, serving as attractive "eye candy," doting admirers, damsels in distress, and, far too frequently, as Simone notes, vic-tims of violence.[14] This began to change somewhat in the 1970s. During that decade the number of superheroines substantially increased, but despite being featured more regularly, most superheroines were—and for the most part still are—relegated to the periphery, with male superheroes still getting more ink on the pages of comic books and graphic novels and more celluloid frames in film. Black Widow is a good example of this slighting. Although she is the most prominent female member of the Avengers, and that team's sole female at the start of the narrative arc that began with 2012's *Marvel's the Avengers,* it was not until 2021 (admittedly delayed a year because of the COVID-19 pandemic) that she was finally featured in her own eponymous film, and only after the conclusion of the same narrative arc with 2019's *Avengers: Endgame.* This is quite a contrast to Black Widow's male team-mates. Black Panther, Captain America, Iron Man, Thor, and Dr. Strange all had feature films with their names in the title during the theatrical run of the Avengers film franchise, while Black Widow was scandalously relegated to the role of supporting cast member. Interestingly, one female member of the Avengers, Captain Marvel, did have her own eponymous film released

13. Bongco, *Reading Comics,* 113.
14. Simone, "Front Page."

in 2019, as a way of introducing her to the mainstream audience prior to *Avengers: Endgame,* but this is the exception that highlights the general rule.

Throughout much of her career, the character of Black Widow has been exploited for prurient purposes through visual depiction, provocative dialogue, and sexually suggestive situations. This is to be expected given the genre's long history of sexually objectifying female characters and subjecting them to the male gaze. What is truly telling, however, is the fact that such sexual objectification is so pervasive that it can be found even in such presumably pure and innocent places as a children's television show. To illustrate, we point to an episode of *The Super Hero Squad Show,* which first aired on October 31, 2009, entitled "Deadly Is the Black Widow's Bite!" The simple story lines, straightforward animation style, juvenile humor, absence of graphic violence, and uncomplicated characters clearly indicate that the cartoon series featuring that episode is geared toward a viewing audience presumably composed of young children and their protective, "captive" parents and is thus distinctively different from more mature superhero fare such as the R-rated Deadpool films. In keeping with generic convention, both the male and female superheroes wear colorful, skintight, form-fitting costumes that showcase their buff bodies. There are, however, significant differences between the visual depictions of the costumed men and that of Black Widow. For example, and significantly, none of the men are drawn in a manner that emphasizes their posterior by delineating the dividing line separating their butt cheeks. Instead, the male heroes' rears are asexually depicted as a flat, solid color without definition. In contrast, a line distinguishes the division of Black Widow's buttocks, and in doing so attracts attention to her derrière. She is often shown from behind, with the "camera angle" pointedly focused on her provocatively posed posterior.[15]

Another notable difference is the way the episode's male superheroes behave as contrasted with the behavior of female characters. The men are ostensibly held up for mockery—in a satirical and subtle, G-rated fashion—as hapless slaves to their sexual appetites. They fall all over themselves and compete with one another whenever Black Widow is near, and they pine for her when she is absent. But slaves or not, openly appealing to their lusty natures is a primary plot device that privileges their masculine prurient interest and places it at center stage. Ironically, however, although the male members of Squad thought they were interacting with Black Widow, the character they encountered was actually Mystique, a shapeshifter in disguise. Mystique / Black Widow found her attempts to spy on the Squad thwarted by

---

15. "Black Widow's Bite!"

the mens' behavior, leading her to complain, "They won't give me a chance to gather any info. They won't act normal around a Black Widow." Silver Surfer summed up the male's rather embarrassingly flirtatious behavior by asking, "Did she really fool us all just by being pretty?"[16] Indeed, their weakness in the face of flaunted feminine beauty was exploited, allowing them to be used and manipulated by Mystique in her guise as a sexually alluring Black Widow imposter. That it was actually Mystique, and not Black Widow, to whom they were attracted and over whom they made fools of themselves is not materially relevant to our discussion of Black Widow's objectification, as it does not matter at whom they were leering. What is relevant is that they were leering—and lusting and longing, preening and pining.

Later MCU films continue to objectify the character. Romanoff entered *Marvel's the Avengers* tied to a chair in a warehouse, a salacious situation reminiscent of the soft-core bondage imagery associated with William Moulton Marston's classic Golden-Age version of Wonder Woman. Responding to Black Widow's calculated exploitation of her sexuality in functioning as a spy, her captor commented, "This is not how I wanted this evening to go," to which Romanoff replied, "I know how you wanted this evening to go. Believe me this is better."[17] Later in that same film, provocatively dressed in a tank top and wrap skirt, Romanoff persuades Bruce Banner / The Hulk to come out of hiding and join the epic battle for the survival of Earth and its inhabitants that was brewing, and for which she and her Avengers colleagues were preparing.

Other films in the series continue to exploit Romanoff as an object of sexual interest. For instance, in *Captain America: Winter Soldier* (2014), Romanoff ended a description of an encounter with a Russian assassin, during which she was shot through the abdomen, with the line "Bye-bye bikinis." Steve Rogers / Captain America responded, "Yeah, I bet you look terrible in them now."[18] It is difficult if not impossible to imagine male heroes of any stripe making such a statement about the lasting aesthetic impact of their own injuries. They are depicted as indifferent to their wounds and scars, or they wear them as badges of honor. This verbal exchange is not the only scene in the same film in which Black Widow's sexual appeal is exploited. At one point, Romanoff distracts their pursuers by kissing Rogers while on an escalator and then teases him about his lack of sexual experience.[19] In another film, *Avengers: Age of Ultron* (2015), Romanoff uses a seductively quiet voice

16. "Black Widow's Bite!"
17. Whedon, *Avengers*.
18. Russo and Russo, *Winter Soldier*.
19. Russo and Russo, *Winter Soldier*.

and sensually soft touch to trigger The Hulk to transform back into Bruce Banner, essentially employing her feminine wiles—cultivated by her Soviet handlers in order to transform her into a seductive super spy—as a means of taming the green beast.[20] Thor's unintentionally comical attempt to use the same tactics in *Thor: Ragnarok* (2017) failed miserably.[21] Black Widow's success with these tactics, and Thor's failure, reinforces traditional expectations regarding gender roles.

Nowhere is the depiction of Black Widow's adherence to traditional patriarchal gender-role tropes more evident than in the previously mentioned *Avengers: Age of Ultron* (2015), when she described the "graduation ceremony" from her spy and assassin training, which included the graduates' being sterilized. She described the procedure, with a remarkable display of seemingly callous indifference, as "efficient. One less thing to worry about. The one thing that might matter more than a mission. Makes everything easier, even killing. You still think you're the only monster on the team."[22] By tying the loss of reproductive capability to the ability to kill, and calling herself a monster, Romanoff uncritically expressed traditional gender norms regarding motherhood and family. In commenting on that scene, Jen Yamato notes, "The result is an overdue character exploration for Black Widow that still manages to reduce the baddest bitch in the MCU to a shell of a superheroine who's sad she can never be a complete woman."[23] In commenting on this focus on Black Widow's infertility, Alyssa Rosenberg states:

> Natasha's not a super-powerful woman suddenly brought low by a reckoning with her biological clock or the fact that putting the hurt on intergalactic baddies led her to put off developing a personal life. She's a hero reckoning with what it means to be both female and merely human in a testosterone-heavy, super-powered environment. Natasha may not be able to have her own children, but she's built a family of her own—in a late shot in the movie, we see her waving at baby Nathaniel via video chat. And if most men are easily and lazily dazzled by her most readily apparent qualities, she'll find one who responds to the darkness in her.[24]

Linda Holmes notes the connection of Black Widow's experience to that of other "real life" women:

---

20. Whedon, *Age of Ultron*.
21. Waititi, *Thor: Ragnarok*.
22. Whedon, *Age of Ultron*.
23. Yamamoto, "Avenger's," para. 12.
24. Rosenberg, "Strong Feminism," para. 14.

But standing alone, this is (1) a story about a woman subjected to institutional interference with her fertility and (2) a story about a woman who was told they didn't trust her to take on an important job because they believed she secretly would always care about babies more. Neither one of those two things, historically, has happened only in fiction. Those themes are well worth exploring.[25]

In contrast, masculine procreational potency, or its lack, is not a driving concern on the part of creative teams in their development and depiction of the characters of male superheroes.

This is a sad commentary not only on the current state of film and other narratives featuring costumed superheroes but on society in general. We are not saying that all women should be mothers, or even have the potential to do so, but rather that females should not be expected to deny the maternal in order to achieve success. The two are not mutually exclusive. Women should have the right to choose the path in life that is best for them. We suggest that this is the most salient critical concern about Black Widow's sterilization: the choice was made for her, and not by her, so she can work to achieve the objectives of others rather than her own goals. Her accepting and remarkably positive attitude toward being robbed of that choice speaks volumes about the continued hegemonic influence of the traditional patriarchal order still permeating American popular culture. This should not be surprising. As Randy Duncan and Matthew Smith point out, "given the prevalence of male creators, male characters, and male themes in contemporary comics, it would be erroneous to assume that the dominant ideology has relinquished its hold on the audience's thinking entirely."[26] Women in positions of power over film development (directors, producers, etc.) influence the stories told and how they are related.[27] For that reason, we are encouraged that more women are being given power in the filmmaking business, as for example Cate Shortland, who directed the *Black Widow* film.

Conclusion

Throughout nearly sixty years of existence, and through a wide variety of media, Black Widow has proved difficult to define. She has undergone many physical changes—she debuted with short, black hair before transitioning to

25. Holmes, "Black Widow," para. 6.
26. Duncan and Smith, *Power of Comics*, 258
27. Smith, Choueiti, and Pieper, "Gender Inequality."

the iconic red—including her much publicized different hairstyles throughout the Avengers franchise. Her backstory has changed, becoming more
traumatic and complicated with each iteration. Yet the creators who write
her stories continue to focus on her alluringly dangerous Slavic sexuality,
which she exploited as a spy and continued to employ after that career, as
her primary defining characteristic. Darren Franich notes:

> Black Widow is a consummate supporting character. Unlike Hawkeye,
> who's basically an eternally genial dudely dude, Widow has a livewire per-
> sonality that has let her serve as a great utility player in various capacities
> for decades. She's been a double agent and a stern commanding officer. She
> has the attitude of someone who can eat men alive, which oddly makes her
> a great go-to love interest. In stark contrast to the other Avengers, who are
> all defined with very vivid characterizations, Widow has managed to out-
> live her original Soviet context specifically by being a kind of chameleon.[28]

In the end, despite her character's popularity and ubiquity within the Marvel Multiverse, Black Widow, in many ways, remains a traditional female
comic book figure: bigger than life, sexualized, objectified, and frequently
out of the spotlight. And, chances are, she will also remain one of the few
Slavic superheroes so long as creative teams prefer to depict Slavs, and especially Russians, as villains whenever they deign to depict them at all. However, given current trends, we are cautiously optimistic about the prospect
of Black Widow and other female superheroes assuming their rightful places
within an increasingly demographically diverse MCU.

Bibliography

Bongco, Mila. *Reading Comics: Language, Culture, and the Concept of the Superhero in
  Comic Books*. New York: Garland, 2000.

Cink, Lorraine (a), and Alice X. Zhang (i). *Marvel: Powers of a Girl*. Los Angeles: Marvel
  Press, 2019.

Coggan, Devan. "Black Widow's Breakout." *Entertainment Weekly*, no. 1586 (April 2020),
  26–31.

Cornell, Paul (w), Tom Raney (i), and John Paul Leon (i). *Black Widow: Deadly Origin* 1.
  New York: Marvel, 2017. Kindle.

Duncan, Randy, and Matthew J. Smith. *The Power of Comics: History, Form and Culture*.
  New York: Continuum, 2009.

---

28. Franich, "Avenger," para. 4.

Franich, Darren. "Avenger: Black Widow File." *Entertainment Weekly*, May 3, 2012. https://ew.com/article/2012/05/03/avengers-files-black-widow/.

Holmes, Linda. "Black Widow, Scarce Resources and High-Stakes Sources." *NPR*, May 12, 2015. https://www.wnyc.org/story/black-widow-scarce-resources-and-high-stakes-stories/.

IMDb. "The Super Hero Squad Show." Accessed September 2, 2020. https://www.imdb.com/title/tt1388589/.

Jewett, Robert, and John Shelton Lawrence. *The American Monomyth*, 2nd ed. Lanham, MD: University Press of America, 1988.

Lawson, Corrina. "Comics Spotlight on Black Widow: Deadly Origin." *Wired*, February 2011. https://www.wired.com/2011/02/comics-spotlight-on-black-widow-deadly-origin/.

Rosenberg, Alyssa. "The Strong Feminism Behind Black Widow, and Why the Critiques Don't Stand Up: Feminist Critics Who Are Going After Joss Whedon for Giving Natasha Romanoff a Story Line about Her Fertility Miss the Measure of the Character's Heroism." *Washington Post*, May 5, 2015. https://www.washingtonpost.com/news/act-four/wp/2015/05/05/black-widows-feminist-heroism/.

Russo, Joe, and Anthony Russo, dirs. *Captain America: The Winter Soldier*. Marvel Studios, 2014.

Simone, Gail. "Front Page." *Women in Refrigerators*, March 1999. https://lby3.com/wir/.

Smith, Stacy L., Marc Choueiti, and Katherine Pieper. *Gender Inequality in Popular Films: Examining On Screen Portrayal and Behind-the-Scenes Employment Patterns in Motion Pictures Released between 2007–2013*. Annenberg School of Communication and Journalism, University of Southern California, 2013.

Stevens, Mathew. "Ruskie Business: The 15 Most Dangerous Russians in Comics." *CBR*, June 17, 2017. https://www.cbr.com/ruskie-business-the-15-most-dangerous-russians-in-comics/.

The Super Hero Squad Show. "Deadly Is the Black Widow's Bite!" Season 1, episode 13. November 7, 2009.

Waititi, Taika. *Thor: Ragnarok*. Marvel Studios, 2017.

Whedon, Joss, dir. *The Avengers*. Marvel Studios, 2012.

———. *The Avengers: Age of Ultron*. Marvel Studios, 2015.

Yamato, Jen. "The Avengers' Black Widow Problem: How Marvel Slut-Shamed Their Most Badass Superheroine." *The Daily Beast*, April 14, 2017. https://www.thedailybeast.com/the-avengers-black-widow-problem-how-marvel-slut-shamed-their-most-badass-superheroine.

CHAPTER 11

Pepper Potts

Performance as Partner, Professional, CEO, and Superhero

Mildred F. Perreault and Gregory P. Perreault

At the end of the climactic battle in 2019's *Marvel Avengers Endgame: Part 2*, Virginia "Pepper" Potts cradles the head of her dying husband. As the looming catastrophe lifts, Tony Stark looks sadly into her eyes, and Pepper says, "We will be okay." Pepper's stoic face changes for a second as she looks into his eyes and he closes his. The scene fades and changes to Tony's funeral, where Pepper is seen holding her daughter Morgan's hand, bringing twelve years of Marvel movies to a close. In just those twelve years, Potts' character evolved more across comics and film than in the forty-five years of her existence leading up to them, mirroring an age in which women in pop culture moved from token female character to female lead.

In the comics, Pepper Potts is involved in a complex love triangle with Tony and his handler, Happy Hogan. But Marvel took a different approach with the films. In the movies, Pepper Potts, depicted by actress Gwyneth Paltrow, is not only a romantic partner to Tony Stark but also his office manager and later the chief executive officer of Stark Enterprises. Her help and planning are integral to Tony's success. She also dons pieces of the Iron Man suit in several of the films and finally is presented in the guise of the superhero Rescue in *Avengers: Endgame*. Throughout her stories, her depictions are feminine at their heart but speak to the changing role of women in both professional and intimate relationships.

The female superhero has morphed from niche to mainstream alongside the development of social media. For example, most recent news coverage by women's blogs and magazines of the newest iteration of the character Captain Marvel, Carol Danvers, features a female superhero as the primary protagonist. This role, depicted by Brie Larson in *Captain Marvel* (2018) and *Avengers: Endgame* (2019), received coverage in niche publications and mainstream entertainment media. But this is not where the story of gender in the Marvel Cinematic Universe begins.

The most recent Marvel movie universe began in 2008 with Iron Man and his female assistant Pepper Potts. Pepper Potts is sometimes jealous and impulsive, but she's also sharp, poised, professional, and even daring. Her character starts out as a love interest, then girlfriend and business partner. However, her character's development over time eventually presents her as an equal partner to husband Tony Stark / Iron Man. Her story perhaps mimics the time in which she was created, but also the time in which she goes from woman to superhero.

Pepper Potts's Background

While Pepper does not take on a superhero role initially, she has a consistent role. She is identified either as Virginia (in comics and Marvel's *Iron Man* [2008]) or as Patricia (*Iron Man: Armored Adventurers*) and is consistently a support character for Tony Stark. In her earliest depictions in both comics and film, Pepper is presented as a secretary at Stark Industries. Over the arc of her character story, she becomes more invaluable both to Stark Industries and to Tony Stark—at times operating as executive assistant of the company, as CEO of Stark Industries, and running the business in the absence of Tony Stark. She becomes the superhero Rescue after receiving a custom arc reactor that combines the Stark and Rand technologies. The name denotes the main purpose of her armor—search and rescue. Notably, Pepper feared wearing armor with weapons (as was the case with Iron Man and War Machine armors); hence, she acts as a character who can rescue but not go to war. This departs slightly from Rescue's depiction in *Avengers: Endgame,* which shows Pepper using a fully weaponized armor.

Performativity and Pepper

In her theory of performativity, Butler argues that gender is socially constructed through shared speech, nonverbal communication, and images.[1]
These signifiers are often used by society and culture to define and maintain the role of women and gender minorities within that culture. As Butler
puts it, any deviation or subversion of these norms and signifiers is seen as
gender "troubling," or the means through which subjects "fail to do their
gender right."[2] Butler suggests that gender is constructed through the continual repetition and ritualistic performance of gender norms. This repetition
serves to "establish what will and will not be intelligibly human, what will
and will not be considered to be 'real.'"[3] It consists of repeated acts, gestures,
and enactments of "socially established"[4] meanings that bring the discursive subject into the materialist realm. It also reveals the gender binaries
by which subjects are constrained. Although her theory has been criticized
for denying agency to subjects, who are continually constituted by existing
power relations, Butler developed her ideas in later work, suggesting opportunities for resistance. Even so, critical theorists have continued to grapple
with the potential of applying Butler's theory within critical assessments
of texts. Allen found that Butler's theory is problematic if understood only
within a dominating/empowering dialectic.[5] Butler's suggestion that power
can be neither withdrawn nor refused, Allen argued, does not provide an
opportunity for power relations to be changed. Similarly, Schep suggested
that Butler's theory attempts to "account for all gender relations,"[6] which is
problematic for those who resist an essentialist determination of gender and
desire theories offering emancipatory potential.

Scholars, though, have suggested a means through which performativity
can be understood in particular contexts, including narrative understandings. Morison and Macleod outlined a performativity-performance approach
to qualitative inquiry, suggesting that although Butler's theory was initially
understood within a discursive framework, applications have moved into

---

1. Butler, *Gender Trouble*.
2. Butler, *Gender Trouble*, 178.
3. Butler, *Gender Trouble*, xxiii.
4. Butler, *Gender Trouble*, 178.
5. Allen, "Power Trouble."
6. Schep, "Limits of Performativity," 865.

the materialist realm.[7] As a result, they suggest, the notion of performativity should be supplemented with narrative performance as a means of examining "relational specificities and the mechanisms through which gender, and gender trouble, occur."[8] Addressing performance allows scholars to consider how elements of performativity theory, such as reflexivity and active imagination, contribute to gender construction. We suggest that digital games, in particular, are important sites of not only critical inquiry but also assessments of how female characters, through performativity, reinforce and subvert gender norms. For example, in one study of video game depictions of women, female characters are put in leadership roles, but often in relation to paternal male counterparts.[9] This is noteworthy not only given Pepper's video game appearances but also given that such appearances persist as a part of the broader transmedia narrative of Pepper Potts—a character commonly put in relation to counterpart male figures such as Tony Stark and Happy Hogan.

Transmedia Storytelling

Transmedia storytelling is central to granting characters mainstream visibility. Research concerning transmedia portrayals has found that digital participatory media provide a cohesion of interactivity and identity for those who identify with particular characters and story lines. Jenkins defines transmedia storytelling as "a process where integral elements of a fiction get dispersed systematically across multiple delivery channels for the purpose of creating a unified and coordinated entertainment experience."[10] Experiencing distinct yet familiar stories can help people identify with a story or character within the bounds of a new reality. This active storytelling and creation are increasingly interactive as a result of what Jenkins calls *convergence culture*.[11] Other research indicates that the carriers of this culture are the characters who appear across a number of different media or platforms.[12] Marvel has done this by copyrighting its material, and now that Disney owns Marvel, the control over the copyright has increased even more. Another term used to describe transmedia storytelling across platforms is *echo stories* of

7. Morison and Macleod, "Performative-Performance."
8. Morison and Macleod, "Performative-Performance," 567.
9. Perreault et al., "Female Protagonists."
10. Jenkins, *Fans, Bloggers, and Gamers*, 123.
11. Jenkins, "Future of Fandom."
12. Kinder, *Transmedia Frictions*.

stories, which describes the action of telling a story using multiple platforms, media, and varied degrees of audience involvement.[13]

Women Characters in Pop Culture: Movies, Video Games, and Comics

Even as society reflects less defined gender roles, media representations of gender often present a stubbornly static picture of it. The traditional measures of female representation need to be broadened, and other contextual elements of a more progressive view of gender roles should be included in representational analysis.[14] In transmedia, the idea of representation must include not only biological gender identity, it must also include many forms of gender identity. Therefore, "representation" is not nearly so important to those invested in the narrative as solid, nuanced characters and narratives.[15] Often video games allow for what may be considered gendered male and female character development through characters of both genders. Thus, it is accurate to assume that adding nuanced female characters will attract female players to gaming. The hurdles feminist theories have to overcome in the face of newer, male-dominated technological spaces like video games (mobile games among them) challenge how we are thinking about and interacting with character identities.[16] Gender identity has traditionally emphasized women as "other," and men as dominant.[17] Feminist theory, Shaw argues, is just as applicable in a space that is lacking females as it is in a space that is not. Like in movies, when women have been the main characters in mainstream video games, they have taken on supportive roles to a male character or have a father figure present as part of the game plot.[18] In many cases, this is a gender presentation that has proved resistant to change even as the media systems and ways of involvement have progressed.[19]

Thus, a feminist perspective is particularly important for this chapter since digital spaces are so contentious regarding nuanced, plot-driving female characters despite the increase of transmedia stories and interactive media.

---

13. Emmerson, "Great Examples."
14. Ross, *Gendered Media*.
15. Shaw, "The Internet."
16. Shaw, "The Internet."
17. Chess, *Ready Player*.
18. Perreault et al., "Female Protagonists."
19. Perreault et al., "Female Protagonists."

A powerful female narrative, unicorn that it is, is worth consideration not only as a unique occurrence in a world of male-dominated plotlines but also as a means of eliminating barriers and heralding progress for more developed female voices in digital spaces.

Cosplay and Social Media

The image and likeness of Pepper Potts on social media is common in both audience and professional social media accounts. Individuals share memes of Pepper with quotes from the movies and use the hashtag #pepperony to show their love of the character couple. The images Gwyneth Paltrow (the actress who plays Pepper Potts in the Marvel movies) posts on social media often have a #pepperpotts hashtag included with a number of other hashtags to get traction and attention from her fans. This idea of recreating a character or sharing the character's likeness is not unusual for fans of superheroes. Transmedia intertextuality encourages this, as it remains popular with younger consumers who have access to new digital technologies, and who are increasingly moving happily between different kinds of media while engaging with a consistent story world throughout. Many scholars see the trend toward transmedia storytelling and branding as consistent with brand management and marketing but also as a natural use of social media applications.[20]

Narrative Theory and Analysis

Narratives run through video games, movies, and pop culture mediums with plots, characters, and central decisions rippling across these. Stories inform the way we think about the world and help culture reflect on how it understands certain groups or even experiences.[21] Narrative theory elaborates on the relevance and application of piecing plots and stories together to understand greater meanings. Video game storytelling, for example, often mixes textual and visual; therefore, narrative theory is an apt way to examine the development and interactions between visuals and texts. Narratives can help game players connect to characters, circumstances, and experiences. Human beings often understand more through stories than they do through

---

20. du Plessis, "Prosumer Engagement."
21. Berger, *Narratives in Popular Culture.*

reality,[22] and fictional video games fit that description. Narratives shape how people view certain groups, institutions, and ideas—hence, the presentation of Pepper Potts as the first visible female character in the Marvel Cinematic Universe provides her the opportunity to embody the female story. Narratives tell and bring attention to what a society sees as fitting, but they may also challenge what parts of society deem appropriate.[23] Narrative also helps place women within society and helps assess their agency in shaping their own narratives.[24] Generally, the trend in media has been toward granting more explicit agency to women through narrative,[25] even while their role is still often associated with that of men and puts them in positions to which men are rarely subjected. This of course reflects so much of the story of Pepper Potts, who, as a damsel in distress or as an assistant, is presented in a role rarely placed on men in superhero narratives.

Hence, a study of narrative provides a platform for a critique rooted in the components of narrative: settings, characters, narrators, heroes, villains, and themes, as well as the interaction of these elements.

Narrative theory has been used to evaluate and interpret depictions of gender.[26] Narrative theory emphasizes how human beings tell stories and view the world according to heroes, villains, and plotlines.[27] However, while stories can challenge cultural norms, humans rarely tell new stories. Stories are retold in new ways and through new mediums—and stories told about superheroes are no different.[28] Narrative theory helps identify how applying previous contexts to culturally ingrained stories can help explain what's happening (i.e., campaign horse race coverage may be narrated as a "tortoise and the hare" story). Therefore, we use narrative theory as a normative lens to examine the ways women are presented in these three games, and perhaps in recent gaming culture.

In this chapter, we seek to understand how Pepper Potts's gender is performed and narrated across Marvel transmedia. Studying the presentation of women provides context for how women's stories are narrated in society. These representations serve a sort of double duty: informing men on the nature of women while reaffirming and challenging the nature of women for a female audience.

22. Juul, *Half-Real.*
23. Cooper Berdayes and Berdayes, "Information Highway."
24. Perreault and Perreault, "Symbolic Convergence."
25. Perreault, Perreault, and McCarty, "Marketing Gaming."
26. Perreault et al., "Female Protagonists."
27. Foss, "Narrative Criticism."
28. Bascom, "Forms of Folklore."

The narrative analysis applied here reflects a "family of methods for interpreting texts that have in common a storied form."[29] This makes narrative analysis a sensible method to apply here given that Pepper Potts is essentially a fictional character in a set of fictional stories. Yet she's a character who has obtained remarkable prominence through the Marvel Cinematic Universe. Hence, it is worth considering Pepper Potts as a way to contextualize how future stories about women may be understood and interpreted within a culture,[30] given that such narrative analysis will allow us to contextualize her stories.[31] "Identities are narratives,"[32] and through that lens, it is then worth considering the nature of the female identity presented to more than 54 percent of the US population.[33] Narrative brings the imagined into the real world because "narrative is the proverbial ferry between the abstract and the concrete, between cognition and behavior, and between symbolic and the material."[34]

To properly understand the narratives presented regarding Pepper Potts, we conducted a close reading of all presentations of the character—beginning with the crowdsourced discussions of her on wikis for Marvel films and Marvel comics, then proceeding through presentation in the Marvel Cinematic Universe films, and YouTube presentations of Pepper Potts from her appearance in various video games. We took concurrent notes using the narrative analysis framework on plotlines, settings, characters, time, dialogue, and power presentations. After each close reading, we compared notes on the analytical elements in order to understand the chronological narration of the Pepper Potts story, but also to understand the performance of gender in the Pepper Potts story.

In the next section, we address the research questions in turn and then place the findings in the context of extant literature and theories of narrative and performativity.

Pepper Potts across Transmedia

While often characters are created with a certain role in mind, they often take on a life of their own as new authors, directors, actors, fans, and even

29. Riessman, *Narrative Methods*, 11.
30. Foss, "Narrative Criticism."
31. Foss, "Narrative Criticism."
32. Yuval-Davis, "Theorizing Identity."
33. Watson, "Share of Consumers."
34. Riessman, *Narrative Methods*, 16.

social media audience members identify with them. These were the four areas where we observed the characters of Pepper Potts and Rescue, and each medium provides a different framework for understanding the character, her femininity, agency, and role in the overall Marvel Universe. We look at them separately in order to better understand them both distinctly and holistically.

Marvel's portrayal of women is often postfeminist, a term used by scholars to describe the reactions to the contradictions and absences of feminism in cultural depictions. Postfeminism is a form of feminism that accepts popular culture instead of rejecting it, as was typical with second-wave feminists. Pepper Potts is definitely a character that fits that pattern, as she is often independent but also subjective to Tony Stark and Iron Man.

Considering performativity, the presentation of Pepper Potts and her female gender occurs through the repetition of gender norms associated with the character. While these are consistent across the Marvel Avengers and Iron Man films, they are not consistent with transmedia storytelling. However, while the younger iteration of Pepper appears to be more empowered and independent, her dependency on male characters, specifically Tony Stark, is an indicator of who she is and how she acts in the Marvel universe.

COMICS

The comic presentation of Pepper Potts progresses more slowly from the newer Marvel depictions of Pepper Potts in movies and video games. Further, given the age of the character, the comics display more narratives reliant on the damsel-in-distress characterizers that were more culturally common at the time of the character's introduction in the 1960s. Studies of women in comics have focused on how women were absent from comic books or were often "invisible" characters before the 1970s.[35] However, research has consistently found that female comic book characters push traditional gender representation boundaries and that while they often "imitate gross stereotypes," they allowed women and minorities to be more and more present over time.[36]

Consistent with the portrayals of other women in comics, the feminine portrayal of Pepper Potts emphasizes her intelligence from the beginning. Early on in the comics she is a secretary at Stark Industries, although her

35. Dunne, "Representation of Women," 89.
36. Dunne, "Representation of Women," 89.

story is often shaped by her romantic interest in Tony and other male characters like Happy Hogan.[37] Over the course of the comic narratives, Pepper grows more self-sufficient and direct in her interactions with Tony and other members of the Avengers team. As we discuss more in the conclusion to this chapter, in many ways the comics begin to change how she is portrayed in response to the Marvel movies and television series in 2009 and beyond, as readers were possibly seeking more information and back story for the character they were introduced to on the screen.

The journey toward Pepper becoming a superhero in her own right in the comics emerged following the events of *Civil War*,[38] during which Pepper joined the Fifty State Initiative as Hera.[39] Throughout the comics, Pepper exhibits agency in her interactions with Tony, often giving him advice and guidance and cleaning up his missteps as needed. In 2008 she began to have her own story lines that included separate love interests and scenes with characters other than Tony. She also becomes close with Natasha Romanoff, Black Widow, and Bethany Cabe (a female member of the Iron Man Team) in several of the story lines. She is first introduced as Rescue in 2009, when she is gifted an arc reactor that merges Stark and Rand technologies[40] and that is geared primarily toward search-and-rescue—hence, it includes no weapons. This points to a distinctly feminized portrayal of Pepper in a "support" role, even when she has her own version of Iron Man armor.

In the comic book 2008–20 iteration of Iron Man, Pepper Potts—at times as Rescue—takes on newer, more significant roles. Nevertheless, Rescue remains in a primarily support-oriented role, often engaged in nurturing, rehabilitative activities—helping Tony return to health[41] or finding a family member[42]—as opposed to battle. This is in contrast to the presentation of Pepper in the films, where she participates actively in battle by *Iron Man 3*.

MOVIES

From the start of the 2008 Marvel Cinematic Universe, the character develops from an assistant in the early movies to the eventual CEO of Stark Enter-

37. Bernstein (w), Lee (w), Heck (p, i), *Tales of Suspense* 1, no. 45; Lee (w), Kane (p), and Colan (p), *Tales of Suspense*, no. 91.

38. Millar (w) and McNiven (i), *Civil War*, nos. 1–7.

39. Fraction (w), Kitson (p), Morales (i), and White (c), "Henry—or—The Next Right Thing."

40. Fraction (w) and Larroca (i), "World's Most Wanted, Part 3."

41. Fraction (w) and Larroca (i), "Stark Resilient, Part 8."

42. Schwartz, 2020 *Rescue*, no. 1.

prises, Tony's partner, and mother to Morgan. Later she is seen as a tandem superhero and a member of the Avengers. Her development as a character also aligns with the introduction of more female characters that are introduced in the Marvel Universe movie world. The following are observations of the character role, feminine portrayal, and agency of Pepper Potts in the movie plots.

Pepper in *Iron Man* is really a character with very little pull who gets more screen time and speaks more as the plot develops. Tony Stark shows little interest in her from the beginning of the film and is portrayed as a womanizer. Pepper is seen as a professional woman, in her designer suit and stiletto heels. She often rolls her eyes at Tony, or points to his flaws, only to be greeted with "Oh Pepper" or other actions where he requests her forgiveness. Sometimes these are followed by opulent gifts or fancy dinners. She has a taste for the finer things, and although she accepts his gifts, she is not easily manipulated. Throughout the film the in-movie news media critique the choice of Pepper as the new head of Tony's company, saying that she is not leadership or management material for a multinational corporation.

In *Iron Man* (2008), Pepper Potts appears to be nothing more than Iron Man's assistant until a pivotal moment: Tony must replace his arc reactor (thus causing cardiac arrest) and cannot do it alone. He asks Pepper to help him. She replaces the reactor, teaching Tony—for the first time—that his life is safe in her hands. He gives her the old reactor when they are done. Pepper returns it, enshrined like a trophy with the words "Proof that Tony Stark has a heart"—an indication that Pepper sees Tony's failings but cares about him nevertheless.[43]

Many Marvel women exhibit this idea of different feminisms that create power divisions between women and even police each other's performance. For example, in *Iron Man 2* (2010), when Natasha Romanoff becomes Tony Stark's new personal assistant, it is clear Pepper distrusts her, saying she is a "potential lawsuit." Pepper accuses Natasha later of manipulating Tony and not looking out for his best interests. When Tony exhibits terrible behavior at a birthday party, Pepper even reprimands Natasha, even though she makes it clear to Pepper that she had requested that he reschedule the party. Later, Pepper realizes that Natasha is not a threat and they become friends, eliminating their competition to serve Tony, and are bonded through their frustration over his juvenile and risky behavior.[44]

In *Avengers* (2012), Tony talks about Pepper throughout the film, although the character makes only a few on-screen appearances. Tony says he is sav-

43. Favreau, *Iron Man*.
44. Favreau, *Iron Man 2*.

ing the world but points out that Pepper is busy back at Stark Enterprises managing his life and work, in addition to being the CEO of the company. One scene includes a conversation between Tony and Pepper where she asks to be on the lease of the next building—although Tony has appointed her to make the decision, she is not on the lease for the building.[45]

In *Iron Man 3* (2013), Pepper interacts with one of the villains, Aldrich Killian, and rejects his Extremis project for funding from Stark Enterprises because Tony would not approve of it. This is odd because Tony is not part of the interaction. It is clear, however, that although Tony is not present, she is required to consider his perspective and input when making decisions. Later in the film, Pepper is transformed into Extremis, which helps her body heal under extreme heat. When Killian kidnaps Pepper, the main goal is to hurt Tony and defeat him. At the film's climax, when Killian and Tony battle, Pepper appears to plunge to a fiery death. But because she was injected with the Extremis (heat/fire resistance and super strength) her life is saved, and she rushes in to defeat and kill Killian. Tony then destroys all the Iron Man suits that Pepper has told him are "distractions" throughout the film and surgically removes the effects of the serum on Pepper. Pepper calls herself a "hot mess" in reference to who she was when she was affected by the serum, and Tony again is the superhero.[46]

In her final appearance, *Avengers: Endgame*, Pepper joins other female superheroes in the final battle. Here, she dons the Rescue armor (in blue and gold), a gift from Tony. She is seen in the armor with a group of female superheroes, in the scene where Tony kills Thanos, and then in the final scene at the funeral where she holds daughter Morgan's hand at Tony's funeral. Here, she is seen in her classic Pepper Potts black dress and heels, looking solemn as his original arc reactor, bearing the words "Proof that Tony Stark has a heart," is sent out on a lake. It's a solemn portrayal of a woman who grew up with the Marvel Cinematic Universe and is likely departing the franchise as surely as the character she memorializes.[47]

TELEVISION

In contrast to the solemn, serious portrayal of Pepper in film, Pepper was depicted in more playful narratives in television. The youngest version of Pepper Potts debuted with the show in Pepper's only television portrayal, the animated *Iron Man: Armored Adventures* (2009–12). In this show Pep-

45. Whedon, *Avengers*.
46. Black, *Iron Man 3*.
47. Russo and Russo, *Avengers: Endgame*.

per "Patricia" Potts (voiced by Anna Cummer) is the daughter of an FBI agent, Virgil Potts (also affiliated with S.H.I.E.L.D.). She is presented as a red-haired teenage girl with brown eyes and freckles. She is a computer genius who aspires to become an agent of S.H.I.E.L.D. as well. At the beginning of the series, Pepper is introduced to Tony by Rhodey. When she meets him for the first time in episode 1 of season 1, she shares everything she knows about him, including information about the death of his father, Howard Stark, his affiliation with Stark Enterprises, and other information she has gained from hacking into the FBI computer files with her father's password. Sometimes Tony and Rhodey tell Pepper that she is overexaggerating, but her biggest weakness is presented as her propensity for risk taking. After episode 3, Pepper, Tony, and Rhodey work together to save the world from the influences of villains as "Team Iron Man." The trio work together to keep people from taking over Stark Enterprises—later Stark Solutions—before Tony is old enough to run the company himself. This teenage version of Pepper is a friend and confidant to Tony but also his primary love interest. In the season 2 episodes "Hostile Takeover" and "The Dragonseed," Pepper wears some of the stealth armor designed by Tony and the team in order to defend Tony.[48] Pepper finally dons her very own Iron Man suit as Rescue—which she names herself because she is always rescuing Tony and Rhodey. While Pepper does not possess any superhuman qualities without the suit, *in* the suit she exhibits traits similar to those of Iron Man (Tony) and the War Machine (Rhodey). Her suit has superhuman strength, enhanced durability, the ability to fly, repulsor beams that shoot from the palms, a hot-pink unibeam, energy bombs or projectiles that can shoot from the shoulder and arms, and the ability to enter stealth mode. Tony and Pepper develop a romantic relationship in "The Makluan Invasion Part 2: Unite," where Pepper attempts to reveal her feelings to Tony.[49] After the battle, Tony interrupts her trying to share her concerns with him and gives her a kiss on the cheek and a hug. In short, their love story, which is a primary narrative in the comics and films, is reduced to a footnote in the television narrative.

VIDEO GAMES

In video games, which are typically far more interactive narratively, Pepper benefits little from that interactivity. In *Marvel: Strike Force*, for example, Pepper Potts is a late addition, appearing in the game only after the success

---

48. "Hostile Takeover"; "The Dragonseed."
49. "The Makluan Invasion Part 2: Unite."

of *Avengers: Endgame.* Yet she's widely considered one of the most valuable characters in the early game. She operates as a "tank"—a traditionally male role that denotes taking damage on behalf of others in a team—and in that her character excels.[50] This of course is a small nod to the story of Pepper Potts, who is often the first line of defense for Tony Stark. Rescue appears in the *Lego Marvel* games as well as the mobile game *Marvel: Future Fight.* Worth noting is that all these game presentations include character collecting as a feature, with Pepper then being an item to be collected (e.g., Pokémon). Such games provide less room for narrative in the collection, and Pepper's portrayal is no exception.

It is also worth noting that Pepper Potts's portrayal in video games is less than one might expect given her prominence in the Marvel Cinematic Universe. From a narrative perspective, this somewhat reflects the structure of the storytelling medium: gaming has been critiqued for years for unidimensional portrayals of women.[51] Few video games allow Rescue, or Pepper Potts, to be a playable character; hence, nowhere is there an indication that she was "integral to the games' narratives" or could "change the direction of the stories."[52] Given the portrayal of Pepper Potts throughout the rest of transmedia, it would seem worthwhile to consider her as a marquee game character given the possibility that strong, capable, and attractive—as opposed to oversexualized—women have the potential to draw more women to gaming.[53]

SOCIAL MEDIA

On social media, Pepper Potts is inseparable from her depiction in media (movies, television show, and comics), and this depiction is more iconic to the character, which is consistent with the practice of other depictions on social media around the Iron Man story line and characters. Pepper is rarely seen separately from Tony Stark or Iron Man, although a growing number of cosplay images of fans dressed in the purple-and-silver Rescue suit are popping up on Instagram, as are the hashtags #pepperpotts, #Rescueironman, #pepperpottsrescue, #pepperony, and #Iloveyou3000, a phrase shared by

---

50. FoxNext and Scopely, *Marvel Strike Force.*
51. Lynch et al., "Sexy, Strong, and Secondary."
52. Perreault et al., "Female Protagonists," 857.
53. Lynch et al., "Sexy, Strong, and Secondary."

Tony with Pepper and Morgan at several key moments in the series, including when he is dying at the end of *Avengers: Endgame.*

TRANSMEDIA

Across these media, although how the character is portrayed and interpreted changes based on her interactions with other characters, as well as the specific story in which she exists, Pepper Potts, and her superhero embodiment of Rescue, says something about the ways women have been presented in pop culture and society at large.

Pepper Potts's gender is performed across Marvel's transmedia in a way that often aligns with the story progression and cultural norms expected in the Marvel Universe. She doesn't break boundaries but allows other female characters to push them and benefits from that push. As a dependent character, her gender is coupled with the sometimes overly masculine character of Tony Stark, a self-described "philanthropist, millionaire and playboy." The adult version of Pepper is quiet and serious. Whereas Tony is volatile and drastic, she is often grounded and consistent. But the teenage Pepper Potts is almost the complete opposite. She is impulsive and risky, much more like the adult version of Tony. What is consistent is that she is a caretaker and confidant in all the storylines. Tony trusts her with things he is reluctant to trust others with, and he even sometimes trusts her more than himself. Concerning performativity and gender identity, these are stereotypes that female characters often face. The difference for Pepper lies in the fact that she does support Tony both at home and at work, and much like traditional female characters in earlier comics, she, for the most part, has an invisible personal identity separate from him.

Pepper Potts's story, narrated across Marvel transmedia, is inconsistent and attempts to open up the way gender is viewed, but perhaps this is because of the time in which the media are published. For example, as Marvel introduces more women into their universe, the women already present are given more significant roles, screen time, and story line development. For Pepper, this means a new iteration of her character in *Iron Man: Armored Adventures* who can hold her own, grow up independently, and often rescue her male counterparts. For Pepper Potts in the Disney films, this means that she is not only CEO, Tony's wife, and a mother but also a member of the Avengers team. Similarly, in the comics, Pepper is not dependent on Tony for her character development, and in a few more recent plot lines she is even removed from romantic obligation to him. But because Iron Man is the main character, for the most part he still drives the story.

Summary

While Pepper pushes the understanding of female gender identity concerning women and business, she is still dependent on the story line for the main character Iron Man and rarely has a scene without him or talk of him. The analysis here also reveals something of the structural biases written into the medium. It would seem odd merely from the lens of progress that Pepper would have had more appearances in the comics than in the films, yet it was the presentation of Pepper in film that motivated stronger appearances of the character in the comics. And while certainly Pepper's role remains largely supportive in the films as well, it is noteworthy that when introduced as Rescue, Pepper's armor is fully weaponized, with all the gadgets one would expect to find in the Iron Man or War Machine armors. This, of course, is in contrast to the presentation in the comics in which Rescue lacks weaponry as a result of Pepper's aversion to weapons.

However, when looked at as a cohesive narrative across transmedia, it does raise the question of the degree to which the role of a superhero is a place where new gender roles may be explored. After the first presentation of Pepper Potts in the film *Iron Man* (2008), the comics then put Pepper in stronger roles, granting her the role of Hera in the Fifty State Initiative and then of Rescue, with her own armor, shortly after. By the release of *Avengers: Endgame*, Pepper appears in the climactic final battle with armor that is on a par with Tony's own. Yet would Pepper be viewed in the same narrative light if she had not been granted armor in transmedia? Also noteworthy is that the root of the Rescue armor remains Tony Stark—it was made by him with the agency of her superhero power, then granted by him. In other words, similar to other studies of narratives, women often display their most leadership in connection/collaboration with male figures.[54]

As the Marvel Cinematic Universe puts Iron Man in its shadow, does this leave Pepper Potts behind with him, as an image of the transmediated female—empowered, skilled, intelligent and . . . incidental?

---

54. Perreault et al., "Female Protagonists."

Bibliography

Allen, Amy. "Power Trouble: Performativity as Critical Theory." *Constellations* 5, no. 4 (1998): 456–71.

Bascom, William. "The Forms of Folklore: Prose Narratives." *The Journal of American Folklore* 78, no. 307 (1965): 3–20.

Berger, Arthur Asa. *Narratives in Popular Culture, Media, and Everyday Life*. London: Sage, 1997.

Bernstein, Robert (w), Stan Lee (w), and Don Heck (p, i). *Tales of Suspense* 1, no. 45. New York: Marvel Comics, 1963.

Black, Shane, dir. *Iron Man 3*. Marvel Studios, 2013.

Bold, Christine. "Transforming Practice through Critical Reflection." In *Supporting Learning and Teaching*, 157–72. New York: Routledge, 2011.

Butler, Judith. *Gender Trouble: Feminism and the Subversion of Identity*. New York: Routledge, 1990.

Chess, Shira. *Ready Player Two: Women Gamers and Designed Identity*. Minneapolis: University of Minnesota Press, 2017.

Cooper Berdayes, Linda, and Vicente Berdayes. "The Information Highway in Contemporary Magazine Narrative." *Journal of Communication* 48, no. 2 (1998): 109–24.

du Plessis, Charmaine. "Prosumer Engagement through Story-Making in Transmedia Branding." *International Journal of Cultural Studies* 22, no. 1 (2019): 175–92.

Dunne, Maryjane. "The Representation of Women in Comic Books, Post WWII through the Radical 60's." *PSU McNair Scholars Online Journal* 2, no. 1 (2006): 81–91.

Emmerson, Shannon. "Great Examples of Multiplatform Storytelling." *Echo Stories*, March 12, 2018. http://www.echostories.com/great-examples-multiplatform-storytelling/.

Favreau, Jon, dir. *Iron Man*. Marvel Studios, 2008.

———. *Iron Man 2*. Marvel Studios, 2010.

Fisher, Walter R. "The Narrative Paradigm: In the Beginning." *Journal of Communication* 35, no. 4 (1985): 74–89.

Foss, Sonja K. "Narrative Criticism." In *Rhetorical Criticism: Exploration and Practice*, 3–9. Prospect Heights, IL: Waveland Press, 1996.

FoxNext and Scopely Inc. *Marvel Strike Force*. Scopely, 2018. Mobile.

Fraction, Matt (w), Barry Kitson (p), Mark Morales (i), and Dean White (c). "Henry—Or—The Next Right Thing." *The Order* 1, no. 1. New York: Marvel Comics, 2007.

Fraction, Matt (w), and Salvador Larroca (i). "Stark Resilient, Part 8: Drones Scream Down." *The Invincible Iron Man* 2, no. 32. New York: Marvel Comics, 2011.

———. "World's Most Wanted, Part 3: No Future." *The Invincible Iron Man* 2, no. 10. New York: Marvel Comics, 2009.

Gurevitch, Michael, and Mark R. Levy, eds. *Mass Communication Review Yearbook*, vol. 5. London: Sage, 1985.

Iron Man: Armored Adventures. "The Dragonseed." July 11, 2012.

———. "Hostile Takeover." March 7, 2012.

———. "The Makluan Invasion Part 2: Unite!" July 25, 2012.

Jenkins, Henry. *Fans, Bloggers, and Gamers: Exploring Participatory Culture*. New York: NYU Press, 2006.

———. "The Future of Fandom." In *Fandom: Identities and Communities in a Mediated World*, edited by J. Gray, C. Sanvoss, and C. L. Harrington, 357–64. New York: NYU Press, 2007.

Juul, Jesper. *Half-Real: Video Games between Real Rules and Fictional Worlds*. Cambridge, MA: MIT Press, 2011.

Kinder, Marsha. *Transmedia Frictions: The Digital, the Arts, and the Humanities*. Berkeley: University of California Press, 2014.

Lee, Stan (w), Gil Kane (p), and Gene Colan (p). *Tales of Suspense*, no. 91. New York: Marvel Comics, 1967.

Lynch, Teresa, Jessica E. Tompkins, Irene I. van Driel, and Niki Fritz. "Sexy, Strong, and Secondary: A Content Analysis of Female Characters in Video Games across 31 Years." *Journal of Communication* 66, no. 4 (2016): 564–84.

Millar, Mark (w), and Steve McNiven (i). *Civil War* 1, nos. 1–7. New York: Marvel Comics, 2014.

Morison, Tracy, and Catriona Macleod. "A Performative-Performance Analytical Approach: Infusing Butlerian Theory into the Narrative-Discursive Method." *Qualitative Inquiry* 19, no. 8 (2013): 566–77.

Perreault, Mildred F., Gregory Pearson Perreault, Joy Jenkins, and Ariel Morrison. "Depictions of Female Protagonists in Digital Games: A Narrative Analysis of 2013 DICE Award-Winning Digital Games." *Games and Culture* 13, no. 8 (2018): 843–60.

Perreault, Mildred F., and Gregory Perreault. "Symbolic Convergence in the 2015 Duggar Scandal Crisis Communication." *Journal of Media and Religion* 18, no. 3 (2019): 85–97.

Perreault, Mildred F., Gregory Perreault, and Michael McCarty. "Marketing Gaming for Girls: Narrative Framing of Princess Zelda in American and Japanese Commercials." In *Beyond Princess Culture: Gender and Children's Marketing*, edited by Katherine A. Foss, 51–72. New York: Peter Lang, 2019.

Riessman, Catherine Kohler. *Narrative Methods for the Human Sciences*. London: Sage, 2008.

Ross, Karen. *Gendered Media: Women, Men, and Identity Politics*. Lanham, MD: Rowman & Littlefield, 2010.

Russo, Joe, and Russo, Anthony, dirs. *Avengers: Endgame*. Marvel Studios, 2019.

Schep, Dennis. "The Limits of Performativity: A Critique of Hegemony in Gender Theory." *Hypatia* 27, no. 4 (2012): 864–80.

Schwartz, Burrows. *2020 Rescue*, no. 1. New York: Marvel Comics, 2020.

Shaw, Adrienne. "The Internet Is Full of Jerks, Because the World Is Full of Jerks: What Feminist Theory Teaches Us About the Internet." *Communication and Critical/ Cultural Studies* 11, no. 3 (2014): 273–77.

Watson, Amy. "Share of Consumers Who Have Watched Selected Marvel Studios Superhero Films in the United States as of February 2018, by Age." *Statista*, August 9, 2019. https://www.statista.com/statistics/807367/marvel-movie-viewership-age/.

Whedon, Joss, dir. *The Avengers*. Marvel Studios, 2012.

Yuval-Davis, Nira. "Theorizing Identity: Beyond the 'Us' and 'Them' Dichotomy." *Patterns of Prejudice* 44, no. 3 (2010): 261–80.

CHAPTER 12

Eating Nuts, Kicking Butts, and Becoming a Feminist Icon

Squirrel Girl's Subversion, Commodification, and Fractured Feminist Nature

CarrieLynn D. Reinhard

Debuting in a 1992 Iron Man story written by Will Murray and drawn by Steve Ditko, Squirrel Girl began life as a satirical character intended to subvert superhero tropes.[1] Marvel Comics never revisited the canonical event wherein she beat Doctor Doom in her first appearance, meaning that victory remained canon. This shocking victory helped the character become an underground fan favorite who repeatedly popped up in various Marvel comic book titles thanks to the actions of fans turned creators.[2] In 2005 Dan Slott brought the character increased visibility by including her in a Great Lakes Avengers (GLA) miniseries. This portrayal added to her canonic position as a vanquisher of supervillains and helped her transition from a satirical to a more serious figure (at least compared with the rest of the ill-fated GLA). This mixture of subversive satire and empowered feminism became fundamental to Squirrel Girl's characterization with the launch of her solo title in 2015, written by Ryan North and drawn by Erica Henderson, which then led to her appearance in various media texts, including comic books, young adult novels, animated series, and even a theatrical play. The analysis

---

1. Goodrum, "'Oh C'mon.'"
2. Sims, "That's What's Up."

in this chapter considers whether the transition to a transmedia character also turned Squirrel Girl into a feminist icon.

This question confronts the fractured status of feminism during the span of Squirrel Girl's existence. She emerged during a period contesting second-wave feminism through the rise of third-wave feminism and co-opted discourses such as commodity feminism, choice feminism, power feminism, postfeminism, and marketplace feminism, pushing back against perceived problems with the second wave.[3] While second-wave feminism focused on collective agency for change, feminist scholars perceived the discourses that immediately followed as less revolutionary.[4] Commodified and sanitized feminisms focus more on individual choice and empowerment,[5] capitalizing on the more popular aspects of feminism (such as sexual liberation) while maintaining control over the less popular aspects (such as true equality).[6] As Rosalind Gill noted, being feminist became just another identity choice, one that was "stylish, defiant, funny, beautiful, confident" and that also "'champions' women" while being used to sell goods.[7] Such hegemonic control of feminism seeks to divide "feminists in hopes of conquering the movement."[8] Although the commodification continues, fourth-wave feminism appears to bring focus back to collective agency for change, albeit using the digital tools not readily available for the previous two waves.[9]

Later in this period, Disney acquired Marvel Entertainment in August 2009[10] to appeal more to boys,[11] but in the case of Squirrel Girl they also tried to address the underserved female comic book audience with a third-wave feminist role model. Squirrel Girl truly becomes a transmedia character following this merger, and Disney/Marvel continue to present the character as empowering by equally embracing feminine and masculine traits. Such a presentation seeks to appeal to the largest possible audience, but it also creates inconsistencies along the way. This essay seeks to understand how Marvel Comics, and later Disney, developed Squirrel Girl from a vision of subversion to a corporate business model meant to appeal to an under-

---

3. See Gill, "Postfeminist Media"; Gill, "Post-postfeminism?"; Hains, "Power Feminism"; Zeisler, *We Were Feminists*.
4. Gill, "Post-postfeminism?" 623.
5. Gill "Post-postfeminism?" 624.
6. Gill "Postfeminist Media," 149.
7. Gill "Post-postfeminism?" 625.
8. Hains, "Power Feminism," 109.
9. Zeisler, *We Were Feminists*, 250.
10. Walt Disney Company, "Marvel Entertainment."
11. Roberts, "Disney Bought Marvel."

represented comics audience—girls and young women—by presenting an empowering role model.

Through a feminist analysis, Squirrel Girl as a transmedia character operates as both a subversion of superhero tropes and a commodification of girl power that allows Disney/Marvel to develop the largest possible consumer base / fandom around her. Further, the contradictions allowed to co-exist in the character's portrayal suggest that Disney/Marvel is further commodifying other aspects of fourth-wave feminism, namely intersectionality and the movement to undo gender binaries, in the hopes of appealing to younger audiences. Essentially, Squirrel Girl as a transmedia character reflects the fractured state of feminism from the 1990s to today, and the continuance of this fractured feminist portrayal can be read as both undermining feminism and normalizing its fractured state.

Introducing Squirrel Girl

Doreen Green hails from Los Angeles, where she was bullied in high school and called "Rodent" after developing her squirrel powers.[12] She spent time in local forests bonding with squirrels as an escape, and she eventually encountered Iron Man. Doreen tried to impress Iron Man to become his sidekick, and even defeated Doctor Doom, but Iron Man suggested that she finish school first. After completing high school, Doreen moved to New York City to attend college, only to meet Flatman and Doorman of the Great Lakes Avengers (GLA), who asked her to join the team and relocate to Milwaukee. S.H.I.E.L.D. tried recruiting Squirrel Girl after recognizing her "as one of the nation's most formidable Super Heroes" for taking down foes like Maelstrom, M.O.D.O.K., Thanos, and Deadpool,[13] but Squirrel Girl stayed in Milwaukee and saved her crush, Speedball. After some time-travel shenanigans revolving around Speedball, Squirrel Girl returned to NYC and worked for the New Avengers as a nanny to Luke Cage and Jessica Jones. She later enrolled in Empire State University, where she befriended Nancy Whitehead, Chipmunk Hunk, and Koi Boy.[14]

With her origins in bullying, Marvel presents Squirrel Girl as a model for handling adversity. The introduction to Marvel's online profile for Squirrel Girl emphasizes her personality over her appearance or superpowers, describing her as having a "fun-loving, goofy persona" that "is also a great

12. "Doreen Green."
13. "Doreen Green."
14. Cink (w) and Zhang (i), *Marvel*, 67–68.

way to keep fear and anxiety at bay when the fate of the world hangs in the balance."[15] From the start, the character is framed as "silly" and as desiring respect from her peers but unwilling to "give up the positivity."[16] Positivity is a common trait used to describe Squirrel Girl, a character originally intended as satirical but who has since emerged as a role model for girls and boys.

Marvel's biography includes this recognition of her power: "One of the most beloved heroes in the Marvel Universe, Doreen Green also stands out as among the most surprisingly formidable."[17] Marvel details her powers as involving "enhanced strength, speed, agility, and reflexes" that result in acrobatic abilities, high jumping, claws and knuckle spikes on her hands, enlarged incisors, and "a bushy, semi-prehensile tail, roughly six feet long, which enhances her sense of balance."[18] Doreen hides her tail by folding it "into the shape of a bodacious behind."[19] She also possesses empathic abilities, can communicate with any squirrel by mimicking their speech, and uses them "to distract, disorient, or even assault her opponents, [as] these animal allies often chew through circuitry, wiring, clothing and other materials, attacking targets with their teeth and claws."[20] With these rather dubious—originally intended as comical—abilities, Squirrel Girl's primary claim to fame is the canonical ability to single-handedly defeat some of the Marvel Universe's most dangerous supervillains.

This contradictory nature of being a joke yet powerful is furthered in how Marvel describes her appearance and background. Squirrel Girl is female, with brown eyes and hair, stands five feet, three inches tall, and weighs one hundred pounds.[21] Yet that height and weight means she has a BMI of 17.7, which is underweight and does not align with how she is visually portrayed as larger than other superheroines. I discuss this in more detail below. Further, the Marvel 101 video indicates that her attempts to first impress Iron Man resulted in her endearing "herself to the super hero community instantly," which is not the case canonically, as I will elaborate.[22] The video further indicates that she is unaware of where her powers come from, although she claimed to be a mutant when she first met Iron Man[23]

15. Cink (w) and Zhang (i), *Marvel*, 67–68.
16. Cink (w) and Zhang (i), *Marvel*, 67–68.
17. "Doreen Green."
18. "Doreen Green."
19. Cink (w) and Zhang (i), *Marvel*, 68.
20. "Doreen Green."
21. "Doreen Green."
22. "Squirrel Girl (Doreen Green) | Marvel 101."
23. Ditko (w, i) and Murray (w), "The Coming of . . . Squirrel Girl!"

and during her time with the GLA,[24] and it also mentions that she learned to embrace her mutations.

The video then presents the largest schism in the character's portrayal. It presents her compassionate approach—"Often she'll befriend the villain instead of confronting him directly; with Doreen in the picture, everyone feels the conflict has been positively resolved, without anyone getting too hurt"—yet also touches on her adeptness and willingness to engage in combat: "If there's one thing you can count on, it's the [sic] Squirrel Girl is always ready to eat nuts and kick butts."[25] The book *Fearless and Fantastic! Female Super Heroes Save the World* categorizes her as a compassionate superhero without really explaining why she is placed there.[26] In a different Marvel book, Lorraine Cink described her as "one of the most POWERFUL characters in the Marvel Universe" and positions her as "cute and fluffy" as well as powerful, although "she does often rely on her head and heart instead of her fists and a horde of adorable rodents to win the day."[27] Thus, this description furthers the dichotomy, as it presents how before resorting to violence she will more likely ask questions to understand her foe, to thereby "win a fight by defusing it" and perhaps "make unlikely friends."[28] Again, Squirrel Girl is largely presented as a dichotomy: cute, funny, and compassionate, but one of the most formidable combatants in the Marvel Universe.

To describe her superpowers, Cink draws on language the character commonly uses: "All the powers of a squirrel; All the powers of a girl."[29] Marvel characterizes Squirrel Girl as feminine and masculine, with neither necessarily suppressing the other as Doreen embraces the negatives and positives of her life. Marvel has said: "We all have anxieties, but—and this may sound crazy—they're actually kinda what makes us awesome!"[30] In highlighting how Squirrel Girl overcome bullies by embracing her abilities and remaining positive, Marvel has embraced a character originally intended as satirical and positioned her as an example of an empowering character for their female readers and consumers, whose embracing of Squirrel Girl helped Disney/Marvel realize they could capitalize on this underserviced fan base. It appears that over the past thirty years, Squirrel Girl's characterization has come to encapsulate what Andi Zeisler would argue is a more

---

24. Slott (w) and Pelletier (a), "Countdown to a Miscount."
25. "Doreen Green."
26. Maggs, Grange, and Amos, *Fearless and Fantastic!*, 83.
27. Cink (w) and Zhang (i), *Marvel*, 67; emphasis in original.
28. Cink (w) and Zhang (i), *Marvel*, 67.
29. Cink (w) and Zhang (i), *Marvel*, 67.
30. "Doreen Green."

"media friendly" version of third-wave feminism as embodied in other action heroines such as Buffy Summers and Xena.[31]

Squirrel Girl as Transmedia Character

As a transmedia character, Squirrel Girl's depiction comes largely from her portrayal in print, in both comic books and young adult literature. She first appeared in a one-off Iron Man comic, then with the GLA, and then in more formal appearances in various Avengers titles as well as her own. Squirrel Girl emerged as a favorite character for comic book creators because of her humorous beginnings and undermining of hypermasculine superhero tropes by existing outside of Marvel Universe continuity while being an effective fighter.

Her first appearance with Iron Man is in "The Coming of . . . Squirrel Girl," in *Marvel Super-Heroes* volume 2, issue 8, *Marvel Super-Heroes Winter Special* (Winter 1991). She appears in the shadows watching Iron Man and is properly introduced to readers by tackling him to show how "rough and tough" she can be. Her appearance is scrawny, with a long tail, buckteeth, and black diamonds around her eyes that make her resemble a harlequin. She presents herself as fourteen years old and as a mutant. When Doctor Doom attacks, she calls on squirrels to defeat him. She blames herself for causing the problem, but Iron Man credits her for handing Doctor Doom "one of the most inglorious defeats of his career." While Squirrel Girl is keen to begin her superhero career, Iron Man advises her to finish high school and attend college, and if she still wants to be a superhero after all that, he will put in a good word with the Avengers.

Squirrel Girl was intended as a one-off character, as evidenced by her second appearance: one panel in *Marvel Year-In-Review '92* with a joke about how Marvel would never publish a "Squirrel Girl: 2099" title. These comical appearances, even in her initial outing with Iron Man, suggest that the character was simply meant to highlight the ridiculous nature of superheroes and their powers and not to be taken seriously. Rather than endearing herself instantly to her fellow superheroes, she was meant to highlight how superpowers can come from anything and become credible if they can defeat the toughest foe. Thus, Murray and Ditko, and by extension Marvel, meant the character to reflect on the contrived nature of superheroes and the absur-

---

31. Zeisler, *We Were Feminists*, xv, 16.

dity of characters able to run faster than a speeding locomotive or leap over buildings in a single bound—as the original superhero, Superman, could.

Squirrel Girl remained unseen for over a decade, but she was not forgotten—at least not by those comic book fans who became creators in the industry. When Dan Slott wrote a four-issue miniseries in 2005, *Great Lakes Avengers Misassembled*, he returned Squirrel Girl to the Marvel Universe. The intent of this miniseries was to satirize superhero deaths by having a superhero die each issue. Rather than kill Squirrel Girl, however, Slott brutally dispatched her squirrel companion, Monkey Joe. This event highlighted how, during the GLA run, Squirrel Girl became more aware of her position as a comic book character. She began each issue by directly addressing the readers from a stage. Even before appearing as a character, she warned that the miniseries was not necessarily for kids. When Monkey Joe dies, she laments that comic books should be fun and says she no longer wants to do this, while also basically wondering what is wrong with comic book readers that they would read something so violent. This postmodern presentation aligns her with other superhero characters meant to satirize superhero comics, such as Deadpool,[32] whose penchant to break the fourth wall is juxtaposed with his violent behavior to provide comic relief.

These appearances, however, could be considered outside the Marvel Universe's continuity, which would render them unimportant and explain their comical nature.[33] They also all occurred before the Disney-Marvel merger, after which Doreen became less satirical as she was folded into the continuity. Squirrel Girl became a supporting character in issues 7 through 34 (February 2011–January 2013) of *New Avengers*. On January 7, 2015, Marvel launched *The Unbeatable Squirrel Girl*, issue 1. From there, Squirrel Girl routinely appeared in *The New Avengers* and then *US Avengers*. Marvel published the graphic novel *The Unbeatable Squirrel Girl Beats Up the Marvel Universe!* in October 2016 as a result of the title's success at school book fairs;[34] Marvel further capitalized on this success by publishing the YA novel *The Unbeatable Squirrel Girl: Squirrel Meets World* in February 2107 and its sequel, *The Unbeatable Squirrel Girl: 2 Fuzzy, 2 Furious*, in 2018. The success of Squirrel Girl and other newer superheroes led Disney/Marvel to produce the Marvel Rising franchise, which began as a series of comics in summer 2018 (*Marvel Rising: Alpha, Marvel Rising: Squirrel Girl & Ms. Marvel, Marvel Ris-*

---

32. Which is even emphasized when the two introduce the *Deadpool / GLI Summer Fun Spectacular.*

33. See Goodrum for more.

34. McMillan, "'Unbeatable.'"

ing: *Ms. Marvel & Squirrel Girl,* and *Marvel Rising: Omega*). All these issues
were collected in November 2018 as *Marvel Rising,* with a second five-issue
miniseries released in March 2019.

The franchise would then spawn animated specials, but Squirrel Girl
began appearing in action before then. Beginning in June 2007, during
the satirical period, Squirrel Girl appeared on the animated series *Fantastic Four: World's Greatest Heroes,* auditioning to join the team in the episode
"The Cure." Following the merger, Disney/Marvel presented the character
in more video games and animations, thus aligning these appearances with
the print portrayals. Squirrel Girl appeared in video games, massively mul-
tiplayer online games, and mobile games, some of these treating her and all
superheroes more comically (e.g., *Marvel Super Hero Squad: Comic Combat*
and *Marvel Super Hero Squad Online* in 2011, *Lego Marvel Super Heroes* in 2013,
Lego Marvel's Avengers in 2016, and *Lego Marvel Super Heroes 2* in 2017), while
others portrayed the characters more seriously (e.g., *Marvel Heroes* in 2013,
Marvel Contest of Champions in 2014, and *Marvel Future Fight* in 2015). Importantly, she was not a featured character in any of these games, but the ability
to play as her increased over the years, demonstrating her rise in stature.

Additionally, she appeared in the Disney XD series *Ultimate Spider-Man*
starting in September 2014 but largely as a background character—although
her squirrel army does defeat Juggernaut in "The Next Iron Spider." As a
result of the success of her eponymous series, the animated TV film *Marvel
Rising: Secret Warriors* premiered on the Disney Channel and Disney XD on
September 30, 2018, to showcase younger, more diverse superheroes who
team up as the Secret Warriors.[35] The TV film was preceded by six 4-minute
animated shorts on Disney XD called *Marvel Rising: Initiation* in August
2018 to advertise the film.[36] Five more animated TV specials followed on
Disney XD and YouTube: *Chasing Ghosts, Heart of Iron, Battle of the Bands,
Operation Shuri,* and *Playing with Fire.* Disney/Marvel also developed a live-
action pilot featuring Squirrel Girl called *The New Warriors,* but no television
network bought it. Milana Vayntub voiced Squirrel Girl in *Marvel Rising*
and played her in the pilot. The actress believes that young women would
"feel represented and impassioned by this badass young woman who wants
to make the world a better place" and "doesn't exist solely 'for the male
gaze.'"[37] Vayntub's interpretation of the character aligns with Marvel's official presentation: Disney/Marvel apparently seized on Squirrel Girl's subversive nature to forward her as a representative of the company's support

35. Yeoman, "Secret Warriors Review."
36. Yeoman, "Initiation Review."
37. Cheng and Flaherty, "Marvel's Launching."

for empowered women. This corporate support, however, created a transmedia character full of contradictory features.

Squirrel Girl as Contradictory Transmedia Character

Nicolle Lamerichs theorizes transmedia characters as business models that can present problems across a fan base and thus to a corporation if the character is portrayed inconsistently.[38] Corporations intentionally construct transmedia characters for fans to consume on numerous, interconnected platforms, and the increased consumption furthers the producer's profit. However, because fans may approach such a character on one platform more than others, Lamerichs argues that fans will have different affective relationships with these characters, including different types and amounts of emotional ownership. It may be that if people need to spend more (e.g., time, money) to know and enjoy the complete transmedia character across all the different media contexts, they will come to feel that they in some way have ownership over how the character is represented, which can cause problems if the transmedia character is portrayed inconsistently across these contexts. Additionally, fandoms can fracture over these different emotional ownerships if one subset prefers a specific portrayal over the others. Corporations, then, need to strategize how they portray such transmedia characters to ensure consistency.

Yet Squirrel Girl has not been portrayed consistently during her three decades as a transmedia character. Before the Disney/Marvel merger, Squirrel Girl was treated largely as a joke or as a figure intended to satirically mock superheroes. Even then, however, her capabilities combined with her humor endeared her to fans, and Disney/Marvel appears more interested in furthering this contradictory nature than resolving it.

Squirrel Girl's jovial nature persists across her comic book, gaming, and animated portrayals but is combined with her complete competence in handling problems. For two decades, Marvel perpetuated Squirrel Girl's satirical nature while building her power and effectiveness, thereby appealing to fans who possess more insider knowledge of comics and superheroes. Squirrel Girl was meant to lampoon both comic book characters and fans who treat such entertainment too seriously. In 2007 Fabian Nicieza and Slott portray her as the most competent GLA member in combat and even reference her taking down Doctor Doom with her new squirrel companion, Tippy-Toe:

---

38. Lamerichs, "Insights."

"Yeah, that's right. Squirrel Girl totally *pwns* Doc Doom. Know why? 'Cause of somethin' that happened in a story by *Steve*-freakin'-*Ditko!* That's *so* in continuity. So just deal with it, fanboy."[39] At the same time, Squirrel Girl undermined hypermasculine superhero tropes by being "just a girl" who possessed the "silly" powers of a squirrel and who could single-handedly defeat foes that even the most muscular, masculine, and violent superheroes could not overcome without the help of a team composed of similar superheroes.

After Disney acquired Marvel, while no longer presented as a joke herself, Squirrel Girl continued to crack jokes; simultaneously, she became adept at combat, computer programming, and world-saving—even if the threats are more comical than serious. In *Unbeatable Squirrel Girl,* the portrayal maintains its subversive nature through her comedy, appearance, and powers and adds to it through her use of computer skills to solve problems, the author's comments at the bottom of each page, and, more importantly, Squirrel Girl's tactic of talking to villains potentially to avoid combat. In more recent titles, however, her postmodern humor is not as obvious as in her GLA appearances, in which she even criticizes the hypersexualization of women in superhero comics.[40] Yet she engages in combat and is portrayed effectively solving problems and averting disasters, with her noncontinuity battles accepted as fact and thus as canon. In *Playing with Fire,* she both builds a facial recognition software program to locate the villain and is more than willing to jump into action when she and her teammates find the culprit. In *Lego Marvel Super Heroes 2,* she cracks jokes and manages to defeat M.O.D.O.K. with her "Nut Buster."

Although she is effective in combat, her portrayal in *Unbeatable Squirrel Girl* focuses more on talking to, and even befriending, supervillains to resolve problems. Ryan North, writer of the *Unbeatable Squirrel Girl* comic book series, saw the character's core as "someone who's there to help people. She has superpowers, but you can't solve every problem by punching it, and she's totally there to explore ideas that don't involve punching someone in the face."[41] In a way, North saw this portrayal as a response to her satirical origins: "'The joke with Squirrel Girl before we got her was that she beats up villains who are outside her power range, but it always happened off-panel.'"[42] Indeed, Michael Goodrum argues that never showing Squirrel Girl in action in these initial appearances was meant to control her subversive

39. Nicieza (w), Slott (w), and Dwyer (i), "Squirrel Girl Interludes."
40. Slott (w) and Pelletier (i), "Mistaken Identity Crisis."
41. McMillan, "'Unbeatable.'"
42. McMillan, "'Unbeatable.'"

nature and focus on making her a joke. She could claim all she wanted about defeating huge foes, but if no one sees it, it does not threaten the hypermasculine stereotypes embedded in superheroes.

However, more recent portrayals highlight Squirrel Girl's combat skills, especially in the animations and video games. In *Lego Marvel 2*, Squirrel Girl is a playable character unlocked via a Gwenpool mission where she is joined by the characters Chipmunk Hunk and Koi Boi from *Unbeatable Squirrel Girl*. In the scenario, M.O.D.O.K. interrupts the fundraiser she is hosting. Squirrel Girl says that she has seen this type of thing before, that it could get messy, and that she's "kinda digging this action."[43] She then leaps into battle without trying to talk to anyone to dispel the situation. Similarly, in the Marvel Rising animations, Squirrel Girl rarely tries to talk down a supervillain and instead willingly fights them alongside her teammates. Additionally, she continues to score victories over well-known, powerful supervillains.

Squirrel Girl also fights in the comic books, but often only after a compassionate approach fails. In *Unbeatable Squirrel Girl*, issue 1, the first supervillain she confronts is Kraven, who abducts her squirrel companion, Tippy-Toe. Squirrel Girl first asks him nicely to release her friend, but when Kraven refuses, they exchange blows until she tosses him high into the air, thus giving herself enough time to think of a plan. In this contemplation she realizes that it is more effective to find out what he wants; when she learns his motivation, she sends him down a different path in life, that of hero, and he thanks her for that insight. Later issues reveal that the two characters have become friends who work together to escape a sinister game, and she even defends Kraven in a courtroom following his arrest.

Squirrel Girl also befriends Galactus after convincing him to not eat the planet Earth, negotiates galactic peace with Silver Surfer, and defeats Ultron, only to give him a second chance to become better than his programming. Indeed, when she first meets Brain Drain, she learns "that she cannot be the one to strike first. She not only recognized her mistake, but admitted it and took actions to make amends."[44] Such stories and official accounts focus on her compassion, reflection, and creative problem-solving and describe the character as more willing to help someone turn their life around and to make a friend than fight. This portrayal continues outside of *Unbeatable Squirrel Girl*. In the second Marvel Rising comic series, she discusses how important communication skills are for a superhero, because "not every battle is won with *fists*, ya know."[45] When confronting Morgan Le Fay in the

---

43. From *Lego Marvel Super Heroes 2*.
44. Cink (w) and Zhang (i), *Marvel*, 69.
45. Magruder (w) and Di Salvo (i), "Heroes of the Round Table!"

story's climax, Squirrel Girl asks her to stop fighting and start conversing, and she only continues fighting when Le Fay refuses to do so.

This preference for compassionate communication over violent combat appears to demonstrate more feminine stereotypes in the character; yet her willingness to engage in combat aligns her with the stereotypically masculine superheroes. Squirrel Girl thereby appears to possess stereotyped aspects of both genders. This duality presents third-wave feminism, at least as popularized by the "girl power" movement: she retains the "girl" nature of femininity while drawing on masculine power, in combat and in self-determination. In *Playing with Fire*, when the culprit mocks her name, powers, and computer abilities, Squirrel Girl responds with the "genius comes with the girl part," thereby aligning computer skills with her femininity. She further represents feminist ideals in *Unbeatable Squirrel Girl* and the Marvel Rising franchise through her willingness to work with friends and team members as a collective crime-fighting unit, whereas in the past, although a member of different teams, she often fought supervillains alone, representing a more masculine approach to combat.

She also represents a more body-positive approach to female superheroes. In both *Unbeatable Squirrel Girl* and the Marvel Rising franchise, her character is depicted as larger than other superheroines, including those on the Secret Warriors, but she is never chastised for having a larger body[46] or "bodacious behind." Her size also does not undermine her combat effectiveness. Indeed, Squirrel Girl largely survives being portrayed as hypersexualized as other characters—except for one time. During her time with the Great Lakes team, her combat capability is undermined by increasing feminization and sexualization in her visual representation and her actions. For example, in "First Kiss," by writer Fabian Nicieza and illustrator Paco Medina, Squirrel Girl becomes smitten with the mutant Speedball.[47] She displays stereotypical teenage-girl reactions to a crush and is also hypersexually drawn with a narrow waist and large bust. She saves her crush from a villain, and receives her first kiss for doing so, but the story reinforces stereotypes in how superheroines both act and look. Indeed, even in *Lego Marvel 2*, when she just stands awaiting the player's commands, her posture is rather coy, with her hip cocked and her back arched to stick out her chest and butt. This pose appears less common for the game's female heroes, many of whom affect battle readiness in their stance, some with weapons drawn like Nebula, Kate Bishop, and Okoye.

---

46. Stevens and St. John, "Corporate Affirmations."
47. From *I Heart Marvel: Masked Intentions*, "First Kiss."

This hypersexualization represents a common feminist critique of the "girl power" approach to third-wave feminism, although it is also contradicted by Squirrel Girl's lack of both a sexual and a romantic identity. In *Unbeatable Squirrel Girl*, she initially has a crush on the man she would learn is Chipmunk Hunk, but the crush never materializes as anything but a collegial relationship. Her only apparent romantic interest was with Speedball, as more contemporary portrayals depict her as rather asexual and aromantic and as focused on her education and superhero work. While this portrayal allows for a unique representation of a nonbinary identity, it also becomes worrisome given that she also represents a nontraditional superhero body type, which may suggest that she is being excluded from such romantic and sexual relationships. This contradiction represents a small aspect of her overall character, but it nonetheless demonstrates the inconsistencies that define her fractured feminist nature.

Squirrel Girl as Feminist Transmedia Character

Squirrel Girl's characterization involves many inconsistencies across the media texts in which she appears. Because of these inconsistencies, Squirrel Girl demonstrates different aspects of feminist thought and embraces an intersectional both-and instead of an either-or approach to identity. She exists because of these inconsistencies, as they appear to attract fans. She began as a satirical joke people loved and wanted to see more of, which led to a more serious portrayal that nevertheless retains the subversive spirit that first drew people to her; in her more empowered portrayal, her fandom has only grown. In a sense, she exists because people like the co-existing, unresolved contradictions. Her portrayal, then, demonstrates more fluidity than binary rigidity. As that of a transmedia character, Squirrel Girl's contradictory nature and inconsistent portrayal deconstructs binaries, as she presents opposing features as intersecting and making her stronger and better equipped to handle different situations, problems, and foes.

Feminist theorists have argued that agency is collective whereas empowerment is individual, suggesting that popularized versions of feminism like "girl power" focus on empowerment in personal lives instead of collectively acting to bring about political change. Rosalind Gill and Shani Orgad argue that focusing on improving self-confidence for empowerment comes at the expense of addressing structural inequalities.[48] Rather than improving insti-

---

48. Gill and Orgad, "The Confidence Cult(ure)."

tutional structures that further the oppression of women, the focus on self-confidence argues that girls and women need to focus on regulating their self-esteem instead of sociocultural changes.

If this is true, Squirrel Girl was more empowered to control her own destiny before Disney acquired Marvel as she seeks to solidify her position as a superhero. And after the acquisition, she acts more as a collective agent for change: she becomes more of a team player, albeit perhaps more of a leader within the team, in *Unbeatable Squirrel Girl* and the Marvel Rising franchise. At least in the *Marvel Rising: Secret Warriors* TV film, this focus on collective agency could be due to the involvement of Mairghread Scott, who penned the screenplay and may have brought focus to communal identity.[49] In analyzing *Marvel Rising*, J. Richard Stevens and Burton St. John III concluded that the franchise "stresses the value of community" as Squirrel Girl and her team members offset "each other's strengths to coordinate their fighting prowess."[50] This collective agency, however, applies only to crime-fighting: at no point do Squirrel Girl and her allies represent actions to challenge patriarchal status quos ingrained in the structures around them. Thus, while being more of a collective agent, the character embodies a postfeminist approach to change: focus on the little improvements you can make yourself rather than organize the public to make progress.

Thus, the earlier portrayal aligned more with second-wave feminism in terms of career-focused self-determination and with third-wave feminism in terms of individualized empowerment, as well as reactionary, commodified, and sanitized versions of feminisms due to the character's individualism, sexualization, and malleability as a commodity. The current messaging, however, aligns with younger-generation political ideology, such as fourth-wave politically active feminism where "those who work together become powerful members of supportive communities."[51] Readers can emulate Squirrel Girl to empower their lives through computer and compassionate communication skills, but they can also learn about the need to work with a team and become collective agents of change. Across these portrayals, then, Squirrel Girl presents how to be both collectivist and individualist: she knows when to be subversive, when to be individually empowered, when to be a collective agent, when to fight, when to love; she demonstrates an understanding of the nuances needed to negotiate a complex, interconnected, diverse world.

---

49. Stevens and St. John, "Corporate Affirmations," 383.
50. Stevens and St. John, "Corporate Affirmations," 383.
51. Stevens and St. John, "Corporate Affirmations," 383.

The both-and approach continues when considering the feminist nature of the other contradictions. Squirrel Girl's combative nature reflects both second- and fourth-wave feminism, while her compassionate approach presents more of a commodified feminism, but this approach is simultaneously also subversive within the hypermasculine, patriarchal tropes of superhero comics. Steven and St. John reach the same conclusion with the Marvel Rising comics: they present "a collective of mostly young female heroes, negotiating the patriarchy of their surroundings to form communities of support and assert their identities in ways that transcend classic gender role expectations."[52] Again, the character acts with both approaches and reflects different feminisms. She reflects more third- and fourth-wave approaches to body positivity, but the sexualization of and disconnect between appearance and official statistics aligns more with commodified feminisms. Finally, even her subversive nature is contradicted and controlled in different ways, reflecting tensions between the different waves of feminism and commodified feminisms; she simultaneously subverts gender-role stereotypes while her compassionate nature undercuts any threat that her power presents to patriarchy.[53] When she is considered holistically as a transmedia character, then, the contradictions reflect the fractured state of feminism and suggest the intentionality of Squirrel Girl's both-and as a business model.

Squirrel Girl's portrayal allows Disney/Marvel to appeal to the largest possible audience. Whether people like the satire or the combat, the compassion or the computers, the sexualized or the realistic, Squirrel Girl demonstrates a polysemous nature as a transmedia character. The Marvel acquisition sought to give Disney more access to boys and young men, but they also discovered an underserved market in girls and young women. Their rebuilding and rebranding of Squirrel Girl allowed for an increased connection to the girls and young women Disney had already reached through their princess lines. Further, including Squirrel Girl in a franchise focused on diversity, with clearly defined "prosocial messaging,"[54] suggests their willingness to use the character's portrayal of fractured feminism for financial gain. Marvel framed Marvel Rising with a message that Marvel characters exist for every Marvel fan and even recognized Squirrel Girl as a rising star and fan favorite.[55] Per Sana Amanat, Marvel's director of content and character development in 2015: "You start having all different types of readers and a divergent fanbase because of the fact that our content sort

52. Stevens and St. John, "Corporate Affirmations," 383.
53. Hains, "Power Feminism," 101.
54. Stevens and St. John, "Corporate Affirmations," 381.
55. McMillan, "Marvel"; Rothman, "Marvel to Launch."

of reflects that, reflects the diversity that's out there."[56] Of course, Disney/Marvel is in the business of making money, not changing politics, and their focus with Squirrel Girl seeks to create the largest possible fan base for the character, even if it means creating an inconsistent transmedia character. If the fans were not buying the comics, asking for more appearances of the character, and supporting her throughout these transmedia portrayals, Disney/Marvel would not employ this business model.

At the same time, because the corporation is not moving to resolve obvious contradictions, they are commodifying not just feminism but the more specific ideas of intersectionality and nonbinary gender identities. From a critical perspective, such commodification could potentially undercut feminist political action for revolutionary change. The character may have commented on representation of women in comic books in the beginning, but she no longer makes such pointed observations. Disney/Marvel celebrates itself for strengthening the diverse offerings of the Marvel Universe, in the face of reactionary conservativism like Comicsgate;[57] however, such diverse portrayals could undercut people's desire to engage in political action: if people see themselves represented, they may feel that they are heard and seen and that no further action is necessary. Of course, such portrayals would also hopefully normalize the characterization among the audience and fans consuming it. The more such portrayals cultivate normality through consistency, the more people may act on those portrayals in considering what is appropriate and real, thus impacting their interactions with each other, from the personal to the political. Both implications are nebulous, whereas the most obvious implication remains Disney/Marvel's profiteering from fractured feminism.

Conclusion

Throughout the years, fans have managed to keep Squirrel Girl alive and have even increased her presence, power, and popularity within the Marvel Comic Universe. As a transmedia character, Squirrel Girl suggests that the comic book industry has listened to the desires of female fans, something

---

56. Bennett, "Growing Female Audience."

57. ComicsGate, like its predecessor GamerGate, involved online discourse around forced diversity in Marvel comics with the introduction of characters like Ms. Marvel and the gender bending of Thor.

the fans have long sought.[58] Yet the perpetuation of an inconsistent portrayal indicates that Disney/Marvel is commodifying other identity politics issues, which could undercut those issues' ability to impact our political world. After all, Squirrel Girl never really utters the "f-word" or discusses feminist issues; while she may embody them, she does not preach them. She had elements of the postfeminist sensibilities, such as her individualized agency in overpowering villains, while languishing in relative obscurity before Disney acquired Marvel. At that time, the fans turned creators kept her active, yet in a subversive way that also undercut her power. After the merger, and in an attempt to reach an underserved audience, Squirrel Girl became more of a collective agent for good and change, suggesting more pure feminist sensibilities while maintaining her humor, espousing a body-positive postfeminism, and embodying feminine stereotypes around compassion in her crime-fighting. As a transmedia character, then, Squirrel Girl reflects a corporate feminism, one meant to inspire but perhaps not completely empower her fans.

With an inconsistent representation across portrayals, Squirrel Girl serves as a model for how a transmedia character can exist as a feminist while allowing a multinational media conglomerate to profit from fans' desires for such a superhero. In a world where different feminist ideologies vie for challenging and changing patriarchal institutions and norms, Disney/Marvel's Squirrel Girl appears to embody the contradictions between these ideologies to become an empowered collective agent who models compassion, body positivity, and self-confidence while failing to fight the oppressive crimes of patriarchy. Indeed, Squirrel Girl represents the contradictory nature of postfeminism itself as it exists as a complex intermingling of feminist and antifeminist discourses.[59] As Gill notes regarding the complex nature of postfeminism, "cultural transformation" perhaps exists as a "complex and nuanced process in which new ideas do not simply displace existing ones."[60] In this way, Squirrel Girl potentially represents a best-fit approach to developing feminist characters for transmedia purposes. Rather than simply embody one feminist discourse, her transmedia nature allows her to embody simultaneously occurring contradictory discourses, thereby expanding her appeal by aligning with this morass of discourses.

---

58. Lauriello, "Searching for Superwomen."
59. Gill "Postfeminist Media," 149, 163.
60. Gill "Post-postfeminism?" 625.

Bibliography

Bennett, Alanna. "With a Growing Female Audience, Marvel Hopes to Invite Every-one In." *BuzzFeed*, October 1, 2015. https://www.buzzfeed.com/alannabennett/marvel-wants-you.

Cheng, Susan, and Keely Flaherty. "Marvel's Launching a New Franchise of Won-derful, Diverse Superheroes." *BuzzFeed News*, December 7, 2017. https://www.buzzfeednews.com/article/susancheng/marvel-rising.

Cicci, Matthew Alan. "Turning the Page: Fandoms, Multimodality, and the Transforma-tion of the 'Comic Book' Superhero." PhD diss., Wayne State University, 2015.

Cink, Lorraine (w), and Alice Zhang (i). *Marvel: Powers of a Girl*. New York: Marvel Press, 2019.

Ditko, Steve (w, i), and Will Murray (w). "The Coming of . . . Squirrel Girl!" *Marvel Super Heroes* 2, no. 8. New York: Marvel Comics, 1992.

"Doreen Green: Squirrel Girl." *Marvel.com*, 2020, https://www.marvel.com/characters/squirrel-girl-doreen-green.

Gill, Rosalind. "Post-postfeminism?: New Feminist Visibilities in Postfeminist Times." *Feminist Media Studies* 16, no. 4 (2016): 610–30.

———. "Postfeminist Media Culture: Elements of a Sensibility." *European Journal of Cul-tural Studies* 10, no. 2 (2007): 147–66.

Gill, Rosalind, and Shani Orgad. "The Confidence Cult(ure)." *Australian Feminist Stud-ies* 30, no. 85 (2015): 324–44.

Goodrum, Michael. "'Oh C'mon, Those Stories Can't Count in Continuity!' Squirrel Girl and the Problem of Female Power." *Studies in Comics* 5, no. 1 (2014): 97–115.

Hains, Rebecca C. "Power Feminism, Mediated: Girl Power and the Commercial Poli-tics of Change." *Women's Studies in Communication* 32, no. 1 (2009): 89–113.

Lamerichs, Nicolle. "An Introduction to Character Studies." *NicolleLamerichs.com* (blog), November 10, 2019. https://nicollelamerichs.com/2019/11/10/character-studies.

Lauriello, Sophia. "Searching for Superwomen: Female Fans and Their Behavior." Mas-ter's thesis, University of Missouri-Columbia, 2017.

Maggs, Sam, Emma Grange, and Ruth Amos. *Fearless and Fantastic! Female Super Heroes Save the World*. London: DK Children, 2018.

Magruder, Nilah (w), and Roberto Di Salvo (i). "Heroes of the Round Table!" *Marvel Rising* 2, no. 1. New York: Marvel Comics, 2019.

McMillan, Graeme. "Marvel Launching Animated Property 'Marvel Rising' in 2018." *The Hollywood Reporter*, December 7, 2017. https://www.hollywoodreporter.com/heat-vision/marvel-launching-animated-property-marvel-rising-2018-1065463.

———. "'Unbeatable Squirrel Girl' Creators Explain How to Beat Up the Marvel Universe (Kind Of)." *The Hollywood Reporter*, October 4, 2016. https://www.hollywoodreporter.com/heat-vision/unbeatable-squirrel-girl-creators-explain-934736.

Niceza, Fabian (w), Paco Medina (a) and Juan Vasco (i). "First Kiss." In *I (Heart) Marvel: Masked Intentions 1*, no. 1. New York: Marvel Comics, 2006.

Nicieza, Fabian (w), Dan Slott (w), and Kieron Dwyer (i). "Squirrel Girl Interludes." *Deadpool / GLI Summer Fun Spectacular 1*, no. 1. New York: Marvel Comics, 2007.

Roberts, Johnnie L. "Why Disney Bought Marvel." *Newsweek*, August 30, 2009, https://www.newsweek.com/why-disney-bought-marvel-78573.

Rothman, Michael. "Marvel to Launch Animated Series Focused on Young, Diverse Heroes." *ABC News*, December 7, 2017. https://abcnews.go.com/Entertainment/marvel-launch-animated-series-focused-young-diverse-heroes/story?id=51653391.

Sims, Chris. "That's What's Up: The Slightly Improbable Rise of Squirrel Girl." *Looper*, March 29, 2019. https://www.looper.com/149074/thats-whats-up-the-slightly-improbable-rise-of-squirrel-girl.

Slott, Dan (w), and Paul Pelletier (i). "Countdown to a Miscount." *GLA* 1, no. 4. New York: Marvel Comics, 2005.

———. "Mistaken Identity Crisis." *GLA* 1, no. 3. New York: Marvel Comics, 2005.

"Squirrel Girl (Doreen Green) | Marvel 101" [Video]. *Marvel Entertainment*, October 17, 2019. https://www.youtube.com/watch?v=3-P-TBrQnRo.

Stevens, J. Richard, and Burton St. John III. "Corporate Affirmations of Self-Identity and Mutual Self-Help: Transmedia Rhetorics of Marvel Rising." *Journal of Communication Inquiry* 44, no. 4 (2020): 376–95.

Traveller's Tales. *Lego Marvel Super Heroes 2*. Warner Bros. Interactive Entertainment, 2017.

Walt Disney Company. "Disney to Acquire Marvel Entertainment." August 31, 2009. https://thewaltdisneycompany.com/disney-to-acquire-marvel-entertainment.

Yeoman, Kevin. "Marvel Rising: Initiation Review." *ScreenRant*, August 9, 2018. https://screenrant.com/marvel-rising-initiation-review-spider-gwen-ms-marvel-squirrel-girl.

———. "Marvel Rising: Secret Warriors Review." *ScreenRant*, September 24, 2018. https://screenrant.com/marvel-rising-secret-warriors-review-animated.

Zeisler, Andi. *We Were Feminists Once: From Riot Grrl to Covergirl®, The Buying and Selling of a Political Movement*. New York: PublicAffairs, 2016.

CHAPTER 13

Symptoms or Resistance?

The Feminist Trauma Theory Framework in *Captain Marvel*

Annika Hagley

Although the character of Carol Danvers has existed since the Silver Age of Marvel Comics, she was not widely known or commercially powerful until Marvel Comics made her Captain Marvel and rebooted her origin story in the series *The Life of Captain Marvel* (2018). What followed was a blockbuster movie in 2019 and a pivotal appearance in *Avengers: Endgame*, the culmination of the Marvel superhero franchise since 9/11.

In nearly two decades of superhero movies—beginning with 2005's *Batman Begins* and culminating in Marvel's 2019 *Avengers: Endgame*—in which masculinity, war, the military industrial complex, revenge, and terrorism were front and center, *Captain Marvel* offered a significant and importance break from the obsessive reliving of 9/11 and turned its focus on the character herself to create a tortured yet empowering narrative of personal trauma, healing, and recovery. In one of the most psychologically complex superhero plots of all time, Carol Danvers goes through a clear stage-based recovery from interpersonal trauma based on the feminist trauma framework and one that women all over the world recognized as eerily similar to their own experiences.[1]

---

1. Without such an obsessive dwelling on the white, militaristic, macho, and at times racist narrative that was drilled into the American public post 9/11 and filtered out through mass-produced media forms, movies like *Black Panther*, *Wonder Woman*, and *Captain Marvel* would have been unthinkable. It was within the oppressive post-9/11 pop culture and societal narratives that movements like Me Too and Black Lives Matter

Marvel's version of Captain Marvel came to be in 1967 after years of infighting within the comic book publishing community over the trademark of the name. The first Captain Marvel, known as Mar-Vell, was sent to Earth by the Kree to protect the human race. This was followed by the Monica Rambeau version (1982—a black female cop from New Orleans), Genis-Vell (1993—the son of Mar-Vell), Phyla-Vell (2004—his sister) and even a Skrull imposter, posing as the Captain after having kidnapped the real one. The comics never enjoyed the mainstream success of *Captain America, Spider-Man*, and *X-Men*, but, knowing that they would lose the rights to the name if they stopped publishing the series, Marvel wound through several versions of the character from the 1970s to 2012 before settling on the most well-known version, Carol Danvers, who had first appeared as Mar-Vell's love interest in the original series. As with many female superheroes written by men in a decade when the feminist movement was burgeoning with full force, the Carol Danvers version of Captain Marvel was both empowered by her superheroic gifts and restricted by issues like appeasement of the male gaze and a fundamental misunderstanding of the ways in which feminism hoped to adjust societal expectations of women and their roles. One example of this was her original costume (later reconfigured), a skin-tight breast-, leg-, and thigh-revealing number that would have been more suitable at the Moulin Rouge than as the combat outfit of a leading female superhero. Another example came in the long-running saga of Carol's personality "splitting" and eventual psychiatric treatment, which enabled her to consolidate her memories and powers to become Captain Marvel. Like Wonder Woman's, Danvers's ascension to status as a superhero was unlike that of her male counterparts. She was shown to be powerful, unstable, tortured, doubtful, and at the mercy of the male characters around her long before she was allowed to assume the role she played in the Hollywood film version in 2019, which finally settled some of the tensions of gender, trauma, and power in an empowering manner.[2]

The Feminist Trauma Framework

Feminist trauma theory is a recent development within the field of psychology regarding the treatment of women who have suffered from interpersonal trauma. Its lodestone is the notion that, too often, practitioners and

---

began to retool, percolate, explode into mainstream American life and be represented on the big screen for the first time in twenty years. For a more detailed analysis of this phenomena, see Hagley and Harrison, *Reborn of Crisis*.

2. Smith, "Brief History."

wider society have viewed women's symptoms as a sign of inherent mental instability brought out by trauma. Feminist trauma theory posits that they are, instead, a powerful resistance women have been forced to manifest in response to trauma. Such trauma is experienced at an interpersonal level and created by a violently misogynistic society. That society then sustains the antifeminist narrative of hysterical women with mental illnesses rather than examine the role the patriarchy plays in the destruction of women's mental health.

As far back as Charcot and Freud, a great tension has existed in the fact that women have traditionally been forced to turn toward a patriarchal and violent system as a means of addressing the symptoms they are experiencing as a consequence of living within such a system. At the Salpêtriére, Charcot was progressive in being one of the first researchers of human behavior to listen to the narratives of his traumatized female patients and to make connections between their traumas and their symptoms. He was also regressive in the sense that he paraded the suffering women as spectacles for Parisian society to behold.[3] Freud brought forth similar issues in his painstaking investigations of women's symptomology, concluding that such symptoms manifested in response to sexual abuse and degradation. He later retracted *The Etiology of Hysteria* because his findings were too much for polite society to bear.[4]

The American Psychological Association has both advanced the humane treatment of women with encouragement to look beyond the traditional Freudian notions of hysteria and arrested progress with the addition of borderline personality disorder to the DSM, which, owing to the symptom clusters that define it, has become both a gendered and a loaded way of labeling women with a negatively viewed and difficult-to-treat mental health diagnosis.[5]

The first and most foundational point of feminist trauma theory is that women's mental health struggles be recognized as symptoms emerging from an attempt to resist the annihilating effect of men's physical, sexual, and emotional violence against them. Meera Atkinson argues that a historical tendency has always existed in which society views violence against women as an aberration instead of acknowledging the reality that the patriarchal structure of every civilization has created: "unsustainable gardens of grandeur" that have "grown on the blood and bones of subjugated women, children, slaves, invaded and colonialized peoples and non-human animals."[6]

---

3. Schneck, "Jean-Martin Charcot."
4. McOmber, "Silencing the Patient."
5. Skodol and Bender, "Diagnosed Borderline."
6. Atkinson, "Patriarchy Perpetuates Trauma."

The system on which such subjugation was built was—for obvious reasons—unlikely and unable to recognize its own complicity in the destruction of women's mental health, and it created a seemingly well-structured system of help (psychotherapy) in which male therapists were viewed as guardians of knowledge and healing. The reality is, of course, that until women reset the psychological practices of trauma treatment in the 1970s, the impulses of practitioners like Charcot and Freud (and those that followed) were paternalistic, short-sighted, retraumatizing, and centered around the notion that women were entirely or somewhat responsible for their own "hysteria." It is a foundational hangover within the field of psychology that persists, and, despite the impact of the feminist trauma framework, it is not unusual for women to be viewed in negative ways as they attempt to seek assistance from the very people society urges them to turn to for help.[7]

Feminist Trauma Theory and *Captain Marvel*

The *Captain Marvel* movie (2019) is instantly recognizable as an explicit trauma narrative. The stages of healing that trauma-informed care has centered around in recent decades are very deliberately played out in the course of the action, including the creation of safety and stability, remembrance and mourning, and reintegration into society.[8] The general theme of PTSD has been mediated heavily in the Marvel Cinematic Universe post 9/11, but it has always been situated within stories about male characters who displayed typically masculine symptoms in response to traumas that were mostly war related. *Captain Marvel* picked up the baton of the lingering post-9/11 cinematic traumas within the Marvel universe and injected the series with a feminist consciousness that had never been explored within the superheroic genre. The film was so faithful and at times incredibly complex in its portrayal of the symptoms of trauma that are particular to women that some critics and viewers were unaware of the underpinning sophistication of the plot and viewed it squarely as a typical shoot-'em-up/good-versus-evil superhero story. Those who did recognize the explicitly feminist trauma framework were female survivors of interpersonal violence who wrote in droves on blogs and internet forums about their identification with Carol Danvers as she fought her way through each stage of recovery to reach a point of empowerment. Here was a complex, female superhero carrying the lead in a cinematic blockbuster resting on a theoretical framework consid-

---

7. Bjorklund, "No Man's Land."
8. Trauma and Emergency Medicine, "Trauma Recovery."

ered radical only decades previously. She was fulfilling the role of super-hero, fighting villains, uncovering deceptions, and gathering the strength to annihilate those who wronged the weak while forcing herself through a painful process of healing from trauma that she first had to recognize, relive, and reconcile in order to take her place in the world.

A comic series, *The Life of Captain Marvel*, released in January 2019, pre-ceded the release of the *Captain Marvel* movie, which debuted in March that year, and set the foundations of the trauma narrative firmly in place. In the comic event, Carol Danvers is revealed as the daughter of a Kree warrior who decided to stay on Earth and protect her half-human, half-Kree daugh-ter, whose birth resulted in the Kree issuing a death warrant against her for desertion of her mission. There are explicit references and recognizable actions that both describe and mirror the symptoms of lingering trauma, PTSD, and, in particular, the manner in which symptoms manifest differ-ently in women. The first aspect highlighted is familial trauma. Carol's father sinks into an alcoholic depression, always guarding his daughter's life, but ultimately knowing that he cannot possibly protect her or his wife should the Kree discover their whereabouts. Carol's father unleashes his impotent rage on his sons, and Carol is forced to stand by and watch her brothers being beaten without the knowledge that she has the physical ability to help them. In one of the opening scenes, Danvers states: "I tell myself that if I'm strong enough, I'll beat down the memories so hard they'll never come back."[9] She signals here both repression and self-blame (not being strong enough to cope with the memories of violence that feminist trauma theo-rists recognize so easily in their patients) and expands on those symptoms by showing signs of disassociation, flashbacks, panic attacks, and a family tendency toward secrets and shame. Carol experiences constant symptoms of betrayal trauma and interpersonal violence throughout the story and in her work on behalf of the Avengers—a mostly male team who recognize her power, minimize her pain, and comment that her anger seems "excessive" in battle. Because Carol finds no solace or assistance in either the world around her or the superheroic family in which she feels alien, her story arc can only become cathartic by going through the recognizable stages within the trauma recovery framework.

Beginning with the revelation of truth that her mother is Kree, Carol quickly enters a cycle in which pain, anguish, and death are endured but recovery is the only possible outcome. Carol's mother reveals to her that

9. Stohl (w), Pacheco (p), Fonteriz (i), Menyz (c), and Sauvage (i), *Life of Captain Marvel.*

"what humans see as Kree powers are just our biological adaptations to a life of combat." This is a clear nod to the manner in which trauma manifests as interruptions in the bodily rhythms of survivors and is passed on genetically through the generations.[10] It is the joining of forces of both women and the revelation of the truth that allows them to heal from the trauma. Shortly before she is killed, her mother tells Carol, "My mission was you." Breaking the cycle of lies, she explains that her decision to abandon her mission, and therefore her traumatic Kree bodily adaptations, let her break the cycle of trauma and set her daughter free. Carol's tribute to her mother's sacrifice plays out in the development of a feminist consciousness. She proudly tells the audience, "Mine is a warrior's story, told in battle and blood and sacrifice" before devoting her life and powers to saving the world because she recognizes that it is the only way she will save herself. The foundations of Carol Danvers's story were set within the comic series with deliberate and intentional focus on the aspects of trauma, feminism, and recovery that went on to become so recognizable to traumatized women all over the world in the *Captain Marvel* movie.

One of the most distressing reactions women have to being traumatized in violent and misogynistic ways is the tendency to internalize blame and shame and to minimize what has happened to them. It is an observed behavior in psychological practice that women are more likely to turn their pain and shame on themselves and that men are likely to turn it outward and project it onto others.[11] Both states are intolerable and dramatically reduce the capacity for both men and women to build safe relationships marked by mutual respect, trust, and hope. Catrina Brown discusses women's struggle in "speaking and hiding simultaneously" within the therapeutic relationship, alongside their tendency to minimize their distress when they do find the strength to describe what has happened to them.[12]

In the movie, these tendencies are clearly played out in Carol's relationship with both Yon Rogg and the Supreme Intelligence. There are several facets to the *Captain Marvel* movie that speak to the feminist trauma theory framework. The first and most obvious is the kind of trauma Carol suffers with and her relationship with her abuser. In the opening scenes of the movie, we watch as "Vers," Carol in her Kree identity, is subjected to physical, mental, and emotional abuse by the Kree, an alien race she erroneously believes she is part of. She is traumatically bonded to her abuser, Yon Rogg, who urges her to remember her past, control her emotions, and become who

---

10. Yehuda and Lehrner, "Intergenerational Transmission."

11. Dingfelder, "Study Uncovers."

12. Brown, "Women's Narratives."

he wants her to be: "I want you to be the best version of yourself."[13] He calls her oversensitive, convinces her that her failure to control her power is an innate problem unique to her personality, and continues to gaslight her with his own version of the events of her life in relation to the outside world. Against a backdrop of Kree propaganda, such as the citywide announcements of Skrull terrorist attacks, Yon Rogg simultaneously reinforces Carol's dependence on him and tells her that she is out of control. When she fails to control her powers, she is sent to the Supreme Intelligence, who reiterates Yon Rogg's message that she is a victim of the Skrulls, suffers from traumatic amnesia in not being able to remember what they did to her, and, again, cannot control her emotions. The meeting ends with the ominous warning that if Vers does not fall in line and control the symptoms of her trauma for the better of Kree society, her powers and identity will be taken from her.

Yon Rogg reveals that upon her arrival on Hala, Vers was given a transfusion of his Kree blood. The ostensible purpose was to regenerate her powers through an injection of a powerful alien life source. The inference, in trauma terms, is the slow and deliberate possession of a person's body, mind, and being until they are so connected to their abuser that they do not question the abuse. Yon Rogg's destruction of Vers's sense of who she is mirrors the destruction of identity in long-term multifaceted abuse. The difficulty for survivors of such abuse is that they cease to exist in a pretrauma state and are not anchored in a pretrauma identity to which they can easily return, forcing them to build an identity from scratch amid the rubble of uncertainty, self-blame, and shame. In the final scenes of the movie, after Carol has passed through the recognizable stages of trauma recovery, she is finally able to confront Yon Rogg, knowing the truth about who she is, what he is, and what he has done to her: "You lied to me! Everything I knew was a lie!" As they face one another and the truth, Yon Rogg realizes that his power is no match for Carol's, and, in a desperate attempt to psychologically destabilize her, he urges her to fight him without employing her powers to prove that she is capable. After knocking him off his feet with a hand-projected laser to silence him, she looms over him and states simply: "I have nothing to prove to you." As she vanquishes him physically, she completes the severance of the traumatic bond between her and her abuser and, knowing the truth about how he betrayed her and the strengths she has gained from her suffering, blasts him back to Hala in disgrace.

In confronting the Supreme Intelligence (the ultimate symbol of her mental captivity), Carol completes the last stage of healing and emerges as

---

13. Boden and Fleck, *Captain Marvel*.

the most powerful version of herself she can be. This comes as a result not of Kree interference nor the power the Kree had bestowed on her but from deep inside herself as she remembers her previous human life, her connection to her chosen family, and all that she was before she became a victim of abuse. As the Supreme Intelligence taunts Carol, "Without us you're weak, you're flawed, helpless . . . we saved you. Without us you're only human," Carol is dragged through a dimensional vortex and brought to her knees. She lies supine on the ground but is triggered by the words *only human*. A flashback sequence shows Carol at various ages: from a young girl, to the time of the crash, being knocked down, screamed at, pushed over, thrown from go-karts, falling from ropes during basic training, and having a baseball pitched at her face. Each time, she lies on the floor, gathers herself, and stands up; repeatedly, after each abuse and humiliation, she stands up. It is these memories that bring her real power to bear, the fact that she absorbed the power sources on the day of the crash and was able to withstand the years of Kree abuse is where her galactic power exists. Recognizing that the Kree have only sought to control that power because it is superior to their own, she rises to her feet, removes the neck implant that allows the Kree to control her, and, in a final act of recovery, states, "My name is Carol" before destroying the Supreme Intelligence and bursting from the room where she is being held to confront Yon Rogg and save the Skrull refugees.

Implicit in the feminist framework is the idea of holding space for the expert (the women herself) to allow herself to heal: "Our role then as feminist therapists is to hold the space for the body to experience what it knows so it can express, organize and heal from the pain."[14] This is achieved by focusing on a woman's competencies and empowerment and by creating an atmosphere in which focusing on what it means to experience violence within a patriarchal structure is encouraged and acknowledged as an extra burden unique to women. Aside from reassurances that the minimization and self-blame previously discussed are understandable defenses against gendered violence, a woman's capacity to enter the healing process must be accompanied by the "capacity to think critically about dominant culture [and the] unique vulnerability [that] stems from the continuous nature of exposure to the threat."[15] In order to reach a place where the unpacking of trauma can occur without triggering the physical memories that trauma survivors are prone to re-enact, re-engagement with both pre-existing and new areas of support is necessary. The capacity for a survivor of trauma to return

---

14. Menk, "Treatment of Trauma."
15. Brown, "Feminist Paradigms."

to a pretrauma state depends largely on the kind of trauma they have lived through and the extent of the support system they are able to create to reconfigure their lives out of uncertainty. In most cases the process begins when the survivor has reached a place of crisis and a level of symptomatology they can no longer live with. At this point, some will engage the services of a therapist who provides a first layer of safety, guidance, and enough positive regard to stabilize the survivor. In *Captain Marvel* this comes in the form of Nick Fury, former soldier, former colonel, currently deskbound spy, and future founder of both the Avengers Initiative and S.H.I.E.L.D.

In their initial encounters, Fury remains open to Carol's reality even though it is deeply dissonant with his own life experience. When her truth is revealed, he adapts to his new reality (aliens exist, and she is some kind of space warrior) with flexibility and an air of sagacity. Their bond is established in a scene where she interrogates him about his life to prove he is not a Skrull. He answers each question without hesitation, trusts her need to know who he is, and establishes a rapport that deepens as they progress through the story arc. The most important thing Fury offers Danvers is validation—he asks questions, probes at the edges of what she is willing to tell him, and facilitates a sense of safety she has never experienced before. Where Yon Rogg sought control, power, and the destruction of Carol's individuality to make her a "warrior," Fury seeks only the truth and supports her fully in the rediscovery of both her identity and her powers. Fury's nontoxic masculinity is played out in several scenes and is vital to the feminist trauma framework. He displays great physical prowess in terms of fighting while being incredibly sweet to Goose (the Flerken/cat), even after he scratches his eye out. He also recognizes Carol's strength as far superior to his own and encourages her to find and use it to her full capacity while remaining utterly comfortable in his own sense of masculinity. Fury is able to guide Carol through the first stage of trauma recovery, the establishment of safety and stability.

The next stage comes by way of her reconnection with her "chosen family"—the single mother, Monica, and her daughter, Maria, who anchor her confusion with the story of the happiness and sense of connection she once shared with them. In her reconnection with her best friend and her best friend's daughter, Danvers is afforded a look at who she was in the past. Carol states that she has "no idea who I am," to which Monica replies, "You are Carol Danvers. You were the woman on that black box risking her life to do the right thing. My best friend who supported me as a mother and a pilot when no one else did. You were smart and funny, and a huge pain in the

SYMPTOMS OR RESISTANCE?   •   199

ass. And you were the most powerful person I knew, way before you could shoot fire through your fists."[16]

It is clear that Rambeau and Danvers share a deep, years-long bond forged as the only female fighter pilots on the air base and the only two Lawson trusted to work on her top-secret project. As Carol is remembering her previous life, the Skrulls arrive with the missing piece of evidence that allows her the full memory of who she was before the trauma, as well as details of the trauma itself. Learning that she was the pilot for the test flight in which Lawson was attempting to reach her sky laboratory to hide the power source from the approaching Kree, Carol has a memory flashback as she listens to the black-box recording of the flight. She finally recognizes that Lawson was a rogue Kree agent dedicated to science in the name of peace, and that Yon Rogg was the enemy who killed Lawson and attempted to kill Carol before he kidnapped her and began his campaign of abuse against her—and that the Skrulls are innocent refugees from the Kree's imperialistic tendencies. In this scene, the second stage of her recovery (remembrance and mourning) is complete. It is interesting that in the first and second stages of the trauma recovery process, Carol is assisted by a Black man, a Black woman and child, and a group of marginalized and brutalized refugees; literal and figurative "others" to the existing and perverse powers structure within the narrative (the Kree warrior empire). In the intersectional vision of feminist trauma theory and feminism in general, it is the bonding together of survivors of the dominant power structure that gives them both the strength and the "feminist consciousness" to fight the oppression. From the beginning of her journey through the last stage of healing (reconnection and empowerment), Carol asks for Maria's help in choosing a new uniform. In choosing the red and blue colors of the USAF, she reclaims her pretrauma identity and emerges not as who she was before but as someone whose previous identity has been rediscovered, layered with the resilience it takes to withstand gaslighting, abuse, and the symptoms of constant traumatic injury, and who stands ready to assume her next identity: that of Captain Marvel.

The closing loop of the feminist framework is what theorists call the development of "feminist consciousness."[17] Brown suggests that this is the development of a systematic awareness of the particular nature of trauma inflicted on women and an understanding of the unique defenses they

16. Boden and Fleck, *Captain Marvel.*
17. Brown, "Feminist Paradigms."

deploy to survive. This understanding, coupled with Judith Herman's suggestion that, for some, the final part of recovery occurs when the survivor re-engages with the world and helps others suffering from trauma to survive themselves, is underscored in Carol's decision to help the Skrulls find a new home and then to seek more survivors of the Kree's destruction and help them as well.

The *Captain Marvel* movie works both within its superheroic genre convention and as a complex narrative about the stages of trauma recovery and that which is particular to the way in which women are subjected to and recover from being traumatized within patriarchal systems. As the narrative proceeds, recognizable stages of the recovery process are shown, characters are introduced who represent those who would be in positions of support for women in real life, and Carol is able to progress through the trauma recovery process within a truly empowering and feminist framework. Further evidence of the presence of a feminist trauma narrative is revealed in the reactions of women who watched the movie, had suffered with the effects of traumatic symptoms and self-blame, and chose to write about how they recognized themselves within the character on various internet blogs.

Several uniting themes were recognized in blog responses to the *Captain Marvel* movie, including its being an important representation of "parallels to our current, real life struggles for gender equality,"[18] the slow and destructive force of emotional manipulation and gaslighting as the usual beginning of further abuse within interpersonal relationships (her relationship with Yon Rogg), and the visceral physical symptoms of trauma itself: "Flashbacks have been my life recently. I've lived my whole life not knowing my entire past but dealing with the symptoms of trauma."[19] The authors also saw the reconnection and re-establishment of bonds in clear terms of their own recovery and situated the relationships Carol developed with Fury and her chosen family as ultimate mechanisms of healing. Finally, and most importantly in terms of a testament to what the complex plot and production team were trying to achieve, female survivors of abuse signified that they not only recognized themselves in the Captain Marvel character but felt seen, represented on the big screen, and able to draw strength and hope from the narrative. One blogger described feeling "seen and empowered" by the end of the action and of having the realization that she was "ready to fight my own battles too."[20] Another stated that watching Carol get support from others and fight both her enemies and her own traumatic symptoms

---

18. Talusun, "Captain Marvel's Trauma."
19. Richardson, "Someone with CPTSD."
20. Talusun, "Captain Marvel's Trauma."

"gave me the strength to keep fighting. It made me see that my pain could make me strong."[21]

The reboot of Captain Marvel situated her as a traumatized female character operating under the extreme stress of posttraumatic symptoms. She had been subjected to the types of abuse that are often recognizable as uniquely gendered, and Marvel's creative team rebooted their entire franchise and repositioned it to take on the new important themes of the coming decade (equality and sexual violence against women). That they did this using a traditionally hypermasculine genre convention served as something of a Trojan horse of truth and gave validation and inspiration to women whose voices and stories are rarely if ever seen on the big screen. Signaling that the obsessive re-creation of American masculinity in the post-9/11 superhero films was coming to a conclusion, it seems that the new stable of Marvel characters will be centered around contemporary issues in American society and, potentially, more ground-breaking than ever before.

Bibliography

Atkinson, Meera. "Patriarchy Perpetuates Trauma: It's Time to Face That Fact." *The Guardian*, April 29, 2018. https://www.theguardian.com/commentisfree/2018/apr/30/patriarchy-perpetuates-trauma-its-time-to-face-the-fact.

Bjorklund, Pamela. "No Man's Land: Gender Bias and Social Constructivism in the Diagnosis of Borderline Personality Disorder." *Issues in Mental Health Nursing* 27, no. 1 (2006): 3–23.

Boden, Anna, and Ryan Fleck, dirs. *Captain Marvel*. Burbank, CA: Marvel Studios, 2019.

Brown, Catrina. "Women's Narratives of Trauma: (Re)storying Uncertainty, Minimization and Self-Blame." *Narrative Works: Issues, Investigations, & Interventions* 3, no. 1 (2013): 1–30.

Brown, Laura S. "Feminist Paradigms of Trauma Treatment." *Psychotherapy: Theory, Research, Practice, Training* 41, no. 4 (2004): 464–71.

Dingfelder, S. "Study Uncovers a Reason behind Sex Differences in Mental Illness." American Psychological Association. Accessed June 2020. https://www.apa.org/monitor/2011/11/sex-differences.

Hagley, Annika, and Michael Harrison. *Reborn of Crisis: 9/11 and the Resurgent Superhero*. London: Routledge, 2020.

McOmber, James B. "Silencing the Patient: Freud, Sexual Abuse, and the 'Etiology of Hysteria.'" *Quarterly Journal of Speech* 82, no. 4 (1996): 343–63.

Menk, Carrie. "Feminism and the Treatment of Trauma." *MN Trauma Project*, March 1, 2016. Accessed June 2020. https://web.archive.org/web/20200924092849/https://www.mntraumaproject.org/post/2016/02/29/feminism-and-the-treatment-of-trauma.

---

21. Richardson, "Someone with CPTSD."

Richardson, Kaitlyn. "Why I Relate to Captain Marvel as Someone with CPTSD." *The Mighty*, April 30, 2019. Accessed June 2020. https://themighty.com/2019/04/captain-marvel-ptsd/.

Schneck, Jerome M. "Jean-Martin Charcot and the History of Experimental Hypnosis." *Journal of the History of Medicine and Allied Sciences* 16, no. 3 (1961): 297–305.

Skodol, Andrew E., and Donna S. Bender. "Why Are Women Diagnosed Borderline More Than Men?" *Psychiatric Quarterly* 74, no. 4 (2003): 349–60.

Smith, John. "A Brief History of the Captain Marvel(s)." *Alamo Drafthouse Cinema*, March 13, 2019. Accessed January 25, 2021. https://drafthouse.com/news/a-brief-history-of-the-captain-marvels.

Stohl, Margaret (w), Carlos Pacheco (i), Rafael Fonteriz (inker), Marcio Menyz (c), and Marguerite Sauvage. *The Life of Captain Marvel.* New York: Marvel Comics, 2019.

Talusun, Roslyn. "I Can't Stop Thinking about Captain Marvel's Trauma." *Fashion*, March 19, 2019. Accessed June 2020. https://www.flare.com/tv-movies/captain-marvel-brie-larson-trauma/.

Trauma and Emergency Medicine. "Phases of Trauma Recovery: How to Reclaim Normalcy after a Crisis." University of Pittsburg Medical Center, August 30, 2019. Accessed June 2020. https://share.upmc.com/2019/08/phases-of-trauma-recovery-50ph/.

Yehuda, Rachel, and Amy Lehrner. "Intergenerational Transmission of Trauma Effects: Putative Role of Epigenetic Mechanisms." *World Psychiatry* 17, no. 3 (2018): 243–57.

CONTRIBUTORS

Editors

BRYAN J. CARR is an Associate Professor in the Communication and Information Science departments at the University of Wisconsin–Green Bay, where he specializes in mass media and critical studies of popular culture. Dr. Carr's research focuses primary on critical questions of identity and its intersection with social and economic forces, primarily in superhero media and video games. He is the author of *The Transmedia Construction of Marvel's Black Panther: Long Live the King,* and his work has appeared in books such as *Parasocial Politics, What Is a Game?,* and *From Jack Johnson to LeBron James.* He also hosts and produces the podcast *Serious Fun* on the Phoenix Studios podcast network.

META G. CARSTARPHEN, APR,[1] is a Gaylord Family Professor in the Gaylord College of Journalism and Mass Communication at the University of Oklahoma and a Gaylord Family Professor in Strategic Communication. Her research interests explore how media can affect social change. Carstarphen received the 2020 Lionel C. Barrow Jr. Award for Distinguished Achievement in Diversity Research and Education and the 2022 Félix F. Gutiérrez and Clint C. Wilson II Award for Teaching Excellence and Innovation, both

---

1. APR stands for Accreditation in Public Relations and is a designation given to those who complete a voluntary international certification process affirming a commitment to professional excellence and ethical conduct in public relations.

from the Association for Education in Journalism and Mass Communication (AEJMC). Her publications include five books, more than fifty peer-reviewed articles in books and journals, and numerous newspaper commentaries and book reviews. Carstarphen currently serves as editor in chief for the *Communication Booknotes Quarterly* journal, published by Taylor & Francis, which highlights in-depth and concise reviews about books relevant to media and communication fields. She is currently finishing a book manuscript for Peter Lang Publishing Group titled *Writing Home: Race, Newspapers and the Culture of Place in Oklahoma.*

Contributors

JULIE A. DAVIS is an associate professor of communication at the College of Charleston. Her research interests include the way comics both reflect and affect American culture, with an emphasis on comic heroes' evolution from printed page to other media and the intersection of marginalization and superhero narratives.

RACHEL GRANT is an assistant professor in the University of Florida's College of Journalism and Communications in Gainesville. She is an affiliated faculty member with UF's Center of Gender, Sexualities and Women Studies and UF's African-American Studies program. Her research focuses on historical and contemporary social movements, media activism, and media studies of race, gender, class. Grant previously served as an assistant professor in Xavier University of Louisiana's Mass Communication Department, teaching classes in strategic communication, social media management, and media law. She received her PhD from the University of Missouri's School of Journalism as well as a graduate minor in Black Studies. Her professional career includes newspapers, magazines, and corporate advertising.

ANNIKA HAGLEY is an associate professor of Politics and International Relations at Roger Williams University in Rhode Island. She completed her PhD in Political Science at the State University of New York at Buffalo in 2010 and has published work on post-9/11 representations of superheroes in *PS: Political Science & Politics,* written an analysis of the geographical ramifications of Proposition 83 in the California 2006 election in *Politics and Public Policy,* and co-authored several book chapters. Most recently, Dr. Hagley co-authored the book *Reborn of Crisis: 9/11 and the Resurgent Superhero* (Routledge) with Dr. Michael Harrison.

AMANDA K. KEHRBERG is an instructor and writer from Phoenix, Arizona. She has a master's in American Media and Popular Culture from Arizona State University and has worked in higher education for more than ten years, creating and teaching courses on film and television, writing, and digital media. She has published on topics including sports films and musicals, fandom and public relations, and celebrity interaction on social media. Find her at heymandakate.com.

GREGORY P. PERREAULT is an assistant professor of Multimedia Journalism at Appalachian State University. He is a media sociologist who examines how journalism narrates difference. He does this through exploration of norms and practices in journalism and the values that shape content in emerging technologies in journalism. His work has been published in *New Media & Society, Journalism: Theory, Criticism & Practice, Journalism Practice, Journalism Studies,* and *Games & Culture.* His research has been widely discussed in publications including *VICE, Le Monde, Kotaku,* and *Yahoo! News.* He holds a doctorate of philosophy from the University of Missouri School of Journalism, and a masters of arts from the department of Communication, Culture and Technology at Georgetown University.

MILDRED F. PERREAULT is an assistant professor of Media and Communication at East Tennessee State University. Perreault has written about the roles of news, social media, and public relations in forming cultural narratives. She has researched gender dynamics, local journalists, public relations practitioners, and disaster communicators. Before entering academia in 2011, Perreault worked as a journalist and public relations professional in Washington, DC, and South Florida. Perreault has been published in *Games and Culture, Disasters, Communication Studies,* and *Journalism Education.* She holds a doctorate of philosophy from the University of Missouri School of Journalism, a master of arts from the Department of Communication, Culture and Technology at Georgetown University, and a bachelor's of arts in journalism from Baylor University.

CARRIELYNN D. REINHARD is an associate professor at Dominican University in River Forest, Illinois, where she teaches classes in digital communication technologies, game design, communication research methods, and persuasion. She published numerous articles and book chapters on reception studies, primarily concerning digital communication technologies. She has edited anthologies, co-authored *Possessed Women, Haunted States: Cultural Tensions in Exorcism Cinema* (Lexington Books, 2016), and solo-authored *Fractured Fandoms: Contentious Communication in Fan Communities* (Lexington Books, 2018). She is the editor of *Popular Culture Studies Journal* and inaugural president of the Professional Wrestling Studies Association.

MARYANNE A. RHETT is professor of history at Monmouth University. A world historian by training, Rhett's most recent works are *Islam in U.S. Comics at the Turn of the 20th Century* (Bloomsbury, 2019), "Humans and Gods: Steve Trevor and Etta Candy Navigating *Wonder Woman*'s Universe" in *The Human in Superhuman,* and her co-authored "Diana in No-Man's Land: Wonder Woman and the History of World War" in *Drawing the Past: Comics and the Historical Imagination,* with Bridget Keown; these weave together her scholarly interests in how turn-of-the-twentieth-century history and the nature of comics shape our understanding of the world around us. In addition to other work on Middle Eastern and Islamic representations in comics, Rhett is currently examining the field of history as depicted in Platinum Age (pre-1930s) comics from around the world.

STEPHANIE L. SANDERS is a lecturer and diversity, equity, and inclusion officer in the Gerald R. Ford School of Public Policy at the University of Michigan (Ann Arbor). Through the lens of critical race theory, Sanders's research agenda examines students who transition from urban environments to rural, predominantly white, college environments. Sanders is interested in factors affecting student success. In particular, her research examines contributors (e.g., social, academic, environmental, institutional) to positive student outcomes.

J. RICHARD STEVENS is an associate professor in media studies at the University of Colorado Boulder. He is the author of *Captain America, Masculinity, and Violence: The Evolution of a National Icon* (2015/2018). Dr. Stevens's research delves into the intersection of ideological formation and media message dissemination, comprising studies such as how cultural messages are formed and passed through popular culture, how technology infrastructure affects the delivery of media messages, communication technology policy, and related studies in how media and technology platforms are changing American public discourse.

ANNA C. TURNER is a doctoral student in media studies at the University of Colorado Boulder. Her research interests include hegemonic media practices, framing, and audience effects, with an emphasis on critical theory. Ms. Turner's research focuses on the ideology of media texts in political communication and popular culture, including how ideology is formed through media messages and their effect on audience interaction with such texts. She is specifically interested in the ways in which media texts proliferate political messages and influence audience members' perception of political issues and policies.

KATHLEEN M. TURNER LEDGERWOOD is an assistant professor of English and the Writing Area Coordinator at Lincoln University in Missouri. She researches aspects of popular media and the relationships between literature, film, and television. She has published a variety of chapters on popular media, including "The Betty White Moment: The Rhetoric of Constructing Aging and Sexuality" and "'I'm Your Person': Television Narrates Female Friendships in the Workplace from *Cagney and Lacey* to *Grey's Anatomy*." Dr. TL has loved getting lost in narratives for as long as she can remember, and now she just feels privileged to be able to indulge in the worlds she loves and call it work. She firmly believes that one of the most wonderful things about human nature is how we are absorbed and captivated by stories and how we use stories and writing to make meaning out of life.

ROBERT WESTERFELHAUS earned his BA from Ohio Dominican College (1994) and his MA (1996) and PhD (1999) from Ohio University. He is currently a professor at the College of Charleston, in South Carolina, where he has been teaching in the Department of Communication since 2002. During 2009 and 2010, Dr. Westerfelhaus was a Fulbright fellow at UMCS in Lublin, Poland. Dr. Westerfelhaus has published numerous journal articles, book chapters, and encyclopedia articles about American popular culture viewed through the dual lenses of rhetoric and semiology.

INDEX

abuse, 26, 70, 75, 79, 195–97, 199–201; sexual, 192

activism, 27, 130; hashtag, 127; spiritual, 122, 128, 131–32

advocacy, 130; student, 123

Africa, 25, 29, 92, 94, 100, 102; and Pan-Africanism, 9, 92, 94, 99, 101–2

African diaspora. *See* diaspora

African Americans, 98, 127–28

Afrocentrism, 92–93

Afrofuturism, 89, 90, 93–96, 98, 100, 102–3

agency, 26, 28, 45, 72, 93, 124, 132, 155, 159, 161–63, 168, 183, 187; collective, 172, 183–84

Agent Carter, 9, 51–63; television series, 53–55, 59

Agent Romanoff. *See* Black Widow

Ahmed, Lelia, 115

Ahmed, Saladin, 52

Aisha, 115–16, 119

Aja-Adanna. *See* Shuri

alcoholism, 39, 41–42, 44, 70, 194

Allen, Amy, 155

Alonso, Victoria, 16

Alphona, Adrian, 112

alternate universe, 6, 52, 141

Amanat, Sana, 15, 18, 109, 112–14, 185

America, 75, 142

American culture, 71, 73, 91, 102, 109n9, 113, 116, 137, 138–40, 150, 190n1, 201

American monomyths, 142–46

ancestry, 99, 102, 109–10, 112, 114–17

Anzaldúa, Gloria, 28, 122, 124, 132

Arbery, Ahmaud, 127

archetypes, 4, 8, 73

asexuality, 147, 183

Atkinson, Meera, 192

Atwell, Hayley, 55, 59

Avengers, 17, 38–39, 41, 102, 109, 113, 137, 141–46, 148, 162–63, 167, 176, 194, 198; in anime, 113; in comics, 38–39, 176; in movies, 11–12, 35, 62, 139, 143, 145–49, 151, 153–54, 161, 163–64, 166–68, 190; in television shows, 113, 141; in video games, 18, 75, 113, 178

NEW SUNS: RACE, GENDER, AND SEXUALITY IN THE SPECULATIVE
Susana M. Morris and Kinitra D. Brooks, Series Editors

Scholarly examinations of speculative fiction have been a burgeoning academic field for more than twenty-five years, but there has been a distinct lack of attention to how attending to nonhegemonic positionalities transforms our understanding of the speculative. New Suns: Race, Gender, and Sexuality in the Speculative addresses this oversight and promotes scholarship at the intersections of race, gender, sexuality, and the speculative, engaging interdisciplinary fields of research across literary, film, and cultural studies that examine multiple pasts, presents, and futures. Of particular interest are studies that offer new avenues into thinking about popular genre fictions and fan communities, including but not limited to the study of Afrofuturism, comics, ethnogothicism, ethnosurrealism, fantasy, film, futurity studies, gaming, horror, literature, science fiction, and visual studies. New Suns particularly encourages submissions that are written in a clear, accessible style that will be read both by scholars in the field as well as by nonspecialists.

Printed in the USA
CPSIA information can be obtained
at www.ICGtesting.com
LVHW041505190923
758132LV00011B/12